# CHICKEN SOUP FOR THE SOUL® TEENAGE COLLECTION

# CHICKEN SOUP FOR THE SOUL® TEENAGE COLLECTION

## Stories of Life, Love and Learning

Jack Canfield
Mark Victor Hansen
Kimberly Kirberger

Health Communications, Inc.
Deerfield Beach, Florida

*www.hcibooks.com*
*www.chickensoup.com*
*www.teenagechickensoup.com*

We would like to acknowledge the many publishers and individuals who granted us permission to reprint the cited material. (Note: The stories that were penned anonymously, that are in the public domain, or that were written by Jack Canfield, Mark Victor Hansen or Kimberly Kirberger are not included in this listing.)

*Losing the "Us"* and *My Story*. Reprinted by permission of Lia Gay. ©1996 Lia Gay.

*After a While*. Reprinted by permission of Veronica A. Shoffstall. ©1971 Veronica A. Shoffstall.

*Soul Mates*. Reprinted by permission of Fran Leb. ©1996 Fran Leb.

*My First Kiss, and Then Some*. Reprinted by permission of Mary Jane West-Delgado. ©1996 Mary Jane West-Delgado.

*Changes in Life*. Reprinted by permission of Sheila K. Reyman. ©1996 Sheila K. Reyman.

*First Love*. Reprinted by permission of Mary Ellen Klee. ©1996 Mary Ellen Klee.

*Starlight, Star Bright; The Right Thing* and *The Player*. Reprinted by permission of Kelly Garnett. ©1998 Kelly Garnett.

*Seven Minutes in Heaven*. Reprinted by permission of Andrew Keegan. ©1998 Andrew Keegan.

*A Geek, a Nerd, a Bookworm*. Reprinted by permission of Kimberly Russell. ©1998 Kimberly Russell.

*A Cool Drink of Water*. Reprinted by permission of Camden Watts. ©1998 Camden Watts.

*Unrequited Love*. Reprinted by permission of Rachel Rosenberg. ©1998 Rachel Rosenberg.

*(Continued on page 551)*

Publisher: Health Communications, Inc.
      3201 S.W. 15th Street
      Deerfield Beach, FL 33442-8190

*Cover design by Andrea Perrine Brower*
*Inside formatting by Lawna Patterson Oldfield*

This collection is dedicated
to all the people whose hard work
make these books possible.

# Contents

## 2. ON FRIENDSHIP

## 3. ON LOVE AND KINDNESS

## 4. ON FAMILY

## 7. MAKING A DIFFERENCE

## 8. GROWING UP AND SELF-DISCOVERY

## 9. LETTERS FROM READERS

# Share with Us

Most of the stories in this book were written by teens like you. We would like to invite you to send us stories you would like to see published in future editions of *Chicken Soup for the Teenage Soul.*

We would also love to hear your reactions to the stories in this book. Please let us know what your favorite stories were and how they affected you.

Please send submissions to:

*Chicken Soup for the Teenage Soul*
P.O. Box 936
Pacific Palisades, CA 90272
fax: 310-573-3657
e-mail for stories: *stories@iam4teens.com*
e-mail for letters: *letters@iam4teens.com*

Come visit our Web site:
*www.iam4teens.com*

You can also visit the *Chicken Soup for the Teenage Soul* site at:
*www.teenagechickensoup.com*

We hope you enjoy reading this book as much as we enjoyed compiling, editing and writing it.

# 1

# ON RELATIONSHIPS

*Love means each person is free to follow his or her own heart.*

*Melody Beattie*

"Brian promised to love me forever.
Then he told me about a *Star Trek* episode
where they scientifically proved the possibility that
forever might actually last only a few days."

# Losing the "Us"

*When an emotional injury takes place,*
*the body begins a process*
*as natural as the healing*
*of a physical wound.*

*Let the process happen.*
*Trust that nature*
*will do the healing.*

*Know that the pain will pass,*
*and, when it passes,*
*you will be stronger,*
*happier, more sensitive and aware.*

Mel Colgrove
from *How to Survive the Loss of a Love*

"So does this mean you want to break up?" I asked softly, hoping my question would go unanswered. That is how it all began, or I guess, ended. The months the two of us had shared were some of the happiest, hardest and most educational months I ever experienced. It seemed impossible that this was the last conversation we would have as Ben and Lia, the couple.

I had ignored the fact that the majority of high-school relationships do not last. I guess, in the back of my mind, I always thought that Ben was the only boy I would ever have these feelings for, that he was the only boy who would ever understand me. I never took into account that the last month of our relationship was one of the hardest times I had ever gone through. It just stopped being fun. It stopped being about us and started to be about everything that surrounded him and me.

The next day at school I tried looking great to make him see what he had given up. I even tried to talk to him like my heart wasn't aching, like I was better off and even happier. But inside I looked at him and could only see all the love and time I had given and all the hurt I had received. I walked around school in a complete daze and cried myself to sleep every night. He was the only thing I thought about, dreamt about and talked about. I drove my friends crazy by constantly analyzing the situation. *How could it have ended?* I found my other half when I was with him. I felt like something had been torn from me, like I was no longer whole.

One night, I couldn't stand it. I gave up and called him. I didn't last five minutes before I broke down and started crying. I told him I had forgotten how to be by myself, and that I needed him. I didn't know how to be Lia without Ben. We had been through so much together that I could not imagine getting through this on my own. He told me that he would always care for me, but that it had become impossible to love me.

For weeks I couldn't see him with other girls without thinking that they were dating. I threw myself at different guys.

I don't know at exactly what point things started to change. I began spending time with my friends. I joined clubs and made after-school plans. I was doing all I could to stay busy.

Slowly I began to have fun by myself, without Ben. Beyond that, I discovered things I liked doing, ways I could be of help. I lent a sympathetic ear to others who were hurting.

I began to smile and, finally, to laugh again. Whole days would pass without a thought of Ben. I would see him at school and wave. I was not ready to be friends with him. I was still healing. But I know I didn't cover a big wound with a Band-Aid and forget about it. I let the wound heal itself and felt enough pain to know that I had truly cared for him.

In my rebound stage, I pursued a lot of guys. Once I healed, they pursued me. The wonderful thing that happened was that I learned how to be a whole person, not half a couple. I'm in a new relationship now, and eventually we will probably break up, and it will be hard, and I will cry and feel just as much, if not more, pain. But I had to ask myself if never caring for someone so that I wouldn't feel that hurt was worth it. I know now that the famous quote is true. "Better to have loved and lost than never to have loved at all." Because no matter what, loving yourself can heal anything.

*Lia Gay*

"This is the '90s.
You can't just dump your boyfriend anymore.
You have to recycle him."

# After a While

After a while you learn the subtle difference between
   holding a hand and chaining a soul,
And you learn that love doesn't mean leaning and
   company doesn't mean security,
And you begin to learn that kisses aren't contracts
   and presents aren't promises,
And you begin to accept your defeats with your head
   up and your eyes open, with the grace of an adult,
   not the grief of a child,
And you learn to build all your roads on today
   because tomorrow's ground is too uncertain for
   plans.
After a while you learn that even sunshine burns if
   you get too much.
So plant your own garden and decorate your own
   soul, instead of waiting for someone to bring you
   flowers.
And you learn that you really can endure . . .
   that you really are strong,
   and you really do have worth.
And you learn and you learn . . .
   with every good-bye you learn. . . .

*Veronica A. Shoffstall*
*written at age 19*

# Soul Mates

I have often told my daughter, Lauren, the story of how her father and I met and of our courtship. Now that she is sixteen years old, she is concerned because she realizes that her soul mate might be sitting next to her in a class or might even ask her for a date, and she is not quite ready to make the same commitment her parents made years ago.

I met Mike on October 9, 1964. Our shy eyes met from across the patio at our friend Andrea's party. We smiled and eventually found ourselves in a conversation that lasted the entire evening, to the exclusion of everyone else. I was eleven and he was twelve. We went steady three days later, which ended after a somewhat tumultuous month.

Months later, Mike still invited me to his lavish bar mitzvah and even asked me to dance. (Years later he told me that despite my braces, my skinny legs and my flipped hair, he thought I was beautiful.)

Mike and I had many mutual friends and were in the same social group at school, so our paths constantly crossed throughout the next few years. Every time I broke up with a boyfriend or had my heart broken by another, my mother would say, "Don't worry, you're going to end up with Mike Leb." I would shriek, "Never! Why would you think such a thing?" She would remind me how his name often came up in my conversations and what a nice guy he was.

Finally, I was in high school, and it was packed with new cute guys. I was ready. What did I care if Mike started dating my best friend? Why, I wondered, was this slowly driving me crazy? Why did we find ourselves talking while waiting for our buses? I will never forget the navy blue penny loafers he wore. Nobody else I knew had such great shoes. My mother's words often came to my mind, but I still wanted to erase them.

By the summer after tenth grade, Mike and I had spent more time together—in the company of his girlfriend, also known as my best friend, and others. That summer Mike left for a Spanish program in Mexico. I found I really missed seeing him. When he returned in August, he called and came by my home. He was so adorable with his tan skin and worldly demeanor. He still couldn't speak a word of Spanish but he looked so good. It was August 19, 1968, when we looked at each other outside my home and realized we had to be together. Of course, we had to wait until after the date I had that night with another guy. I told my date that I was going to start dating Mike so I had to be home early. Mike then told his on-again, off-again girlfriend it was off again for good.

We kept our relationship our little secret until we could proudly announce it at the next party. We walked in late and boldly told all of our friends that we were officially a couple. Not a soul seemed surprised as they uttered "finally."

After graduation from high school, I went away to college. I lasted ten weeks before I transferred to a closer college to be near Mike. On June 18, 1972, we were wed. I was nineteen, and Mike was twenty. We set up our love nest in married housing while we both finished our college degrees. I became a special-education teacher while Mike went on to medical school.

Now, twenty-five years later, I smile at our beautiful daughter, Lauren, and our handsome son, Alex. Although their parents' legacy causes them to look at high school relationships a bit differently, they will never have to worry about their parents saying, "Don't take it so seriously; it's only puppy love."

*Fran Leb*

# My First Kiss, and Then Some

I was a very shy teenager, and so was my first boyfriend. We were high school sophomores in a small town. We had been dating for about six months. A lot of sweaty hand-holding, actually *watching* movies, and talking about nothing in particular. We often came close to kissing—we both knew that we wanted to be kissed—but neither of us had the courage to make the first move.

Finally, while sitting on my living room couch, he decided to go for it. We talked about the weather (really), then he leaned forward. I put a pillow up to my face to block him! He kissed the pillow.

I wanted to be kissed sooooo badly, but I was too nervous to let him get close. So I moved away, down the couch. He moved closer. We talked about the movie (who cared!), he leaned forward again. I blocked him again.

I moved to the end of the couch. He followed, we talked. He leaned . . . I stood up! (I must have had a spasm in my legs.) I walked over near the front door and stood there, leaning against the wall with my arms crossed, and said impatiently, "Well, are you going to kiss me or not?"

"Yes," he said. So I stood tall, closed my eyes tight, puckered my lips and faced upwards. I waited . . . and waited. (Why wasn't he kissing me?) I opened my eyes; he was coming right at me. I smiled.

HE KISSED MY TEETH!

I could have died.

He left.

I wondered if he had told anyone about my clumsy behavior. Since I was so extremely and painfully shy, I practically hid for the next two years, causing me to never have another date all through high school. As a matter of fact, when I walked down the hallway at school, if I saw him or any other great guy walking toward me, I quickly stepped into the nearest room until he passed. And these were boys I had known since kindergarten.

The first year at college, I was determined not to be shy any longer. I wanted to learn how to kiss with confidence and grace. I did.

In the spring, I went home. I walked into the latest hangout, and who do you suppose I see sitting at the bar, but my old kissing partner. I walked over to his bar stool and tapped him on the shoulder. Without hesitation, I took him in my arms, dipped him back over his stool, and kissed him with my most assertive kiss. I sat him up, looked at him victoriously, and said, "So there!"

He pointed to the lady next to him and said to me, "Mary Jane, I'd like you to meet my wife."

*Mary Jane West-Delgado*

# Changes in Life

I was sixteen years old and a junior in high school, and the worst possible thing that could happen to me did. My parents decided to move our family from our Texas home to Arizona. I had two weeks to wrap up all of my "business" and move before school began. I had to leave my first job, my boyfriend and my best friend behind, and try to start a new life. I despised my parents for ruining my life.

I told everyone that I did not want to live in Arizona and would be returning to Texas the first chance I had. When I arrived in Arizona, I made sure everyone knew that I had a boyfriend and best friend waiting for me in Texas. I was determined to keep my distance from everyone; I would just be leaving soon anyway.

The first day of school came, and I was miserable. I could only think of my friends in Texas and how I wished I could be with them. For a while, I felt that my life was over. Eventually though, things got a little better.

It was in my second period accounting class where I first saw him. He was tall, trim and really good looking. He had the most beautiful blue eyes I had ever seen. He was sitting just three seats away from me in the same front row of class. Feeling I had nothing to lose, I decided to talk to him.

"Hi, my name is Sheila; what's yours?" I asked with a Texas drawl.

The guy next to him thought that I was asking *him*. "Mike."

"Oh, hi, Mike," I humored him. "What's your name?" I asked again, focusing my attention on this blue-eyed boy.

He looked behind him, not believing that I could be asking him for his name. "Chris," he responded quietly.

"Hi, Chris!" I smiled. Then I went about my work.

Chris and I became friends. We enjoyed talking to each other in class. Chris was a jock, and I was in the school band; in high school, peer pressure demanded that the two groups did not mix socially. Our paths crossed occasionally at school functions; but for the most part, our friendship remained within the four classroom walls of accounting class.

Chris graduated that year, and we went our separate ways for a while. Then one day, he came to see me while I was working in a store in the mall. I was very happy to see him. He went on my breaks with me, and we started talking again. The pressure from his jock friends had subsided, and we became very close friends. My relationship with my boyfriend in Texas had become less important to me. I felt my bond with Chris growing stronger, taking the place of my relationship in Texas.

It had been a year since I moved from Texas, and Arizona was starting to feel like home. Chris escorted me to my senior prom; we triple-dated with two of his jock friends and their dates. The night of my prom changed our relationship forever; I was accepted by his friends, and that made Chris feel more comfortable. Finally, our relationship was in the open.

Chris was a very special person to me during such a difficult time in my life. Our relationship eventually blossomed into a very powerful love. I now understand that my parents did not move the family to Arizona to hurt me, although at the time, it sure felt as though they had. I now firmly believe that everything happens for a reason. For had I not moved to Arizona, I never would have met the man of my dreams.

*Sheila K. Reyman*

# First Love

*Truly loving another means letting go of all expectations. It means full acceptance, even celebration of another's personhood.*

Karen Casey

Michael and I were never really boyfriend and girlfriend. He was three-and-a-half years older than I, which was a lot when I still didn't need to wear a bathing suit top. We grew up around the pool and tennis courts of a country club. He was an excellent tennis player with sure, calm strides and a powerful stroke. When I had to take time out from swimming and diving because my lips had turned blue, I sat on the grass wrapped in a towel and watched the tennis matches. Later in the day, the guys would come to the pool and hoist the girls on their shoulders for water fights. I liked it best on Michael's shoulders, which were broad. I felt safe.

At sixteen his parents allowed him to drive during the day, and he often brought me home in his gray Dodge. The autumn after I turned fourteen, he started asking if I wanted to go to a late-afternoon movie with him. I wanted to say yes, but then I would get this jumpy feeling in my stomach and always change my mind. His dark eyes looked into mine, both pleasing and frightening me.

Gradually I stayed longer in his car, talking about things that troubled me. My older sister had lots of boyfriends, and although I worshipped her, she mostly didn't want anything to do with me. Then there were the intrigues around who was dating whom and which friends I trusted and why. A lot of my pain centered around my relationship with my parents, who had divorced when I was eleven and remarried when I was thirteen. I didn't know anyone else with a broken family, and I felt ashamed and unsure of myself, like I wasn't as good as the other kids. I could talk with Michael about all this. He was reassuring, and I began to trust him.

As time passed, I was ready to go to the movies with him. We also enjoyed hanging out at my house, where we would go down to the television room in the basement. I loved to watch TV with Michael so that I could cuddle with him on the couch. We were a strange pair. He loved sports, while I loved the arts. My sister and others made fun of his sports obsession. I guess I would have preferred it if everyone thought he was cool or if he'd been more artistic, but no one else cared about me the way he did. When he kissed me for the first time, we were at his house during a thunderstorm, watching a baseball game on television. I ran up to my sister's room when I got home. I must have looked goofy as I stood in her doorway and announced, "Michael kissed me."

"So?" she said. "Was that the first time?"

"Yeah," I nodded.

"What have you guys been doing all this time?" she demanded.

Michael dated other girls, and I went out with other boys. But I hated their sweaty palms and was horrified when a blind date tried to put his tongue in my mouth. Only Michael understood that I needed to move slowly, and he was always very patient with me. Even though Michael reassured me many times that our relationship was special by saying, "It doesn't matter whether or not I have a girlfriend or you have a boyfriend; I will always be there for you," I still got jealous when I saw him interested in someone else.

Michael got engaged to a girl from out of town when I was nineteen. I was the only unmarried, unrelated girl at the wedding. As the bride and groom said good-bye to everyone, Michael came over to me and kissed me on the cheek. "I love you," he said.

He remained true to his word. When I needed to talk to someone, he was there. I got jealous sometimes when I thought of him loving and being romantic with his wife, but that changed as she and I became friends. I moved across the country and only saw Michael occasionally, at the club when I returned to visit my family. Now we sat at the pool and watched his kids swimming. Our lives were very different. I thought I probably wouldn't have much more than a half hour's worth of conversation to share with him, but I always felt a current of love go through me when I saw him.

When I was thirty-eight, my father died. The morning before his funeral, I thought to myself, *I wonder if Michael knows.* We hadn't seen each other or spoken for years. After the service the next day, as I was talking with the many friends and family who had come for the funeral, I felt a hand on my shoulder. I turned and saw those dark eyes.

"Are you all right?" he asked. I nodded. Putting both hands on my shoulders, he held me, looking into my eyes.

No one had ever understood the bond between us. I'm not sure that we did. But it was, and will always be, there.

*Mary Ellen Klee*

# Starlight, Star Bright

When I was five years old, I took an extreme liking to my sister's toys. It made little difference that I had a trunk overflowing with dolls and toys of my own. Her "big girl" treasures were much easier to break, and much more appealing. Likewise, when I was ten and she was twelve, the earrings and make-up that she was slowly being permitted to experiment with held my attention, while my former obsession with catching bugs seemed to be a distant and fading memory.

It was a trend that continued year by year and, except for a few bruises and threats of terrifying "haircuts" while I was sleeping, one that my sister handled with tolerance. My mother continually reminded her, as I entered junior high wearing her new hair clips, that it was actually a compliment to her sense of style. She told her, as I started my first day of high school wearing her clothes, that one day she would laugh and remind me of how she was always the cooler of the two of us.

I had always thought that my sister had good taste, but never more than when she started bringing home guys. I had a constant parade of sixteen-year-old boys going through my house, stuffing themselves with food in the kitchen, or playing basketball on the driveway.

I had recently become very aware that boys, in fact, weren't as "icky" as I had previously thought, and that maybe their cooties weren't such a terrible thing to catch after all. But the freshman guys who were my age, whom I had spent months giggling over at football games with my friends, suddenly seemed so young. They couldn't drive and they didn't wear varsity jackets. My sister's friends were tall, they were funny, and even though my sister was persistent in getting rid of me quickly, they were always nice to me as she pushed me out the door.

Every once in a while I would luck out, and they would stop by when she wasn't home. One in particular would have long conversations with me before leaving to do whatever sixteen-year-old boys did (it was still a mystery to me). He talked to me as he talked to everyone else, not like a kid, not like his friend's little sister . . . and he always hugged me good-bye before he left.

It wasn't surprising that before long I was positively giddy about him. My friends told me I had no chance with a junior. My sister looked concerned for my potentially broken heart. But you can't help who it is that you fall in love with, whether they are older or younger, taller or shorter, completely opposite or just like you. Emotion ran me over like a Mack truck when I was with him, and I knew that it was too late to try to be sensible—I was in love.

It did not mean I didn't realize the possibility of being rejected. I knew that I was taking a big chance with my feelings and pride. If I didn't give him my heart there was no possibility that he would break it . . . but there was also no chance that he might not.

One night before he left, we sat on my front porch talking and looking for stars as they became visible. He looked at me quite seriously and asked me if I believed in wishing on stars. Surprised, but just as serious, I told him I had never tried.

"Well, then it's time you start," he said, and pointed to the sky. "Pick one out and wish for whatever you want the most." I looked and picked out the brightest star I could find. I squeezed my eyes shut and with what felt like an entire colony of butterflies in my stomach, I wished for courage. I opened my eyes and saw him smiling as he watched my tremendous wishing effort. He asked what I had wished for, and when I replied, he looked puzzled. "Courage? For what?" he questioned.

I took one last deep breath and replied, "To do this." And I kissed him—all driver's-license-holding, varsity-jacket-wearing, sixteen years of him. It was bravery I didn't know I had, strength I owed completely to my heart, which gave up on my mind and took over.

When I pulled back, I saw the astonished look in his face, a look that turned into a smile and then laughter. After searching for something to say for what seemed to me like hours, he took my hand and said, "Well, I guess we're lucky tonight. Both our wishes came true."

*Kelly Garnett*

# Seven Minutes in Heaven

People say you change many times in the course of
your teenage years, and that your time in school will
teach you lessons you will never forget. I think they were
referring to classrooms and football fields, but one of my
greatest learning experiences began in a parking lot. It
was as I was waiting to be picked up one day that I met
my first girlfriend.

Her name was Brittany. She was pretty, outgoing and
two years older than I was—it seemed too good to be true
that she was interested in me—but not long after we met,
we became an official couple. At our age, "going out" meant
that we talked on the phone every night, and saw each
other at school in between classes. We never really had a lot
of opportunity to see each other or get to know one
another very well. But, never having been in a relationship
before, I thought that this was what they were like. It
didn't seem like a big deal that we weren't that close, that
I didn't get butterflies in my stomach when I saw her.

Not long after we got together, she called me and told
me that she was going to a party with some friends, and
that she wanted me to go with her. I said I would, and

waited somewhat nervously that night for her to pick me up. When the small car packed with teenagers arrived, I squeezed in and wondered what I was getting myself into.

An hour into the party, I was feeling less self-conscious and a lot more comfortable. Though the people at the party were all older than me, they were people I knew, or had seen around school. It all seemed innocent enough—we just sat around eating popcorn, watching a movie and having a good time—until the movie ended.

Someone suggested a game of "Spin the Bottle," and my heart began to beat a little faster. *It can't be that bad,* I thought to myself. *It's just kissing even if it is in front of a bunch of other people.* But after a while, some people wanted to take the game a little further. I heard somebody say "Seven Minutes in Heaven," and everyone answered "Yes!" with knowing smiles. I had no idea what it was, and looked at Brittany for help, but she just smiled and agreed that it was a good idea.

After the first few couples spent their seven minutes in heaven, I figured out what the object of the game was—going into a closet and kissing. My stomach flip-flopped and I felt dizzy as I waited for the inevitable, when it would be my turn with Brittany. I was scared. I had no experience with this kind of thing, and I was about to jump into it head first with a girl two years older than I was. I didn't know what she expected, or what she would tell the other older kids when we got out. I could see a sad reputation of being a lame boyfriend looming in the near future.

I really didn't have a lot of time to think about it, because our turn came, and Brittany pulled me after her into the closet. As it turned out, she was an experienced kisser—I didn't have time to think, or react, she just kind of took over. I was relieved and glad when it was over. When she took me home later, neither one of us said much. I don't know what she was thinking about, but I was still trying to let everything sink in. It wasn't as much fun as I had thought it would be—there was no romance or feeling in it.

It was never talked about, but in the weeks that followed the party, my relationship with Brittany slowly ended, and I returned to doing normal things with kids my own age. I thought it was strange that I didn't feel sad about it. It was almost a relief to not have to worry about another party or situation where I would feel out of my league.

I was at the beach with friends several months later when I started talking to a girl. As we talked, I realized I was strangely happy just listening to her and watching her smile while she told me about her life. There was something about her that made me enjoy just being with her. With no thoughts of what it meant, I knew I wanted to see her again so we planned to meet the following week, same time, same place.

I was completely comfortable as we sat on a blanket that night filling each other in on the events of the long week that preceded our reunion. We sat next to the bonfire and laughed, and suddenly, I wanted to kiss her . . . and I did. A pure, sweet, innocent kiss, one that made me feel warm and happy. And though it was nowhere near seven minutes, it was definitely a piece of heaven.

*Andrew Keegan*
*As told to Kimberly Kirberger*

# A Geek, a Nerd, a Bookworm

*Love is not what we become, but what we already are.*

Stephen Levine

*Stand straight, shoulders back, chin up, eyes forward, smile,* I mumbled to myself. No, it was an impossible task. I put my glasses back on and slouched into my usual character. I immediately regretted this decision as I slid discreetly into my desk. His eyes did not even flicker at my entrance. Clearing my throat in an effort to be acknowledged seemed hopeless.

As I pulled out my organized binder neatly labeled "History," I stole a glance at him as he sat at the desk beside me. He appeared just as he had in my dream last night: flawless. Everything about him was right—his smile, the way a strand of hair always fell in his eyes and, oh, those eyes. He must have felt me staring because suddenly, he turned and looked at me. I quickly dropped my gaze back to my binder and pretended to be intently interested in finding a worksheet. I didn't dare peek to see if he was still studying me. Instead, I shifted my eyes toward the window. The light from the sun made me squint.

Ironically, I'm spending my summer in school. I didn't fail this class, unlike every other student here. I just have an incredible yearning to learn and want to get the most out of my high school career. More simply put, I am a geek. A nerd. A bookworm.

Out of the corner of my eye, I caught his hand ready to tap my shoulder. Every muscle in my body tensed. His touch was so light that I barely felt his fingers. I faced him with my eyes fixated on the tiled floor. I could not bring myself to look at him. In that instant, I just didn't feel worthy.

"The homework, from last night—did you finish it?"

*Of course I finished it! I also finished tonight's assignment. Don't you know who I am? I am only the single most intelligent person in this school. Every night of the week, I spend countless hours in front of a computer screen. The force behind me is pushing me with an even greater force. Someday, I will be so far in the land of outcasts that I will want to carouse with my laptop. No, I have not entered that kingdom yet. For now, I am content knowing that there is something I don't know—what you are thinking right this second.*

I cleared my throat. "Yes, I did the homework."

"Well, I was a little stumped on question thirteen. Do you know the answer?" With one smooth movement he put his pencil behind his ear.

"Me," I said.

"What? You are the answer?" he asked, confused.

"Uh, no." I could feel my cheeks burning. *Ugh! If I am such a brain, how did I just make such an error? I have practiced what I would say to him a thousand times over.* Supposedly, the conversation would lead to an invitation for a rendezvous. He would laugh at my wit and think that no one was more interesting than I.

I took a deep breath. "Franklin Roosevelt's Brain Trust."

"Thanks," he said, taking the pencil from behind his ear. I watched him sloppily jot down the answer and turn from his worksheet to the blond behind him. He tried to impress her by using his humor. She barely chuckled. I would have laughed uproariously. But then I remembered that the joke was not intended for me. I studied her body motions as she leaned forward toward him, twirling strands of her hair around her finger. Any closer and their noses would have touched. I nonchalantly pushed my pencil off the desk.

Distracted, he shifted his attention from her eyes to the floor. He bent down and picked up the pencil that was half gnawed by my nerves. He came up, his nose closer to mine than hers had been to his. My hand brushed against his as I reached for the pencil. Goosebumps ran down my arms and my heart raced. Never before had he shown so much interest.

As if that moment were just a figment of his imagination, without a word, he turned back to his beauty queen. Disappointed, I hunched forward and leaned on my hand, watching in awe as she brought out her lip balm. With much exaggeration, she moistened her lips and pressed them together firmly. He couldn't take those perfect eyes off her. I wanted to scream and shake him and make him wake up. This girl is a complete flake! Behind her beauty queen exterior is wasted, empty space.

*Someday we will save each other,* I silently vowed. *In an unconventional way, we are similar. Both of us are in dire need of being rescued from a fantasy world. This alone is grounds for building a relationship.*

Tonight I could go to Wal-Mart and buy hair dye and lip balm. Or maybe search around the mall until I found the halter top she was wearing. I should take advantage of the summer weather and get a bronze skin tone. Instead, I will end up doing homework.

No, tonight I will practice: practice standing straight, shoulders back, chin up and smiling. Then maybe tomorrow, he will ask me for the answer to number twelve . . . and my name.

*Kimberly Russell*

# A Cool Drink of Water

After brushing my teeth, I stooped to drink the cool water streaming from the faucet, drifting back to that unforgettable summer. It was the summer when life began—the summer I turned sixteen. I had my own car, along with a brand-new soul. It was not the memory of a new privilege that rushed back to me, but that of him looming over me with a laughing grin painted across his lips as he watched me drink from the faucet. It was that memory that rushed back to me.

Our relationship was everything it should have been, almost as if our time together had been written for a novel. We came together through friends of ours, as do most typical high school relationships. We grew closer and closer during the school year, spending time together on weeknights rehearsing for the school's musical production and on the weekends with friends. Soon, with permission from the weather and sometimes despite it, we traveled to the beach with our friends and a cooler of colas. It was on the way home from the beach one Saturday that I realized I was falling for him. Every sign showed love. I could hardly sit still in class just anticipating the next time I would see him and the upcoming weekend we would spend together. Being in his arms were some of the happiest times I had ever experienced. I could look deep into his eyes and be enchanted forever.

Being with him changed my soul. I shared everything with him, even things I kept from my family and my best friend. I felt his love prying apart the hard shell of shyness that encircled me. His trust, his love and his support for me lifted me from the earth and gently sent me into the clouds. He cast off the chains I had given myself. Through him I learned a new insight about the world. It was as if a tall, dark mountain had stood in front of me and, out of nowhere, he provided the wings to fly over it.

Unfortunately, all good things must come to an end. Yes, even for my first love. I had matured a great deal during our time together, which possibly brought me to a clearer understanding of what true love is. Over time, the clouds floated away, replaced with a new sinking feeling that what I was doing was wrong. The eyes that had so lovingly enchanted me soon became those of a dear friend. Somehow, the spell was broken. I wished so dearly that I could return to the long summer nights we had spent together, embracing under the moonlight. But as I longed for those nights, I also longed for a new freedom. The adventure had somehow become a routine.

Sadly, we both acknowledged the separation. We held each other tighter than ever, both roughly accepting the reality that it would be best to say good-bye. He wiped away my tears and held me until it was time for him to leave. My heart was yearning to kiss him good-bye, but my mind and my lips told me no. He walked down the stairs to his black convertible and left. I watched through tear-stained eyes from the window as he pulled out of my driveway. As his headlights faded in the distance, I turned off the light to my first love.

Having satisfied my thirst, I stood up and dried my mouth and chin with the towel at my side. I smiled, once again remembering how he stood by me and protected me in more ways than one. It is impossible to sum up seven-and-one-half months of pure joy and apprenticeship, but if there is one way to do it, a cool drink of water from the faucet would be sufficient.

*Camden Watts*

"He gave me a copy of *The Declaration of Independence*, then he got a tattoo that says *Give Me Liberty Or Give Me Death*. I think my boyfriend wants his freedom."

# Unrequited Love

*Nothing spoils the taste of peanut butter like unrequited love.*

Charlie Brown
*from* Peanuts *by Charles Schulz*

"Guess what?"

I look at Sarah, my best friend since halfway through second grade. We've been through this routine before, and both of us know what's coming. "What?" I ask. I really don't like guessing.

We're walking home together after school. We usually do. It's freezing.

"Guess," she prompts me.

I study her face and then think for a second. What could be making her so happy? "You got another A in biology?"

"Nope."

"Your sister dropped dead?" I suggest.

"I wish," she replies, but shakes her head. "Guess again!"

"Just *tell* me!" I whine.

Her smile grows even broader, and I can see all her braces-covered teeth. "Xander kissed me."

My jaw drops and I turn to her. "Get out!" I gasp. I hit her shoulder. "Don't tell me stuff like that!" But then curiosity gets the better of me, so I meekly ask, "Lips?"

"Cheek."

I hit her shoulder again. "What's wrong with you?" she demands loudly.

I glare at her. I've liked Xander since halfway through eighth grade. Ever since he turned to me one day in class and said, "Alyson, right?" I'd given him my usual witty reply of "Yun-hun." After that we spoke, like, once or twice.

Then this year, Sarah became friends with him and his group. I never used to hang out with Sarah during recess or lunch—her friends were all straight-A students, and I was one of those has-real-potential-but-won't-apply-herself types, so I mostly got Cs. Usually I hung out with my other best friends, Darcy and Mara. But neither Darcy nor Mara had very many friends who were guys, and I wanted some. Sarah did, so I tried to spend lunch with them at least two times a week.

"Why are we still calling him 'Xander'?" she asks, her voice breaking into my thoughts. I look at her, surprised. I had almost forgotten she was there. "No one we know is around here so even if we said his real name, no one would know!"

I shrug. "It's fun."

Xander's name isn't really Xander. I came up with that as a code name for him. All my friends do that. That way they can talk about their crush in front of people and no one will know. I chose to call him "Xander" because I have a deep respect (most people call it an obsession—I can't imagine why) for the TV show *Buffy the Vampire Slayer*. Xander is the name of one of the lead characters. Only three people know that my crush is referred to as "Xander": Sarah, Mara and Darcy. I call him Xander so much, sometimes I think that's his real name. When I talk about him I sometimes have to say "Xander—the untelevised version" so my friends know I'm not talking about Xander from *Buffy the Vampire Slayer*.

"Are you coming with us to see the movie Saturday?" she asks.

I smile. "Is Xander coming?" She gives me a look but says nothing. "Then I'm there!" I say. The last time I went with them to see a movie, I ended up sitting next to Xander. For an hour and forty-three minutes, I thought I'd died and gone to heaven. Okay, maybe heaven is a bit much, but I did feel very, very happy.

But now I think of something and my smile disappears. Nervously I tuck a strand of hair behind my ear. "Sar?"

I begin to crack my knuckles, which I do whenever I'm nervous. Aw, who am I kidding? I crack my knuckles all the time. I really need to stop because it's annoying and it'll give me arthritis when I'm older. "What does he think of me?" I ask.

I hear a click as Sarah turns off her Walkman. I know she'll tell me the truth. Sar isn't the kind of friend who, when you tell her you just messed up in public speaking, says, "I'm sure nobody noticed!" Instead, she'd just laugh. At you. Mockingly. Loudly. So I nervously wait for Sarah to answer.

"He . . . he says you're kinda weird. Like, a depressed, poetry-writing nut. But, like, a nice one," she adds to make it sound better.

"Really?" I sigh, feeling as though fifty midgets have found a way into my chest and have decided to simultaneously perform cartwheels, jumping jacks and handstands on my heart.

"That's a bit harsh," she says. "Look, he likes you—he just thinks you're a bit morbid."

I try to look at the positive, "Nice is good!" I tell her. She nods her head and turns her music back on.

I begin to feel worse every time I think about what Xander had said. "Nice is good," I repeat dejectedly. I stare straight ahead for a moment and then squint because the sun is so bright it hurts my eyes. Nice but insane is probably what he meant. *I am not insane,* I tell myself, *I am depressed. There's a difference.* I kick at a bit of snow on the ground.

"You are not depressed," Mom always tells me. "Right," I reply, "I am just deeply unhappy!" "There is a difference, Alyson," she tells me, then ships me off to therapy.

I pinch Sarah the way she taught me to, back in fifth grade. It's the best way to pinch 'cause it really, really hurts. She squeals and looks at me, annoyed. "What?"

"Am I depressing?"

"Yes, you're negative, morbid, cynical. . . ."

I sigh.

She puts her arm around my shoulders, "But that's why we love you."

I'm also known around school as being depressed.

That's not to say I actually *am* depressed. I'm not; I'm a complete and utter sucker for corny, happy endings (I practically live on films like *While You Were Sleeping* and *Addicted to Love*). A movie can be incredible, but if the ending is sad, I'll immediately despise it. But when people want to know about you, they usually ask certain questions, and my answers sometimes feed their "depressed poet" image of me. *Fave color?* Black. *Hobby?* Writing poetry and stories. *Oh, what kind of poetry? Sad?* Usually.

Of course, I don't exactly dissuade them from the tortured writer concept they have of me, because at least I'm known for something. Maybe it's negative, but it's better than nothing, right? So let them think me forlorn. I have my own friends and I don't really care what any of them think. Except *him.* . . .

But a long time ago, I really was depressed. I'd just been dumped by my first boyfriend and felt really crappy. I thought about death and suicide a lot. I know it was dumb, but I'd never been dumped before and it just . . . hurt. That's the only word I could think of to describe it. And I know it sounds clichéd and all, but my heart actually felt as though it had been broken in two. But I got over it (with the help of my therapist, school guidance counselor, my parents and a really long letter to Mara that I never gave her and ended up gluing into my diary). And now when I think of Xander, I feel so miserable. . . .

Sarah and I reach the street where we split. We stop and I turn to her, "This is where I get off," I say. "I'll call ya later," I begin crossing the street.

She continues on. "Alright. Bye!" she calls.

I turn onto my street and look down at the ground. The snow around here is all white and beautiful. It reminds me of cream cheese. Not like the snow in front of our school. That snow is all gray and dirty and yuck. This snow is nice. Nice. Like how he thinks of me. Nice. The chances of Xander ever liking me are about as good as me passing math. I know that!

I giggle. But hey, maybe I'll get a few poems out of this unrequited love thing. Ya think?

*Rachel Rosenberg*

# Hopscotch and Tears

I watched the blue Toyota speed down my street and listened to the sound of the diesel engine fade. Tears collected in my eyes and trailed down my cheeks until I could taste them. I couldn't believe what had just happened. Making my way into the house, I quickly ran up the stairs, hoping that my brother wouldn't see the frozen look of terror in my eyes. Luckily that rainy day, his eyes were glued to the TV.

Plopping down on my unmade bed, I buried my face in my pillow. Light sniffles turned into cries, and cries into hysterics. I couldn't bear it; the pain was too strong, and my heart was broken.

We had been seeing each other for three months and two days (not that I had been counting). I had never been so happy. We had brought out the best in each other. But that day he threw it all away, out the window of his rusty blue Toyota, in a speech that still rings in my ears.

"I don't think we should see each other anymore . . ." his voice had trailed off. I wanted to ask him why, I wanted to scream at him, I wanted to hold him, but instead I whispered, "Whatever," afraid to look him in the eyes because I knew I would break down.

I lay there crying all afternoon and into the night, feeling so alone, so upset, so confused. For weeks I cried myself to sleep, but in the morning I'd put a plastic smile on my face to avoid having to talk about it. Everybody saw right through it.

My friends were concerned. I think they thought I would recover sooner than I did.

Even months after the breakup, when I heard a car drive up my street I'd jump up to the window to see if it was him. When the phone rang, a chill of hope would run down my spine. One night as I was cutting out magazine pictures and taping photos on my wall, a car came up my street, but I was too preoccupied to notice that it was the car I'd been listening for over the last two months.

"Chloe, it's me, it's . . ." It was him, calling me to come downstairs! On my way down, my heart was pounding and my thoughts were of a reconciliation. He had seen the error of his ways. When I got outside, there he stood, gorgeous as always.

"Chloe, I came to return your sweater. You left it at my house. . . . Remember?" I had forgotten all about it.

"Of course. Thank you," I lied. I hadn't seen him since the breakup and it hurt—it hurt a lot. I wanted to be able to love him again.

"Well, I guess I'll just see ya around then," he said. Then he was gone. I found myself alone in the darkness, listening to his car speed away. I slowly walked back to my room and continued to tape photos on my wall.

For weeks, I walked around like a zombie. I would stare at myself for hours in the mirror, trying to figure out what was wrong with me, trying to understand what I did wrong, searching for answers within the mirror. I'd talk to Rachel for hours. "Rachel, did you ever realize that when you fall in love, you only end up falling. . . ." I'd say before breaking down in tears. Her comforting words did little but give me a reason to feel sorry for myself.

Pretty soon my sadness turned into madness. I began to hate him and blame him for my troubles, and I believed he had ruined my life. For months I thought only of him.

Then something changed. I understood I had to go on, and every day I grew a little happier. I even began to see someone new!

One day, as I was flipping through my wallet, I came upon a picture of him. I looked at it for a few minutes, reading his face like a book, a book that I knew I had finished and had to put down. I took out the picture and stuck it in a cluttered drawer.

I smiled to myself as I realized I could do the same in my heart. Tuck him away in a special place and move on. I loved, I lost and I suffered. Now it was time to forgive and forget. I forgave myself also, because so much of my pain was feeling like I did something wrong. I know better now.

My mom used to tell me, "Chloe, there are two kinds of people in this world: those that play hopscotch and sing in the shower, and those that lie alone at night with tears in their eyes." What I came to understand is that people have a choice as to which they want to be, and that each of us is a little of both.

That same day, I went outside and played hopscotch with my sister, and that night I sang louder than ever in the shower.

*Rebecca Woolf*

# Why Guys Like Girls

One day while reading my e-mails, I came across one of those that you have to scroll down for an eternity just to get to the letter part because it is sent to hundreds of people.

Well, normally, I automatically delete those. But this one intrigued me. It was titled, "A Few Reasons Why Guys Like Girls." The instructions were to read it, add to it and then forward it to at least twenty-five people. If you did not forward it, you would have bad luck with relationships, but if you did send it to twenty-five people or more, you would be the lucky winner of romantic bliss.

After reading the reasons why guys like girls, I had an idea. If I could attain romantic bliss by sending this e-mail to twenty-five people, imagine how lucky I'd be if I sent it to millions. My husband and I are looking forward to marital perfection thanks to each and every one of you who reads this.*

[*References to chain letter results are not meant to be taken seriously.]

## A Few Reasons Why Guys Like Girls

1. *They always smell good, even if it's just shampoo*
2. *The way their heads always find the right spot on your shoulder*
3. *The ease with which they fit into your arms*
4. *The way they kiss you and all of a sudden everything is right in the world*
5. *How cute they are when they eat*
6. *The way they take hours to dress, but in the end it's all worthwhile*
7. *Because they are always warm, even when it's minus thirty degrees outside*
8. *The way they look good no matter what they wear*
9. *The way they fish for compliments*
10. *How cute they are when they argue*
11. *The way their hands always find yours*
12. *The way they smile*
13. *The way you feel when you see their names on the caller ID after you just had a big fight*
14. *The way they say "Let's not fight anymore," even though you know an hour later . . .*
15. *The way they kiss when you do something nice for them*
16. *The way they kiss you when you say "I love you"*
17. *Actually, just the way they kiss you . . .*
18. *The way they fall into your arms when they cry*
19. *Then the way they apologize for crying over something silly*
20. *The way they hit you and expect it to hurt*
21. *Then the way they apologize when it does hurt (even though we don't admit it)*
22. *The way they say, "I miss you"*
23. *The way you miss them*
24. *The way their tears make you want to change the world so that it doesn't hurt them anymore*

*Yet regardless of whether you love them, hate them, wish they would die or know that you would die without them . . . it matters not. Because once they come into your life, whatever they are to the world, they become everything to you. When you look them in the eyes, traveling to the depths of their souls, and you say a million things without a trace of a sound, you know that your own life is inevitably consumed within the rhythmic beatings of their very hearts.*

*We love them for a million reasons. It is a thing not of the mind but of the heart. A feeling. Only felt.*

*Compiled by Kimberly Kirberger*

"Everything about girls makes me really, really nervous. I flunked my algebra test because algebra has the word 'bra' in it!"

*Reprinted by permission of Randy Glasbergen.*

# Why Girls Like Guys

In *Chicken Soup for the Teenage Soul II,* we included "A Few Reasons Why Guys Like Girls." We thought it would be fun to keep the momentum going for this book, so we asked you write to us with more reasons "Why Guys Like Girls" or even "Why Girls Like Guys." And write you did! We had such a good time reading all the imaginative and entertaining responses you came up with.

Since we heard from the guys for *Teen II,* we thought we'd let the girls have their say for this book. The following is a compilation of the sweetest lists we received from the girls:

## A Few Reasons Why Girls Like Guys

1. *They always wear your favorite cologne (which happens to be the one that you bought them for their birthday)*
2. *The way they run their fingers through your hair*
3. *That look they give you that makes you just want to die right then and there*

4. *The way they kiss away your tears*

5. *The way they get mad when they can't make your problem go away*

6. *The way they show off around their friends, even though you know you would love him if he missed a basket or two*

7. *The way they make it their personal mission to ensure that you are never cold*

8. *That confused look they get on their faces when you are mad at them—guaranteed to make your heart melt and the anger fade away*

9. *The way they always let you win any game you play together*

10. *. . . And when you point this out to them they pretend not to know what you are talking about*

11. *That smile they flash that can make your stomach drop to your feet*

12. *The way they call to apologize after you had a big fight*

13. *The way they touch and hold you so gently, as if they are afraid they will break you*

14. *The way they say, "I love you"*

15. *The way they would die before saying "I love you" in front of their friends*

16. *The way they kiss you*

17. *The way they kiss you after making up from a fight*

18. *The way they hold you when you are crying*

19. *The way they think they are your big protector*

20. *The way they say, "I miss you," even though they hate to admit it*

21. *The way you miss everything about them when they are gone*

22. *The way they comfort you when you have had a bad day*

23. *The way they write you love letters even if they think it's uncool*
24. *Regardless of whether you love them, hate them, wish they would die or know that you would die without them . . . it matters not. Because once they enter your life, whatever you were to the world, they become everything to you. When you look them in the eyes, traveling to the depths of their souls and you say a million things without even speaking, you know that your own life is consumed by their love. We love them for a million reasons; it is a thing, an indescribable feeling.*

*Compiled by Kimberly Kirberger*

# Love Is Never Lost

*If our love is only a will to possess, it is not love.*

Thich Nhat Hanh

They say it's better to have loved and lost, than never to have loved at all.

That thought wouldn't be very comforting to Mike Sanders. He had just been dumped by his girlfriend. Of course, she didn't put it quite that way. She said, "I do care about you, Mike, and I hope we can still be friends." *Great,* Mike thought. *Still be friends. You, me and your new boyfriend will go to the movies together.*

Mike and Angie had been going together since they were freshmen. But over the summer, she had met someone else. Now as he entered his senior year, Mike was alone. For three years they shared the same friends and favorite hang-outs. The thought of returning to those surroundings without Angie made him feel—well, empty.

Football practice usually helped him take his mind off his troubles. Coaches have a way of running you until you are so tired, you can't really think of anything else. But lately, Mike's heart just wasn't in it. One day it caught up with him. He dropped passes he wouldn't normally miss and let himself get tackled by guys who had never been able to touch him before.

Mike knew better than to have the coach yell at him more than once, so he tried a little harder and made it through the rest of the practice. As he was running off the field, he was told to report to the coach's office. "Girl, family or school: Which one is bothering you, son?" asked his coach.

"Girl," Mike responded. "How did you guess?"

"Sanders, I've been coaching football since before you were born, and every time I've seen an all-star play like a J.V. rookie, it's been because of one of those three."

Mike nodded. "Sorry, sir. It won't happen again."

His coach patted him on the shoulder. "This is a big year for you, Mike. There's no reason why you shouldn't get a full ride to the school of your choice. Just remember to focus on what's really important. The other things will take care of themselves."

Mike knew his coach was right. He should just let Angie go and move on with his life. But he still felt hurt, even betrayed. "It just makes me so mad, Coach. I trusted in her. I opened myself up to her. I gave her all I had, and what did it get me?"

His coach pulled out some paper and a pen from his desk drawer. "That's a really good question. What did it get you?" He handed Mike the pen and paper and said, "I want you to think about the time you spent with this girl, and list as many experiences, good and bad, that you can remember. Then I want you to write down the things that you learned from each other. I'll be back in an hour." With that, the coach left Mike by himself.

Mike slumped in his chair as memories of Angie flooded his head. He recalled when he had first worked up the nerve to ask her out, and how happy he had been when she said yes. Had it not been for Angie's encouragement, Mike wouldn't have tried out for the football team.

Then he thought of the fights that they had. Though he couldn't remember all the reasons for fighting, he remembered the sense of accomplishment he got from working through their problems. He had learned to communicate and compromise. He remembered making up after the fights, too. That was always the best part.

Mike remembered all the times she made him feel strong and needed and special. He filled the paper with their history, holidays, trips with each other's family, school dances and quiet picnics together. Line by line, he wrote of the experience they shared, and he realized how she had helped shape his life. He would have become a different person without her.

When the coach returned, Mike was gone. He had left a note on the desk that simply read:

*Coach,*

*Thanks for the lesson. I guess it's true what they say about having loved and lost, after all. See you at the practice.*

*David J. Murcott*

# Never Been Dissed—Until Now

What can I say? Sometimes I'm a little dumb. I consider Cheetos a major food group. I play air guitar. I think burping is funny. And, worst of all, I screwed up my chance with Darcy by listening to a bunch of other jerks who were just as clueless as me.

Darcy was kinda like the Jewel CD I loved. I played that thing over and over on the way to school, but the second I pulled into the parking lot, it got stuffed under my seat for, uh, safekeeping and replaced with the Beastie Boys.

Imagine me confessing to my friends that I, captain of the basketball team, was dating Darcy, captain of the debate team. Believe me, I didn't plan on falling for the school brain. But I was blown away by the first words she ever spoke to me.

"Uh, are you lost? This is the li-brar-y. The gym is on the other side of the school, remember?" she said, enunciating the words like she was talking to a toddler. Ouch.

Even though we went to the same school, Darcy and I lived in completely different worlds. She spent her time with the Net nerds, and I roamed the halls like Moses parting the Red Sea of fans who worshipped the guys on my team. I was totally knocked for a loop when she broke the silence.

"Books. I need a book," I stammered, suddenly unable to remember my assignment. She pointed to a row of books on Thomas Edison—just the man I was looking for—and before I could turn to thank her, she was gone.

When I did catch up with her again, she was on her tippy toes reaching for an encyclopedia in the next aisle. "Need a ladder? Or how 'bout some platforms?" I asked giving her a taste of her own sarcasm.

"How about giving me a hand?" she replied. "Oh, that's right. Books are *square*, not round like a basketball. Think you can hold one?" *Cha-ching!* This girl has guts, I thought. When I started laughing, Darcy totally cracked up and started snort-laughing. The number-two pencils holding up her hair were shaking.

"I can't believe I said that to you. I can't believe you're laughing. This is so surreal," she laughed. "Oh, sorry, that's a big word. Do you need a dictionary?" More laughing, more snorting. We went on like that for a while, ripping on each other until I thought my sides would split.

For the rest of the day—okay, the rest of the *week*—every time I thought about her, I felt the same gut-socking, dizzy feeling I get before a big game. Then I found myself taking different routes to get to class just to see if I'd bump into her, and when I did . . . doh! We didn't say a word to each other, but the joke was still going. I'd innocently make gorilla noises, and she'd die laughing. Or she'd take off her glasses and bump into walls, sending her books, pen and protractor flying everywhere. She taped Brain Gum to my locker. I glued a pair of sweaty gym socks to hers. Two weeks into our secret game, Darcy asked me out. Correction: she blackmailed me into a date. I found a ransom note in my locker saying that if I ever wanted to see my lucky jockstrap again, I'd better meet her at a nearby coffee shop. What guy wouldn't love a girl with that sense of humor?

After that first date, we spent nearly every day together talking about everything—cheesy Kung Fu movies (our shared obsession), how I hated being judged as a jock despite my 3.5 GPA, why I hadn't lost my virginity—all of the things I could *never* talk about with the guys or would even think about mentioning to any of the other girls I had dated. Then again, Darcy wasn't like anyone I had ever been with before. She was a lot of firsts for me. She was the first girl who had the guts to ask me out. She was the first girl I didn't judge by her bra size or reputation. She was the first person who made me feel I had more to offer the world than a killer turnaround jumper. She was the first girl I dated who didn't obsess about her hair, her weight or what she was wearing. And she was the first girl I didn't blab about in the locker room when the guys started bragging about their weekend conquests.

It didn't take long for everyone to start wondering why I was flaking on basketball practice or missing the weekly Duke Nukem marathons at Kyle's. I had been making up *the* lamest excuses to cover for hanging out with Darcy and was feeling pretty skanky about it when the guys confronted me about it. So I told them about her.

"Who?" Steve asked.

"Not the girl in overalls and hightops?" Eric asked.

"Why are you wasting time on *that*?" Kyle asked.

I sat there as they teased me about slumming with a "geeky chick," assuming that once they exhausted all of their lame jokes about Darcy, they'd move onto their next target. Wrong. After that day, whenever I told them I was doing stuff with Darcy, they unloaded on her again. At first, I didn't let it bother me. Then one morning, Dave asked, "Have you figured out how to get her to wear a bag over her head to the prom yet?" That really pissed me off and eventually the little things turned into big things, like "accidentally" forgetting to tell me about practice or suddenly not having enough room at the lunch table for me.

After a few weeks of getting the cold shoulder from my friends, I started to doubt my own judgment. Darcy *wasn't* one of the prettiest girls in the school. Was I actually planning to take her to my senior prom? She'd probably wear number-two pencils in her hair *and* those hideous high-tops. Once I finished picking her apart, I was convinced she was totally wrong for me. Darcy didn't like basketball or my friends. She refused to go to any of the team parties. I'd been blowing off practices to be with her, and my game was totally suffering. In my mind, the relationship was doomed.

I tried to be subtle at first by taking different routes to my classes to avoid her. I'd promise to call her but never did. She finally cornered me in the hall one day and demanded an explanation, so I swore I'd meet her after school. Then I blew her off. I was hoping she'd get the hint and go away if I flaked, but she didn't let me off that easily. The next day, in front of the entire school, Darcy let me have it. She yelled at me, called me a coward, a jerk and an idiot, and, worst of all, tossed my friends a box of notes I'd written to her. I stood there speechless as they read each one aloud and laughed like hyenas. The funny thing was that for the first time (*another* first with Darcy) I didn't really care what the guys were saying or who saw me standing there like an idiot, because I knew she was right. When I looked at my friends howling and high-fiving each other, I finally realized that I was going to be the first guy in our pathetic circle to grow up.

I wish I could say there was a happy ending to the story, that I begged Darcy to take me back and she did, but it didn't happen. Well, at least not the part about her taking me back. I begged. I pleaded. I stuffed notes in her locker. I followed her around school. I was practically stalking her by the time I realized it was too late. She had already gotten over slumming with a dummy.

Last I heard, Darcy graduated early and got accepted to an out-of-state college. I still feel a little sad when I think about her and what could have been, but I'm also grateful that I learned what I did, when I did. I know a little bit more about who I am—the *whole* me, not just the big man on campus part—and who I can be, regardless of what my friends think or say. So, Darcy, if you're reading this . . . thanks.

*Shad Powers*

"This time it's *really* over, Jared. I threw out all your pictures *and* deleted all your e-mails."

# A Crush

*I'm not afraid of storms, for I am learning how to sail my ship.*

Helen Keller

"Aaarghhhmmmmm . . . Hello?"

It was about 10:00 on a beautiful July morning, and I had just been woken up from a deep slumber by the untimely ring of the telephone. Little did I know my destiny was on the other end of the line.

"Is Leigh there?" the rich tenor voice asked.

"Yeah. This is." I sat bolt upright, smacking my head on the headboard in the process. I rubbed my forehead and stared in disbelief at the receiver in my hand.

I met Josh while we worked together at the same pizza parlor. It was love at first sight for me, and the whole restaurant knew about it. Never mind that Josh was five years older than I was or that he didn't know my name (or so I thought, until this fateful phone call proved otherwise). I was 100 percent head over heels for the guy, the guy who was at this very moment on the other end of my telephone wire, calling my name. . . .

"Leigh? Hello? Leigh?"

I regained my senses enough to answer. "Yes. I'm here. Um, hi."

"Leigh, I need to talk with you. Can I pick you up in a half hour?"

*Could he?* "Yeah. Sure." I responded, trying to sound casual. We hung up, and I stared at the telephone for another moment, until I realized that I had twenty-eight minutes left before the love of my life would arrive at my front door to confess his undying passion for me.

Thirty-two minutes later, I stood gazing up at Josh's figure in my doorway. This was simply too good to be true. He looked slightly uncomfortable as he stood, his tall, slim frame moving restlessly.

"Let's go," he said.

Josh led the way to his car, and we both got in. As we pulled out of my driveway, I again gazed at his beautiful face. His lips were full but firm, his nose straight and perfect, his hair sun-streaked blond (from a side job landscaping, as a little investigative research had revealed to me), and his eyes, his gorgeous, wide-set, polished mahogany eyes were . . . staring right back at me! I flushed in embarrassment, as I began to say something, but Josh interrupted me. He didn't bother with small talk, but got right down to business.

"I've been hearing some rumors at work," he began.

This was *not* the opening I had anticipated.

"What kind of rumors?" I ventured.

Josh presented me with an accusatory glance. "Oh, just that you and I are dating. That we're practically engaged. All sorts of great stuff." He gave me a pointed look. "Since I have never even *talked* to you until this morning, I don't know how anybody could have gotten that impression. Unless *somebody*," he paused dramatically, "told them."

I stared at him, shocked. I was speechless for a long

minute, my mouth attempting to form denials that wouldn't make it past my throat. A vice took hold of my heart, squeezing painfully. Finally, I managed to collect myself enough to say, "I swear, I never said anything like that. I might have had a"—my throat began to close up, but I was able to continue in a humiliated whisper—"a little crush on you, and some people knew about it, but I promise, I swear to you, I never insinuated anything else. I'm sorry."

Josh looked at me. My shock at his accusation and every ounce of my humiliation were evident on my face. After a moment, he accepted my admission for the truth that it was, and he tried to change the topic to more light-hearted chit-chat, but I was too occupied trying to keep the tears from streaming down my face, to be a good conversationalist.

After about five minutes, I requested that he take me to my friend Annette's house. As he pulled away, the tears overflowed down my cheeks. I turned to see Annette rushing outside. I ran toward her, sobs making my body shake, and she hugged me until I finally began to calm down. When my crying had diminished to random hiccuping sighs, my best friend took my face between her hands and said softly, with wisdom beyond her years, "If it were supposed to feel good, they wouldn't call it a crush."

*J. Leigh Turner*

# Sea Glass

We're sitting on the cold shore combing the sand around us looking for sea glass. It's windy, and the cool mist coming off the waves feels cold and charming. We're bundled up in all our layers, and he gently touches my face and kisses my lips. His blue-green eyes stare deep into mine, and I feel him looking straight into my heart.

The brilliant rays of purple, gold and turquoise start to fade as the sun finishes setting. We stand up, wipe the sand off our pants and start walking to the parking lot. I take a deep breath and smell the salt and seaweed crawling in with the tide.

On our walk home, he holds my hand, and we laugh and talk about nothing of real significance. We walk slowly to savor the moment, to savor the time we have together. The trees seem to make a tunnel, surrounding us and isolating us in our own little world.

When we get back to my house, we take the sea glass and put it in my jar. "It's almost halfway filled," he remarks, as I look at the tiny pieces filling the jar. There must be at least a hundred pieces in there, all of them different shapes and different colors. I suppose that if I counted them, there would be just as many as the days we have spent together, and the nights we have comforted each other on the phone.

Each piece of glass is a different color. I decide that they represent the ordinary days filled with insight and love. They are the most frequent ones, the everyday ones. I notice that I put in a green one today. It is a day like today that we shared together that the green ones represent. The green ones frosted with white specks represent the days in which one of us was upset and confided in the other. Although there are only a few, there are some and they're big. I think those are the ones that help the relationship grow the most. The white pieces are the biggest and the shiniest. They reflect the time one of us accomplished something or was really happy about something. One might represent him winning his car, another might be when I made the team, and yet there are so many I can't remember what each one represents. There are so few dark-brown ones. Those have the sharpest edges and cut your fingertips when you touch them. They cause tears and hurt. They're the ex-girlfriends, the not-too-long-ago crushes, the jealousy, the fights. They are the painful parts of our relationship that will never go away, but have become smoother over time.

There is one brilliant bluish-purple piece of glass. It is very small, and I know exactly what it represents. It is the first time he said those three words that before that night were just tossed around and used carelessly by other guys. It represents the time when he looked deep into my eyes, brushed back my hair and told me he loved me.

All of the pieces of sea glass are strong. No matter how hard you try (and people have tried), they won't break. They may get smoother, maybe a little smaller, but so do all memories. They are strong and will always be there and will never be lost.

Then there's a big rock, a big pink rock in the shape of a heart, down at the bottom. Its shape represents exactly what it is. It's our hearts, with all the sea glass and memories and good times to come piled on top. Our small, pink hearts, learning about each other and ourselves, piling little green days on top of big white ones, avoiding the sharp brown ones and trying to find another blue one. It's our hearts, the ones that have grown to love each other. The ones that have spent over two years piling memories on top, good and bad, to make two different, wonderful people. The glass jar will never break. The jar is our bodies that protect our hearts and memories. Like the sea glass, it is strong and even if one of us goes away, it will still be there with all the memories left behind.

*Stacey Doerner*

# Fading Fast

Looking down at the interior side of my Strawberry Shortcake running shoes, I realize that his name, Forrest David, is fading. I trace my finger over his signature, remembering the day he autographed my shoe with his dad's pen as I sat in the Austin airport, tears blurring my vision.

*That's what he's doing,* I think, *slowly fading out of my life.* And yet, I remember everything and every moment I was with him, savoring his every move, smile and kiss. I never thought a person could be so precious to me. He was so beautiful, it hurt to look at him. But now it hurts to think of him. I memorized his face: dark eyebrows, greenish-blue eyes, tousled hair. His hands, tan and strong, could swallow my own. I had never loved anyone else the way I loved Forrest.

The first time I saw him, I stood there quietly, drinking him in. And when I finally had him, I was almost in tears because I had never felt so alive. I don't know how long I stood there holding him, breathing in his scent with my face pressed against his shirt. I knew I didn't want to let go.

I cried bitterly the day we parted, feeling utterly alone

as I watched him vanish down the airplane terminal. I tasted the salt as I wept, feeling so angry at the world and at life. I had found my love, the one I wanted to be with forever, and life had chosen to be cruel and unfair, keeping us over six hundred miles away from each other. It might as well have been 10 million. I thought my heart would break.

I sigh as I remember these painful memories, but I don't cry. I have no tears left for him.

They say real love is forever. I don't know the exact definition of it, but Forrest is as close as I've ever come to it. He's gone now, and my dreams have been shattered by the harsh reality of the situation. I thought we were meant to be together, and I dearly loved him. Two teenagers living so far away from each other usually can't make it. I thought we would be different, that we were strong enough to make it. I was wrong. When he left, he took a piece of my heart with him. It's now floating somewhere in Austin.

For a while, I couldn't eat or sleep. I felt so sick and empty. I didn't think I'd be able to go on without him. As I look back now, I see that it was a time of mourning—I was mourning the loss of a two-year relationship. I didn't think the hurt would ever end.

Then, one morning I woke up, and the sick feeling in my stomach was gone. I knew then that I was going to be okay, that I no longer needed him. I began to live again. As I look back, the only thing he ever gave me that I'll be able to carry with me forever is the discovery of my inner strength. It will carry me through all the pain, all the hurt, and I will survive. I had it in me the entire time; I just couldn't quite find it. Thank you, Forrest.

I smile as I remember him, and then I gently slip my running shoes off and let go.

*Kendal Kelly*

*Reprinted with permission of Randy Glasbergen.*

# The Mirror

Her name was Jillene Jones. Jillene Jones! The alliteration just added to her mystique. To me, she was a character in the great American novel; the star of a blockbuster movie; the president of my world. She was truly the woman for me. I just knew it. Now if I could only find out something about her.

I asked around. I was Jim Rockford, Sherlock Holmes and Magnum P.I. all rolled into one. First clue: She was into heavy metal. Cool! Well, not so cool. Actually, I couldn't stand heavy metal. My hearing's a little sensitive, especially when the noise level exceeds that of a cannon blast. So what—who needs to hear? A lot of unwanted noise in this world anyway. I started listening to heavy metal.

Second clue: She liked to work out. I joined her gym. The machines in there looked like they were designed for some sort of bizarre psychological testing. Since there didn't appear to be any instruction manuals, I decided to stick to something simple like the treadmill. What fun! What a high! Actually, I felt like a hamster in a wheel. No matter. I was moving closer to my goal.

I decided to make some discreet inquiries among her

friends. The fates were truly on my side because not only did the woman of my dreams, Jillene Jones, know who I was, but she didn't find me totally repulsive. The die was cast. The plot was set. She would be mine. Even though the die was cast and the plot was set, etc., it took me another week to get up the courage to ask her out.

More research. Third clue: She loved Aramis. What an amazing coincidence! I loved Aramis, too—until I smelled it. Yikes. But surely if Jillene Jones loved Aramis, it must be an acquired taste. I bought the econo-size bottle of Aramis and began wearing it every day, everywhere I went. Every time I smelled my unique odor, I thought of Jillene Jones. And strangely enough, I began to notice a change in the way others perceived me. I always found a seat on the bus. If I had to stand in line, people would step aside and let me move to the front. Animals and small children fled in fear as I walked down the street. No matter, because I was on a quest.

A little more research and I would be ready. Clues four, five and six: She loved the color peach, bowling and sushi. I bought a peach-colored bowling shirt, found a bowling alley that served sushi and learned to throw strikes. Finally, I got up my courage and made the call. Luck was in my favor; the most popular head-banging band around was playing at our local college venue. I finagled great seats after draining my meager bank account. I put on my best Barry White baritone (which sounded more like Steve Urkel on a bad day) and asked Jillene Jones out on a date. She said yes.

The stars were aligned. All was right with the world. I saw my destiny and it had a name: Jillene Jones. The day of what would surely be the best night of my life began at the gym. Forty-five minutes on the hamster mill. I saw her out of the corner of my eye. Did she notice my Motley Crue T-shirt? I could only hope. The night finally arrived.

I put on my peach bowling shirt, drenched myself in Aramis, spiked my hair and threw in a fake nose ring for good measure.

Her eyes lit up when she saw that peach bowling shirt. "You know I was watching you today," she said. "You looked pretty cute on that treadmill. I didn't know you were a metal-head!" She saw the shirt!!! My plan was working!!! I walked her to my car and popped in a little Ozzy. She didn't seem to notice that the volume blew out all four of my speakers. She just grooved to the buzzing.

We went to the concert and I screamed at her for three hours until my ears felt like they were bleeding. Then mercifully the band finally stopped and we were able to leave. Sushi. She ordered some really slimy, expensive stuff that slid down my throat like dead goldfish. I had to pretend to use the restroom and sneak out to my car to gather all the spare change from the floorboards to pay the bill.

I drove her home and walked her to the door. She gave me a kiss that should be reserved for sailors going to sea. I had won her over. She was mine!!! Then she said the six words that I had never imagined, in my wildest fantasies, hearing: "Would you like to come in?"

Before my rational mind could answer, something came out from some part of my being that I heretofore did not know existed. "No," I said. I looked around, wondering where that had come from. She looked at me in disbelief and said good night.

I drove myself home in silence. Well, I really had no choice since my speakers were blown. I walked inside and went into the bathroom. I looked at myself in the mirror. There I was with spiky hair, a fake nose ring and wearing a peach bowling shirt. I reeked of dead fish and cheap cologne. My ears were ringing so loud I kept picking up the phone. Who was I? Jillene Jones. I remembered some

*National Geographic* special I had once seen on TV where the narrator described how lions hunt. "They become their prey." But starting a relationship shouldn't be a hunt. That didn't seem right.

I took off the peach bowling shirt and the nose ring. I rinsed out my hair and put on some mellow jazz. I went back into the bathroom and looked again in the mirror. There I was. Me. And somewhere out there was a woman for ME.

Every once in a while I pass an Aramis counter in a department store or smell someone wearing that potent scent and I think of Jillene Jones. The name still rolls off my tongue. I wish her well and hope she found that special peach-shirt-wearing, sushi-loving, treadmill-running, Aramis-drenched, bowling metal-head to love.

*Dan Clark*

# I Dare You!

On the first day of my second year at California State University at Sacramento, I saw the most gorgeous guy! He was standing alone in line at the cafeteria and looked out of place. Turning to my friends, I said, "I have to meet him!"

Challenging my spontaneity, my friends reached into their purses and came up with money for a bet. They then dared me to run up to him, pretend that I knew him and convince him that he knew me. Smiling, I turned and was off to meet the cutie pie.

"Dan, Dan!" I yelled as I ran up to him. "How are you? How's your mom?" He just stood there looking at me. I could tell that he was shy. I liked him immediately.

"I'm not Dan," he said, looking a little confused.

"Sure you are!" I countered. "You lived in Sierra Hall last year, third floor! You were Bob's roommate."

"No, I lived off campus last year," this sweet man replied, still not getting it. I turned and started to leave, and he began asking me a series of questions: "Do I know you from my mom's allergy clinic?" (I hate shots.) "Were you in the parrot class I took last summer?" (I like birds only slightly more than shots.) "Do you eat at Taco Bell? I work there." (Never.)

"Well," he said, "I know I'm not Dan, and I didn't live in Sierra Hall." He reached out his hand to mine. "My name is Tim, and I'm pleased to meet you anyway."

He invited me to his fraternity party that night. I composed myself and informed him that I did not go to fraternity parties. But as I watched him walk away, I had second thoughts. That afternoon, I took the money that I'd won from the bet and bought a black miniskirt. I was going to my first fraternity party.

When I arrived there, I was a little nervous. Would he be there? When I got to the front steps of the frat house, I looked up and saw Tim sitting at the top. He looked at me and smiled.

"I was hoping you would come. I've been waiting for you." I sat down next to him and we started talking. We talked all that night—and for the next three nights—until dawn. Four months later, he asked me to marry him. Four years later, we tied the knot. This year, we celebrated the fifteenth anniversary of the day we met.

Some nights when we are snuggling together, I'm reminded that I found my soul mate on a dare. Now and then, my husband asks, "Am I Dan or Tim tonight?" Having a special place in my heart for both of them, I always laugh and reply, "You decide!"

*April Kemp*

# The Love I'll Never Forget

*The moment you have in your heart this extraordinary thing called love and feel the depth, the delight, the ecstasy of it, you will discover that the world is transformed.*

J. Krishnamurti

My Minnesota hometown is a farming community of eight thousand people, tucked into the northwest corner of the state. Not a lot that is extraordinary passes through. Gretchen was an exception.

Gretchen was an Eickhof, a member of one of the town's wealthiest families. They lived in a sprawling brick place on the banks of the Red Lake River and spent summers at their vacation home on Union Lake, thirty miles away.

But there was nothing snooty about Gretchen. In sixth grade, she broke both legs skiing and for months had to be carried around by her father. After that, she taught herself to walk again. In high school, she tutored students less able than herself and was among the first to befriend new kids at school. Years later, she told me she had also been the "guardian angel" who left cookies and inspirational notes at my locker before my hockey games. She moved through the various elements of high-school society—farm kids, jocks and geeks—dispensing goodwill to all. Gretchen, the Central High Homecoming Queen of 1975, was clearly going places.

I knew her only well enough to exchange greetings when we passed in the halls. I was a good athlete and, in the parlance of the time, kind of cute. But I was insecure, especially around females. Girls were mysterious creatures, more intimidating than fastballs hurled high and tight, which may explain my bewilderment one midsummer night in 1977 when I bumped into Gretchen at a local hangout. I had just finished my freshman year at the University of North Dakota in nearby Grand Forks. Gretchen, whose horizons were much broader, was home from California after her first year at Stanford.

She greeted me happily. I remember the feel of her hand, rough as leather from hours in the waters of Union Lake, as she pulled me toward the dance floor. She was nearly as tall as I, with perfect almond skin, soft features and almost fluorescent white teeth. Honey-blond hair hung in strands past her shoulders. Her sleeveless white shirt glowed in the strobe lights, setting off arms that were brown and strong from swimming, horseback riding and canoeing.

Though not much of a dancer, Gretchen moved to the music enthusiastically, smiling dreamily. After a few dances we stood and talked, yelling to each other over the music. By the time I walked her to her car, Main Street was deserted. The traffic light blinked yellow. We held hands as we walked. When we arrived at her car, she invited me to kiss her. I was glad to oblige.

But where hometown boys were concerned, Gretchen was as elusive as mercury. As passionately as she returned some of my kisses that summer and the next, for her, I was part of the interlude between childhood and the more serious endeavors to come. I, however, was dizzy for her and had the bad habit of saying so. Each time I did, she pulled away from me. These were college summers, not the time for moony eyes and vows of undying devotion.

One night in 1978 when Gretchen and I were together, out of nowhere she spoke the words that guys in my situation dread above all.

"Tim," she said, "I think we should just be friends."

I told her I was tired of her games and was not as much of a fool as she thought. I stormed away. By morning, I had cooled off. I sent her some roses that day, with a note offering an apology and my friendship.

Gretchen and I started dating again about a month later. But this time I had learned my lesson. No more moony eyes. I could be as detached and aloof as the next guy. It worked beautifully, except that after a few weeks Gretchen asked, "What's wrong with you?"

"What do you mean, what's wrong?"

"You're not yourself," she said. "You haven't been for a long time."

"I know," I said, and let her in on my ruse. For the only time I remember, she became angry. Then she proposed a deal.

"You be who you are," she said, "and I won't go any-where, at least for the rest of the summer."

It was a bargain I quickly accepted. She was as good as her word.

Those weeks seemed golden, a bit unreal. One time as we said good night, I discarded the final wisp of my caution and told Gretchen that I loved her. She only smiled.

I came back from college to see her off to Stanford in mid-September. While Gretchen packed, I absently shot pool at her father's table. When she finished, we took a last walk around her family's horse pasture in the gathering September chill. I thought how dramatically our lives were about to diverge and was saddened. But more than anything, I was thankful for the fine, fun times we had spent over the last two summers.

Gretchen planned to find work in California next summer. For her, the serious part of life beckoned, and I knew what that meant.

"Good-bye," I said as we stood at her front door.

"Don't say 'good-bye,'" she replied. "Say 'see you later.'"

A month later, the last of the autumn leaves were falling, but the sky was a cloudless blue, the air crisp and invigorating. Classes were done for the day.

The telephone rang the second I stepped into my dorm room. I recognized Gretchen's friend Julie's voice on the other end of the line, and my heart soared. Julie was to be married the following month, and maybe Gretchen would be returning home for the wedding after all. But hearing the uncharacteristically quiet scratch of Julie's voice, I knew before she told me that Gretchen was dead.

The previous morning Gretchen had collected one of her birthday presents from a college friend: a ride in a small plane. Shortly after takeoff, the craft lurched out of control and pitched into a marsh. Gretchen and her friend were killed instantly.

"Gretchen's parents wondered if you would be a pallbearer," Julie said.

"I'd be honored," I heard myself reply. The word sounded strange even as it left my mouth. *Honored?* Is that what I felt?

I left my dormitory and walked aimlessly. I am told I sought out a campus priest, but eighteen years later I have no memory of that. *How does a person grieve?* I wondered, unable to cry.

The night after the funeral, I sat with my high-school buddy Joel in his Chevy Vega outside the restaurant where Gretchen's mourning friends planned to congregate.

Seeing him was the beginning of both my pain and my consolation, for as Joel spoke of Gretchen, his voice briefly failed. That tiny catch in my old friend's voice dissolved whatever stood between my sorrow and me. My torrents of grief were unleashed.

The next morning, Joel and I joined a procession from the Eickhofs' lakeside summer house into the nearby woods. Gretchen's sisters took turns carrying a small urn that contained her ashes. It was cool and sunny, and the fallen leaves crackled underfoot.

We came to a lone birch tree, its magnificent white bark standing out among the surrounding maples. Scratched into the trunk were the names of Gretchen, her father and her younger sister, as well as a date many years before.

Someone said a prayer. Gretchen's father placed the urn in the ground below the birch. Above us, wind rustled through newly barren branches.

I was among the last to leave. I emerged from the woods that day into a different world, where memories of first love linger but summers always end.

*Tim Madigan*

# Dear Girl

Dear Girl,

I feel that the time has come for me to have a girlfriend. I know you're out there somewhere. Don't worry, I'll find you.

And when I do, I hope that you will love me because I'm Derek, not because I'm Mike's younger brother. I hope you won't be embarrassed when my clothes don't match, or be annoyed when I want to watch the Lakers on ESPN, instead of *Party of Five*.

I hope that you will remember I play soccer, not football, and that I play midfield, not defense, and that every weekend I live with my dad.

I pray that you'll love me despite my tendency to forget birthdays, and if your parents invite me to dinner, please write their names really small on my hand so I can use it as reference.

Please know that I will constantly act strong and in control, but inside I am actually lost and confused. (Just don't tell my friends.) Please don't worry if I hurt myself skateboarding. Instead, be there to mend my wounds with kisses.

Understand that loving each other means being together, but not all of the time. We should never bail on our friends. Also understand that I may at times act jealous and overly protective, but only because *I* have insecurities not because *you* are doing anything wrong.

And if we fall out of love with one another, please don't hate me. And if I cry in front of you, please don't laugh at me. Please know that I am sensitive . . . in a manly, tough kind of way.

Please be honest with me without being hurtful. After all, I am a *boy*. And I promise to always be honest with you, because you deserve honesty. And I promise to open doors for you and buy your ticket when we go to the movies.

And no, you aren't fat, so please don't constantly ask. And you don't need makeup either. Oh, and don't be upset if you cut your hair and I don't notice. I will love you even in Levi's and a T-shirt.

I hope you don't think I'm asking too much of you. I just want to be happy making you happy. I'm coming to find you, so don't go anywhere. Stay where you are, whoever you are. And by the way, my name's Derek.

Yours Always,
Derek

*Derek Whittier*

# Dear Boy

Dear Boy,

I do not know who you are, or where or when we will meet, but I do hope it is soon.

I pray that when we meet and fall in love, you will love me, for me, and not hope for someone who is thinner or prettier. I hope you won't compare me to girls who may have brighter smiles. I hope that you will make me laugh, take care of me if I get sick, and be trustworthy.

I hope you will remember that I prefer daisies to roses, and that my favorite color changes with my mood. Please know that my eyes aren't blue, they're gray, with flecks of navy.

Please know that I might be too shy to kiss you first, but please don't be afraid to kiss me. I won't slap you or push you away. I'm sure your kisses will be perfect. When we go on a date, please don't stress about where to take me; what's important is that I'll be with you.

If I cry, please know it isn't because of you, just hold me close, and I'll heal quickly. And, if it is because of you, I'll heal just the same.

And if we decide to break up, please understand that I

may be bitter, but I'd like to be your friend if you'll let me. I promise to remember that you have feelings too, even though you'll never admit it, and when you are ready we'll have a friendship.

Please tell me if anything I do bothers you, or if something just doesn't sit right. I would like you to always be honest with me. If I have a bad day, I hope you will shower me with confidence and smiles.

I hope you don't think that I'm asking too much of you. I hope you understand that I'm a little bit nervous and very scared. I wish I could tell you how or when we will meet, and if we will be in love forever. Every relationship is a new game of cards, and . . . (sigh) . . . I've never been good at cards. But I will try my best to be kind and love you dearly for all that you are, without expecting too much from you. Thank you for listening; this is all that I ask.

Yours Always,
Sarah

*Sarah Bercot*

# 2

# ON FRIENDSHIP

*Some people come into our lives and quickly go. Some people stay for a while, leave footprints on our hearts, and we are never, ever the same.*

*Flavia Weedn*

# A Simple Christmas Card

*A friend is a gift you give yourself.*

Robert Louis Stevenson

Abbie, shy and reserved, started ninth grade in the big-city high school in the center of town. It never occurred to her that she would be lonely. But soon she found herself dreaming of her old eighth-grade class. It had been small and friendly. This new school was much too cold and unfriendly.

No one at this school seemed to care if Abbie felt welcome or not. She was a very caring person, but her shyness interfered with making friends. Oh, she had those occasional buddies—you know, the kind that took advantage of her kindness by cheating off her.

She walked the halls every day almost invisible; no one spoke to her, so her voice was never heard. It reached the point where she believed that her thoughts weren't good enough to be heard. So she continued to stay quiet, almost mute.

Her parents were very worried about her, for they feared she'd never make friends. And since they were divorced, she probably needed to talk with a friend very badly. Her parents tried everything they could to help her fit in. They bought her the clothes and the CDs, but it still didn't work.

Unfortunately, Abbie's parents didn't know Abbie was thinking of ending her life. She often cried herself to sleep, believing that no one would ever love her enough to be her real friend.

Her new pal Tammy used her to do her homework by pretending to need help. Even worse, Tammy was leaving Abbie out of the fun she was having. This only pushed Abbie closer to the edge.

Things worsened over the summer; Abbie was all alone with nothing to do but let her mind run wild. She let herself believe that this was all that life was cracked up to be. From Abbie's point of view, it wasn't worth living.

She started the tenth grade and joined a Christian youth group at a local church, hoping to make friends. She met people who on the outside seemed to welcome her, but who on the inside wished she'd stay out of their group.

By Christmastime Abbie was so upset that she was taking sleeping pills to help her sleep. It seemed as though she was slipping away from the world.

Finally, she decided that she would jump off the local bridge on Christmas Eve, while her parents were at a party. As she left her warm house for the long walk to the bridge, she decided to leave her parents a note in the mailbox. When she pulled down the door to the mailbox, she found letters already there.

She pulled the letters out to see who they were from. There was one from Grandma and Grandpa Knight, a couple from the neighbors . . . and then she saw one addressed to her. She tore it open. It was a card from one of the guys in the youth group.

*Dear Abbie,*

*I want to apologize for not talking with you sooner, but my parents are in the middle of a divorce, so I didn't have a chance to talk with anyone. I was hoping you could help me with some questions I have about divorced kids. I think we could become friends and help each other. See you at Youth Group on Sunday!*

*Sincerely your friend,*

*Wesley Hill*

She stared at the card for a while, reading it over and over again. "Become friends," she smiled, realizing that someone cared about her life and wanted plain, quiet Abbie Knight as a friend. She felt so special.

She turned around and went back to her house. As soon as she walked in the door, she called Wesley. I guess you could say he was a Christmas miracle, because friendship is the best gift you can give anyone.

*Theresa Peterson*

# Why Rion Should Live

*Believe that life is worth living and your belief will help create the fact.*

William James

High school didn't frighten me. Oh sure, the endless halls and hundreds of classrooms were overwhelming, but I took it in with all the pleasure of starting a new adventure. My freshman year was full of possibilities and new people. With a class of nearly two thousand new-comers, you just couldn't go wrong. So I, still possessing the innocence of a child concealed in a touch of mascara and lipstick, set out to meet them all.

Spanish One introduced me to Rion. By the student definition, he was a "freak": the black jeans, the well-worn Metallica shirts, the wallet chains, the works. But his unique personality and family troubles drew me to him. Not a crush, more of a curiosity. He was fun to talk to, and where interrupted whispering sessions left off, hours of phone conversations picked up.

During one of these evening conversations, "it," as we like to address the incident, unfolded. We were discussing the spectacular height of Ms. Canaple's over-styled bangs when I heard Rion's dad yelling in the background. "Hold on," Rion muttered before a question could be asked. I could tell that he was trying to muffle the receiver, but you could still hear the horror as if his room were a dungeon, maximizing the bellows. Then the line went dead.

Shaking, I listened to the flatline of the phone for a minute before gently placing it in its cradle, too scared to call back for fear of what I might hear. I had grown up in an ideal family setting: a mom and a dad and an older sister as a role model. This kind of situation took me by surprise, and I felt confused and helpless at the same time. A couple of tense hours later, after his father had gone to bed, Rion called me to apologize. He told me his dad had received a letter from his ex-wife, Rion's mom, saying she refused to pay child support. Having no other scapegoat, he stumbled into Rion's room in rage.

"I can't take this anymore. All the fighting . . . it's always there. . . ." His voice had trailed off, lost in painful thought. "All I have to do is pull the trigger, and it will be over."

"No!" I screamed. "Don't talk like that! You know you have so much to live for." It was becoming clearer every second how threatening the situation was. A cold, forced chuckle came from the other end of the line. "Yeah, right," was his response. We got off the phone, but only after promising to go right to sleep.

Sleep, however, was light years away from me. I was so worried and had a feeling I was Rion's only hope. He had told me repeatedly that it was hard to open up to anyone but me. How could someone not want to live? I could literally list the reasons why I loved waking up every morning. Frantically, I racked my brain for ways to convince Rion of this. Then the lightbulb clicked on. I took a piece of notebook paper and entitled it, "Why Rion Should

Live." Below, I began listing every reason I could think of that a person had to exist. What started as a few sentences turned into twenty, then thirty-two, then forty-seven. By midnight, I had penned fifty-seven reasons for Rion to live. The last ten were as follows:

48) Six feet of earth is pretty heavy.
49) They don't play Metallica in cemeteries.
50) Braces aren't biodegradable.
51) God loves you.
52) Believe it or not, your father loves you, too.
53) Spanish One would be so boring.
54) Two words: driver's license.
55) Satan isn't exactly the type of guy you want to hang out with for eternity.
56) How could you live without Twinkies?
57) You should never regret who you are, only what you have become.

Believing that I had done my best, I crawled into bed to await tomorrow's chore: saving Rion.

I waited for him at the door to Spanish the next day and handed him the paper as he walked in. I watched him from the opposite side of the room while he read the creased sheet in his lap. I waited, but he didn't look up for the entire period. After class, I approached him, concerned, but before I could say a word, his arms were around me in a tight embrace. I hugged him for a while, tears almost blinding me. He let go, and with a soft look into my eyes, he walked out of the room. No thank you was needed, his face said it all.

A week later, Rion was transferred to another school district so that he could live with his grandmother. For weeks I heard nothing, until one night the phone rang. "Sarah, is it you?" I heard the familiar voice say. Well, it was like we had never missed a day. I updated him on Ms.

Canaple's new haircut, and he told me his grades were much better, and he was on the soccer team. He is even going to counseling with his dad to help them build a stronger relationship. "But do you know what the best part is?" I sensed true happiness in his voice. "I don't regret who I am, nor what I've become."

*Sarah Barnett*

[EDITORS' NOTE: *Rion was lucky. Everyone isn't as fortunate. If you are depressed or thinking about hurting yourself, (or if you think any of your friends are in this situation),* please call for help, toll-free: **1-800-SUICIDE**. *Remember, you are not alone. People care and can help you.* **WE LOVE YOU!!**]

# She Told Me It Was Okay to Cry

*It takes a lot of understanding, time and trust to gain a close friendship with someone. As I approach a time of my life of complete uncertainty, my friends are my most precious asset.*

Erynn Miller

I saw her last night for the first time in years. She was miserable. She had bleached her hair, trying to hide its true color, just as her rough front hid her deep unhappiness. She needed to talk, so we went for a walk. While I thought about my future, the college applications that had recently arrived, she thought about her past, the home she had recently left. Then she spoke. She told me about her love—and I saw a dependent relationship with a dominating man. She told me about the drugs—and I saw that they were her escape. She told me about her goals—and I saw unrealistic material dreams. She told me she needed a friend—and I saw hope, because at least I could give her that.

We had met in the second grade. She was missing a

tooth, I was missing my friends. I had just moved across the continent to find cold metal swings and cold smirking faces outside the foreboding doors of P.S. 174, my new school. I asked her if I could see her Archie comic book, even though I didn't really like comics; she said yes, even though she didn't really like to share. Maybe we were both looking for a smile. And we found it. We found someone to giggle with late at night, someone to slurp hot chocolate with on the cold winter days when school was canceled and we would sit together by the bay window, watching the snow endlessly falling.

In the summer, at the pool, I got stung by a bee. She held my hand and told me that she was there and that it was okay to cry—so I did. In the fall, we raked the leaves into piles and took turns jumping, never afraid because we knew that the multicolored bed would break our fall.

Only now, she had fallen and there was no one to catch her. We hadn't spoken in months, we hadn't seen each other in years. I had moved to California, she had moved out of the house. Our experiences were miles apart, making our hearts much farther away from each other than the continent she had just traversed. Through her words I was alienated, but through her eyes I felt her yearning. She needed support in her search for strength and a new start. She needed my friendship now more than ever. So I took her hand and told her that I was there and that it was okay to cry—so she did.

*Daphna Renan*

# I Just Wanted to Be Skinny

I couldn't believe that I hadn't let myself see how awful Colleen had become. I was so ashamed of myself at that moment, staring at her in her size zero sundress draped loosely over her. She looked like a little girl swimming in her mother's clothes. It was as if I was seeing her for the first time. Her adorable round baby face had become so gaunt, and her once bright eyes had become dull and faded, now just slightly sunken in as if all her desire for life had been sucked out of her. I began to panic as my eyes frantically scanned the rest of her body. But it was no use. With every glance, I saw skin and bone where there should have been the beginnings of womanly curves. Everything about her was so tiny and frail that she reminded me of a twig that could be snapped with the blow of a harsh winter wind. I was overwhelmed with guilt. I was supposed to be her friend. I was supposed to keep her from doing things like this to herself. I had promised I would always be there for her. And right then, I wanted to run crying from the store because I knew I had failed. Instead, I just stood there next to her, unable to say anything, while she critiqued herself about how fat she looked and how tight the dress was. How had this happened?

I later found out it began in the eighth grade, which was the year when attention on being thin became emphasized. Diets became an obsession for many girls. There was a new one to try every week, each promising better results than the last. They were "in style" the same way green nail polish or jelly sandals were. Colleen was always insecure about being fat, which surprised me because she had such a healthy looking body. But seeing those stick-figured girls talk about their diets only perpetuated Colleen's insecurity.

How could I have been so dumb and so blind? How could I not have realized that her reasoning for all the missed school lunches were just excuses, that she hadn't conveniently just eaten before she came over? And all the times my friends and I invited her to eat with us, how could we not have seen the pattern in her continuous declines, saying she would love to come . . . another time?

Colleen's parents took her to see a doctor, and he confirmed everyone's worst fear: He diagnosed her as anorexic. It sounded so weird to hear her called that; even though everyone knew she was, no one had ever actually said it before. Colleen was anorexic. It was almost as if I had to say it to myself a couple of times before I could really comprehend it. She weighed only eighty-six pounds at a height of 5'4" when she was admitted, and the doctors said that had she continued the destructive pattern much longer, there was a good chance she could have died of a heart attack. Imagine that—dying of a heart attack at age fourteen.

The doctors and psychologists asked Colleen repeatedly, "What made you decide to stop eating?" And she always answered sincerely and simply, "I just wanted to be skinny." This reply frustrated them. I guess they expected to hear a huge psychological reasoning behind her anorexia, like pressure from her parents, school or sports. I'm not really sure what they wanted to hear, but they couldn't seem to accept that Colleen starved herself because she just wanted to be thinner.

It's been a little over a year now, and I'm proud to say that Colleen has only been back to the hospital once. She has worked incredibly hard to gain back her normal, stress-free life, and it's been a difficult struggle. But I know she will win this battle in the end.

It bothers me, though, that Colleen's struggle could have been prevented. What is it that makes girls feel like they must look like waifs before they are considered beautiful? Some people might blame the media, others may fault the girl's lack of self-confidence, or the parents for not providing better examples. Maybe it's a little of all three. If only there were a way to tell each young, impressionable girl that women are *supposed* to be different shapes, that it's all those dozens of unique figures that make our world beautiful. If only there were some way to tell them that it's this variety that makes every woman truly beautiful. Then, maybe, cases like Colleen's could be prevented.

*Laura Bloor*

# The Rift

I sit perched on the edge of my bed, faint smiles drifting across my face, as I sift through all my old photographs. My sleeves pushed up over my elbows, I dig down into all the old memories. I hold each memory briefly in my hands before dropping it onto the pile in my lap and searching for the next happy moment to remember. Each picture evokes feelings long gone, but deep within me. I'm not exactly sure what has prompted this sudden trip to my past, but I feel like I need to stop, and look back.

As I continue to relive the memories, I can't help but notice one photo in particular buried deep in the box. I pluck it from the sea of snapshots and hold it in my hands. The picture at first glance is lovely. The sun was shining with not a cloud to be seen in the bright blue canopy that hung high over my head. I was sitting with my arm around a happy-looking girl, her arm rested casually on my shoulders. As I focus in on the person's face, the warm smile that covers my face is replaced by an agitated frown. It is Amy Soule, my now ex-best friend. A terrible pang of regret flashes through me, and I feel the familiar constriction in my throat.

I'm not sure exactly how, or when our decline as friends started, but it started small. A simple crack that flourished in our awkward adolescence and shameful neglect. It began with simple differences in interest. She wanted to go to the mall and scout for guys, while I wanted to spend the evening watching old movies and talking about nonsense gossip. Suddenly after-school activities took up our usual time together and weekends were spent doing other things. Soon the only time I saw her was when we exchanged a hurried hello in the busy school halls between classes. A far cry from the whispered conversations behind my half-open locker at every spare moment. No more notes were passed behind the teacher's back, and my parent's phone bill became considerably cheaper. She found a new group of friends, and so did I. Before I had a chance to patch the crack between us, she moved away from me, causing the crack to become an uncrossable rift.

I tried to make excuses for not keeping in touch. I couldn't visit, it was too far and I couldn't ask Mom to drive me all that way. I even tried to convince my nagging conscience with the notion that people change, I matured, and that is why. I knew that was not the answer, but I was too nervous to pick up the phone and call. The rift grew too large to bridge. Amy had left, and she had taken a huge chunk of my heart with her.

I stand up and stretch my cramping limbs. Pulling myself back into the now, I let the picture fall from my hand onto my cluttered desk. I glance up at my calendar and remember that Amy's birthday is around the corner. In fact, we were born in the same room, two days apart. It had always been a good-natured joke between us that she was two days older than I. We started so close, and ended up so far. This bittersweet memory causes me to smile despite my feelings of regret. I suddenly have an idea. I hastily drop to my knees and begin to rummage through my desk drawers. At last I lay my hands on an old picture frame I have had around forever. I pick up the fallen photo of Amy and me, and snap it into the frame. I quickly pen a note, and for lack of anything better to say, I simply write,

*Happy Birthday Amy!*
*Erica*


I stick the piece of white paper under the edge of the frame and search for Amy's address. I hold the frame tightly in my arms. I am not going to let this golden chance slip through my fingers. It's not much, but it is a beginning and the space between us has already gotten smaller. Maybe this time I will be strong enough to build a bridge.

*Erica Thoits*
Teen People *contest winner*

# The Right Thing

The counselor was late for our appointment. I sat in one of the hard plastic chairs in her office that, despite a few squirming attempts to rearrange myself, continued to be uncomfortable. I glanced at the boy who sat beside me, my partner in crime. He looked upset and unsure, wounded by the decision that we had finally made out of desperation. Friends for many years, we now offered each other little comfort as we sat lost in our own thoughts and doubt.

My tingling nerves heightened my senses, and I took in everything around me. From the smell of freshly sharpened pencils to the sight of the overly organized desk, the room oozed with the aura of a disciplined junior high school counselor and I found myself again questioning our judgment in choosing this complete stranger to help save our friend.

She entered in a cloud of smiles and apologies for being late. Sitting down across from us, she looked at us expectantly. I felt as if she were waiting for us to announce that she had just won the lottery rather than tell the story of pain and frustration we had both been holding in for so long.

I was overcome for a moment by the fear that had nested in my stomach. It was hard to imagine how my best friend Suzie would react when she found out that the two people she had trusted most in the world had betrayed her. But selfishly, I was also concerned about how this betrayal would affect me. *Would she hate me? Would she even speak to me?* As much as the pain that she would feel, I contemplated whether or not I would have a best friend the next day.

"Why don't you begin, Kelly, by telling me why you're here?" the counselor suggested. I cast one more glance at my friend; his sad eyes confirmed that we were doing the right thing.

As I began to tell Suzie's story, my uncertainty gave way to a feeling of relief. Carrying the emotional burden of a friend who was slowly killing herself was a lot for a fourteen-year-old to handle, and more than I could stand any longer. Like an exhausted runner, I was passing on the baton for someone else to carry.

By way of my emotional and broken telling, Suzie's story came out. How we laughed at her strange habit of breaking all her food into tiny little pieces, not realizing that by splitting her food up, she could take more time to eat less. How we went along with her self-deprecating jokes about how overweight she was, without realizing that deep inside, she wasn't joking.

The guilt rose in my throat as I related fact after fact, knowing now that all these things should have made us aware months earlier that Suzie actually had a very serious problem. We had pushed it away as she had deteriorated a little at a time. It wasn't until it was almost too late that we had finally understood the big picture.

I explained that the depression that typically walked hand-in-hand with anorexia had closed in on Suzie a few weeks earlier. I had sat by her side, avoiding the sight of her dark-circled eyes and gaunt cheekbones as she told me that she now ate practically nothing at all, and that for no explainable reason, she would often cry for hours.

It was then that I too began to cry. I couldn't stop my tears as I explained how I hadn't known how to stop my friend's tears, either. She had reached a point that terrified me, and the terror in my voice was plain as I revealed the last thing I knew, the thing that had cemented my determination to tell someone: She was looking for an escape from the pain, sadness and feelings of inadequacy that were now constant for her. She thought that killing herself might be that way out.

My part completed, I sat back in disbelief. I had just poured out secret after secret that I had been told with the understanding that I would never speak them again. I had shattered the most sacred aspect of our friendship: trust. A trust that had taken time, love, and good and bad experiences to build had just been destroyed in ten minutes, broken out of helplessness, desperation and the burden that I could no longer bear. I felt weak. I hated myself at that moment.

So did Suzie.

She needed no explanation when she was called to the office. She looked at me, at her boyfriend sitting at my side, at the concerned look of the counselor. The tears of fury that welled up in her eyes said that she understood. As she began to cry out of anger and relief, the counselor gently sent Aaron and me back to class, shutting the door behind us.

I didn't go back to class right away, but instead walked the hallways of the school trying to make sense of the emotional ramblings going through my head. Though I had just possibly saved my friend's life, I felt less than heroic.

I still can recall the overwhelming sadness and fear that surrounded me, as I was sure that my actions had just cost me one of the best friends I'd ever had. But an hour later, Suzie returned from the counseling office, and with tears in her eyes, headed straight into my arms for a hug that I, perhaps even more than she, needed.

It was then that I realized that no matter how angry she was at me, she would still need her best friend to help her get through what was going to be a very difficult journey. I had just learned one of my first lessons of growing up and being a true friend—that it can be hard, and even terrifying, to do what you know is the right thing.

A year later, Suzie handed me my copy of her school picture. In it, she had color in her cheeks again, and the smile that I had missed for so long spread across her face. And on the back, this message:

> Kel,
>
> You were always there for me, whether I wanted you to be or not. Thank you. There's no getting rid of me now—you're stuck with me!
>
> I love you,
> Suzie

*Kelly Garnett*

# Choices

*Hold a friend's hand through times of trial,*
*Let her find love through a hug and a smile;*
*But also know when it is time to let go—*
*For each and every one of us must learn to grow.*

Sharon A. Heilbrunn

When I first met Molly, she instantly became my best friend. We enjoyed the same things, laughed at the same jokes and even had the same love for sunflowers.

It seemed like we had found each other at the right time. Both of us had been in different groups of friends that didn't get along or we didn't feel comfortable in. We were thrilled to find each other.

Our friendship grew very strong. Our families became friends, and everyone knew that wherever you found Molly, you found me, and vice versa. In fifth grade, we were not in the same class, but at lunch we both sat in nearby assigned seats and turned around to talk to each other. The lunch ladies did not like this. We were always blocking the aisle, talking too loudly and not eating our lunches, but we didn't care. The teachers knew we were best friends, but we were also a disturbance. Our big mouths got us into trouble, and we were warned that we would never be in the same classes again if we kept this up.

That summer, Molly and her brother were at my house quite often. My mom took care of them while their mom worked. We went swimming, played outside and practiced playing our flutes. We bought best-friend charms and made sure to wear them as often as possible.

Summer went by very quickly, and middle school began. As the teachers had warned us, we were not in the same classes. We still talked on the phone, went over to each other's houses, sang in choir and practiced our flutes together in band. Nothing could destroy this friendship.

Seventh grade started and, again, we were not in the same classes and could not sit near each other at lunch. It seemed as if we were being put to a test. We both made new friends. Molly started to hang out with a new group of people and was growing very popular.

We spent less time together, and we rarely talked on the phone. At school, I would try to talk to her, but she would just ignore me. When we did take a minute to talk, one of her more popular friends would come up and Molly would just walk away with her, leaving me in the dust. It hurt.

I was so confused. I'm sure she didn't know at the time how badly I felt, but how could I talk to her if she wouldn't listen? I began to hang around with my new friends, but it just wasn't the same. I met Erin, who was also a friend of Molly's. She was in the same situation I was with Molly. She and Molly had been close friends, and lately Molly had been treating Erin the same way as me. We decided to talk to her.

The phone call was not easy. Talking and saying how I felt was difficult. I was so afraid that I would hurt her feelings and make her angry. It was funny, though—when it was just the two of us talking on the phone, we were friends again. It was the old Molly.

I explained how I was feeling, and she did, too. I realized I was not the only one hurting. She was alone without me to talk to. What was she supposed to do, not make new friends? I didn't think about this before, but she was feeling left out by me and my new friends. There were times when I didn't even notice I was ignoring her. We must have talked for a long time, because once we were finished I had used a handful of tissues for my tears, and felt as if I had lifted a heavy weight off my heart. We both decided that we wanted to be with our new friends, but we would never forget the fun and friendship we had shared with each other.

Today, I look back on all of this and smile. Molly and I are finally in the same classes, and you know what? We still get in trouble for talking too loudly. Molly is not my best friend anymore, but more like my sister. We still enjoy the same things, laugh at the same jokes and share the same love for sunflowers. I will never forget her. Molly taught me something very important. She taught me that things change, people change, and it doesn't mean you forget the past or try to cover it up. It simply means that you move on, and treasure all the memories.

*Alicia M. Boxler*

"You're my friend, Katie, but we just don't
fight enough to be *best* friends."

# Friends Forever

It seemed as if Chrissy and I had been friends forever. Ever since we'd met on the first day of fourth grade, we had been inseparable. We did almost everything together. We were so close that when it came time to pick partners, it was just assumed that we'd pick each other.

In ninth grade, however, things changed. We had been in the same classes for the last five years, but now we were going to different schools. At first we were as good friends as ever, but eventually we found we had no time for each other. Slowly but surely, we were drifting apart. Promises were broken and important get-togethers postponed. I think both of us knew we were breaking apart, but neither of us wanted to admit it.

Then one day, I finally faced the fact that Chrissy and I weren't close anymore. We'd both grown up, and didn't have much in common any longer. I still missed her, though. We had shared five incredible years together—years I will never forget. Years I don't *want* to forget.

One day, as I was thinking of our great times together, I wrote a poem about our friendship. It was about letting go and growing up, but never forgetting friends.

I still talk to Chrissy sometimes, though now it's hard because we both have such busy schedules.

To this day, I still think of Chrissy as one of my best friends . . . even though by some definitions we aren't. But when I'm asked to list my friends, I never hesitate to add her name. Because as she would always say: "Real friends are forever." When I gave her this poem we both cried, for it's changes like these that make growing up so difficult.

## Changes

*"Friends forever," you promised.*
*"Together till the end."*
*We did everything with each other.*
*You were my best friend.*

*When I was sad, you were by my side.*
*When I was scared, you felt my fear.*
*You were my best support—*
*If I needed you, you were there.*

*You were the greatest friend,*
*You always knew what to say:*
*You made everything seem better.*
*As long as we had each other,*
*Everything would be okay.*

*But somewhere along the line,*
*We slowly came apart.*
*I was here, you were there,*
*It tore a hole in my heart.*

*Things were changing,*
*Our cheerful music reversed its tune.*
*It was like having salt without pepper,*
*A sun without its moon.*

*Suddenly we were miles apart,*
*Two different people, with nothing the same.*
*It was as if we hadn't been friends;*
*Although we knew deep in our hearts*
*Neither one of us was to blame.*

*You had made many new friends*
*And luckily, so had I*
*But that didn't change the hurt—*
*The loss of our friendship made me cry.*

*As we grow older, things must change*
*But they don't always have to end.*
*Even though it is different, now,*
*You will always be my friend.*

*Phyllis Lin*

# I Remember Gilbert

It's been seven months since I last saw the light in Gil's room. Mrs. Blithe waved at me from his bedroom window next door. I smiled, but inside I was numb.

I will never forget the first day I met Gil and his mom. I was seven, and Mom and Dad were taking me to our new house in the suburbs. My mother's employer transferred her, so we'd had to move and leave everything behind.

I missed my room and my best friends back home. I could not believe how my parents were torturing me. The idea of going to a new school was frightening. I didn't have any friends to talk to, and I did not want to make new friends either.

My grandparents were at the new two-story house to welcome us, and I noticed a lady hugging my mother. It turned out that Mrs. Blithe was Mom's best friend from high school and our new next-door neighbor.

Mom took me to my room upstairs, and I let myself fall onto the bed. I must have fallen asleep because the next thing I knew, it was getting dark. The huge window in my room was open, and I could hear loud music coming from outside. I looked out the window, and across from me was another window. A boy in dark clothes was looking through his telescope and into the glittering night sky. Right away, I noticed the white Christmas lights on his ceiling.

"Hi, I'm Gilbert Jim Jonathan Blithe. Call me Gil." He startled me.

"I'm Katharine Kennedy—Katie for short," I shouted back.

It was our beautiful beginning. I realized then and there that I liked this weird neighbor of mine. Gil was like a brother to me. We spent countless hours just talking and telling stories to each other. My dad put a fire escape ladder on my window. After that, Gil used it as an entrance to my room. Funny, he never used the front door. And he had lights on his ceiling because the stars and planets fascinated him.

When school started, we biked there together. He kept me safe and held me back from hurting myself. Sometimes, *I* had to keep *him* out of trouble. Afterwards, we would go to the park and play on the monkey bars. Most of the time my family's backyard was our playground, and the big acacia tree, which had boards nailed to its trunk, held our tree house. It was home, and nobody was allowed in there except us.

Summers passed and I turned thirteen. Gil gave me April blossoms. Then Mrs. Blithe told Mom and me that Gil was sick and needed a heart transplant. When I heard that, I was so distressed, I felt I needed one, too.

The hospital was gloomy. A white-walled prison that had disgusting food. Every day, Gil had to eat mushy-looking meals. I promised him I'd bring chocolate-covered peanuts the next day, and I knew I made him happier.

Whenever Gil sensed I was anxious or about to cry, he would tell me to look out my bedroom window. "Let the light in my room tell you I'm always there," he said softly. He always found a way to make me smile.

After a month in the hospital, Gil came home. It was the first time I had ever been in his room, and it felt peculiar. It was unexpectedly neat. After jumping onto his bed and throwing me a pillow, he said he missed his room. I said I missed him more. It troubled me that things might never be the same, but Gil was up and about after a couple of weeks. I knew he was all right when he climbed up to my room and ate pizza with me.

Before we knew it, Gil and I were in high school. School and girls kept him occupied, but he was always there. Despite our jobs, we spent sunny summers together. As usual, the days hanging out with him passed quickly. But then he got sick again.

During the first semester of our senior year, Gil was taken to the hospital for the second time. At first I thought it was a false alarm, but it was worse than I could imagine. All I could do was hope and pray that he would get better. The unlit room across from mine was the constant reminder of his being away. I visited him in the hospital as often as I could, even though I never knew what to say. To tell him that everything would be all right was a fallacy, yet it comforted us both.

Christmas was spent in a cold hospital room. He was determined that we would go to our graduation together. I assured him we would. I held his hand and looked into his eyes until they stopped looking into mine. No words were uttered; we both knew what we were feeling. He looked peaceful when he said his last good-bye.

I locked his face at that moment in my thoughts, but it wounded my soul. He went away even though I tried my best to keep time from slipping.

How could a friend, someone who was with me and kept me happy, be the one person who would leave me now, forever? There was no one now to console me.

Now, as I stood looking at his bedroom window and

the stars and planets on his ceiling, I knew he would always be there—in my room, in my heart and in my memories. I wiped away the tears on my cheek, and I saw a little boy waving at me. Until this day, I cannot figure why I could not say "I love you" to Gil, even at the last second. Maybe because I knew he felt the same way.

I'm leaving for college soon, and I am sad he won't be there to laugh at my jokes or comfort me when I'm blue. But because of a little boy looking through a telescope into the infinite night sky, I now know that friendship goes beyond time. I will always remember Gilbert, and the light of his love tells me he's always there.

*April Joy Gazmen*

# Colorful Shades of Gray

Moths are very ugly creatures. At least that is what I always thought until a reliable source told me otherwise. When I was about five or six years old, my brother Joseph and I stayed overnight at our Aunt Linda's house, our favorite relative. She spoke to us like adults, and she always had the best stories.

Joseph was only four years old and still afraid of the dark, so Aunt Linda left the door open and the hall light on when she tucked us into bed. Joe couldn't sleep, so he just lay there staring at the ceiling. Just as I dozed off to sleep, he woke me up and asked, "Jennie, what are those ugly things near the light?" (I had always liked that he asked me questions because I was older and supposed to know the answers. I didn't always know the answers, of course, but I could always pretend I did.) He was pointing to the moths fluttering around the hall light. "They're just moths. Go to sleep," I told him.

He wasn't content with that answer or the moths near his night light, so the next time my Aunt walked by the door he asked her to make the ugly moths go away. When she asked why, he said simply, "Because they're ugly and scary, and I don't like them!" She just laughed, rubbed his head, and said, "Joe, just because something is ugly outside doesn't mean it's not beautiful inside. Do you know why moths are brown?" Joe just shook his head.

"Moths were the most beautiful insects in the animal kingdom. At one time they were more colorful than the butterflies. They have always been helpful, kind and generous creatures. One day the angels up in heaven were crying. They were sad because it was cloudy and they couldn't look down upon the people on earth. Their tears fell down to the earth as rain. The sweet little moths hated to see everyone so sad; they decided to make a rainbow. The moths figured that if they asked their cousins, the butterflies, to help, they could all give up just a little bit of their colors, and they could make a beautiful rainbow.

"One of the littlest moths flew to ask the queen of the butterflies for help. The butterflies were too vain and selfish to give up any of their colors for either the people or the angels. So, the moths decided to try to make the rainbow themselves. They beat their wings very hard and the powder on them formed little clouds that the winds smoothed over like glass. Unfortunately, the rainbow wasn't big enough so the moths kept giving a little more and a little more until the rainbow stretched all the way across the sky. They had given away all their color except brown, which didn't fit into their beautiful rainbow.

"Now, the once-colorful moths were plain and brown. The angels up in heaven saw the rainbow and became joyous. They smiled, and the warmth of their smiles shone down on the earth as sunshine. The warm sunshine made the people on earth happy, and they smiled, too. Now every time it rains the baby moths, who still have their colors, spread them across the sky to make more rainbows."

My brother sank off to sleep with that story and hasn't

feared moths since. The story my aunt told us had been gathering dust in the back corners of my brain for years, but recently came back to me.

I have a friend named Abigail who always wears gray clothes. She is also one of the most kind and generous people I've ever met. When people ask her why she doesn't wear more colors, she just smiles that smile and says, "Gray is my color." She knows herself, and she doesn't compromise that to appease other people. Some may see her as plain like a moth, but I know that underneath the gray, Abigail is every color of the rainbow.

*Jennie Gratton*

# My Best Friend Mike

*A friend is one who knows you and loves you just the same.*

Elbert Hubbard

"Hi. It's Mike . . ."

"Hi, Mike, what's the matter?" Mike had been going through a lot lately, and it was not unusual for him to sound upset.

"I need to tell you something, but I'm not sure if I should," he said. Curiosity got the best of me, and I convinced him to let me in on his big secret. "I can't tell you on the phone. Come over." I walked for five minutes around the block, rang his doorbell and followed his mother's instructions to go up to his room.

Mike had been my best friend for the past two years. At first I thought he was weird. We met during our freshman year of high school and soon became inseparable. The summer after that year was the highlight of our friendship. I never had more fun with any other person. We spent every night and every day together. Time flies when you are having fun, however, and we soon found ourselves back in school. I began to notice a change in Mike. The fun ceased, and I felt a strain in our friendship.

Mike was suffering from depression, and I could not understand why. He seemed to have everything going for him. He was doing well in school, there were no problems at home, and he had many friends who loved him. I soon found myself spending every weekend in his bedroom, trying to convince him to cheer up. Nothing seemed to work. His parents became worried and decided to seek professional help.

Mike began to take medication to counteract his depression, and things seemed a little better, but they were not what they used to be. I was still clueless as to what had been causing this change in his behavior. I did not want to give up on my true best friend, so I continued spending painful hours trying to drag him out of his house.

It was one of those weekends, and there I was, sitting on his bed, waiting to hear what he had to say. I had a sense that he was about to tell me something serious. There was a strange look in his eyes, and he would not focus them on me. The silence was overbearing. He finally looked up at me.

"I'm gay." It hit me like a bolt of lightning. I was shocked. "Okay" was all I managed to utter. Silence followed for minutes afterward.

It took some getting used to, but I decided right then and there that I was not going to lose my best friend over it. Mike seems to be back to his normal self these days. We're seniors now, and I still spend a large portion of my time with him and his friends.

A smile comes to my face every time I think back to the first day we met, and the first thought that came to my mind as I approached the bus stop that day: *Who is that weird kid?* That weird kid is my true best friend, Mike, and there is nothing weird about him.

*Brian Leykum*

# My Perfect Friend

Sometimes people look at me like I'm strange. I catch them staring out of the corner of my eye and shudder. Their sideways glances pass through me, and I feel judged, unaccepted. My best friend, Mariah, never looks at me that way, though. Even though we are opposites— I spend my time in the world of books, escaping into other stories, while she spends hers in the world of boys and crushes—we have always gotten along perfectly. Somehow, our differences just seem to work well to create a relationship of comfort and acceptance.

On our first day of high school, Mariah and I walked into school together. It was intimidating, so I was glad that I had Mariah at my side. As we turned the corner toward our first class, we both saw him. He was beautiful. We giggled like little girls and followed him. When we lost sight of him, we both sighed with regret, wishing he had passed our way.

After school, Mariah and I waited at the bus stop together, discussing the day's events, eating whatever snack was left over from our lunch that day, and laughing. In mid-sentence, I looked over, and there he was, standing right next to us! I threw my half-eaten banana to the side and fiddled nervously.

Although I'm painfully shy, Mariah doesn't have that problem. As I stood petrified by his looks, she walked boldly up to him and asked him his name. "Jonathan," he said, while he ran a hand through his hair, brushing it out of his pale blue eyes. That is when my infatuation began, even though I knew nothing about him. And for the first time in our whole lives, Mariah and I had the same crush.

"So, where are you from . . . Jonathan?" Mariah asked, emphasizing his name. As the bus pulled up and we boarded, I caught Mariah's eye. She winked, and I giggled. Jonathan sat across from me on the bus, and as he sat, he smiled. I awkwardly attempted to smile back.

That began the routine that I followed for about a week: seeing him in the hall, nervously sitting near him on the bus, and calling Mariah each night to reconstruct every detail. Our school had a dance planned, and the date was approaching. Mariah was determined to go with Jonathan, but she had a list of guys, just in case he didn't work out. I laughed, the chances of Jonathan asking me were slim to none, but it was fun to fantasize.

Then, one afternoon, we boarded the bus in the same fashion, hoping to sit as close to Jonathan as possible. But this afternoon was different. I didn't have to try to sit near him, for he sat right down beside me. I caught Mariah's eye and shot her a quizzical look. I thought to myself, *No one has liked me before, what is this guy doing?*

Then, my question was answered. He leaned over to me and whispered, "Hey, how about you let me take you to the dance on Friday?" It was more a statement than a question. I nearly choked on my gum.

I barely squeaked out my reply, "Yeah, sure, I guess . . . I mean, if you want to."

He smiled and said, "Cool."

Without words, Mariah motioned for me to get off at her stop. I quickly took inventory of the situation: the same guy who had been plaguing my thoughts just asked me out. I was on cloud nine. We remained calm until the bus was out of sight, and then, as the coast became clear, we grabbed onto each other and started jumping up and down. For once, I didn't feel so different. Mariah screeched, "Danielle, this is s-o-o-o-o-o cool!"

"I know. Was I shaking?" I replied.

She gave me a hug. "No. You were so calm, you did great." We split at the road and left it at that. I had done great.

The night of the dance, I was frantic. Desperately trying to apply my makeup in a hurry while talking to Mariah on the phone at the same time, I heard my mother yell that I was going to be late. Soon Mariah's parents dropped her off.

On our way to the dance, we met up with Mariah's date, Ben. When we reached the school, Jonathan wasn't there yet, so I waited outside and motioned for Mariah and Ben to go on ahead while I waited. I looked up and saw him. There he stood, with those pale blue eyes, that soft hair, that smooth skin and that sweet smile. There he stood, but . . . with another girl! He wasn't alone, and he definitely wasn't waiting for me.

I hid myself behind a tree. *How could I have been so stupid?* I should have known it was too good to be true. He was popular, and I wasn't. I let myself feel ugly and undesirable. But worst of all, worse than the embarrassment and the shame, I felt heartbroken.

I made my way out from behind the tree, just in time to see their backs as they entered the dance together. I walked home and into my room, ignoring my mother's questions of why I had returned so early. Sitting alone on my bed, I was plagued by a voice in my head, the voice that told me I was ugly and unloved.

Later, my phone rang. It was Mariah. I knew she wasn't calling to torture me with the dance details, but, rather, to comfort me. This was my first time playing in her world, and I had been hurt. She knew that, and her soothing words helped mend my aching heart and silence that voice in my head that told me I wasn't good enough. Maybe Jonathan didn't think I was good enough, but who cared? Mariah reminded me that there would always be other guys. She told me I was beautiful, and most of all, that I was loved. The self-deprecating voice quickly faded. Mariah and I may be different, even worlds apart, but she accepts me for who I am, and she is my perfect friend.

*Danielle Eberschlag*

# Sometimes Things Are Never the Same

*I wish they would only take me as I am.*

Vincent van Gogh

Michelle and I had been best friends since the fourth grade. She was a beautiful person inside and out, one of the kindest I'd ever met. We were like paper and glue—completely inseparable.

When we began junior high, the new social life was a tough adjustment. But our friendship endured, and we were there for each other. I took comfort in the fact that I could tell her anything and always trust her.

Sixth grade passed, as did seventh, and soon eighth grade was upon us. It was that year that things slowly started to change between Michelle and me. I became a social butterfly, fluttering around to different cliques of friends, discussing the hottest gossip and relishing my new categorization as "popular." Although I made many new friends that year, I still loved Michelle and wanted her to hang out with my new, fairly large social group. I attempted to drag her along to my social gatherings, but

I soon noticed the disapproving looks and whispers about Michelle—a clear message that she was not "cool enough" to hang out with us.

My new, so-called friends made up lies and rumors about Michelle in order to ruin our friendship. And somewhere along the way, I fell into their trap. I started to believe that I shouldn't be friends with Michelle just because my other friends didn't like her.

One night, one of my new friends, Jamie, came over after school. I was thrilled that she wanted to come over to my house and spend time with me. After a couple of hours of laughing and having a great time, Michelle's name came up in our conversation. Slowly, a mischievous grin formed on Jamie's face. Remembering that Michelle was madly in love with a boy named Zach, Jamie ordered that I tell Michelle that Jamie was going out with Zach, and then rub it in her face. Afraid that my new friends would dislike me if I refused, just like they did Michelle, I picked up the phone, dialed Michelle's number and blurted it out to her. She was more sad, heartbroken and furious than I'd expected, and as I listened to her hysterically cry over the phone, I remembered how close we used to be. At that moment, I realized how much I treasured her friendship, and the cruelty of my actions sunk in. Needing to think about what I had just done, I got off the phone.

I soon called Michelle back and told her the truth. Zach was not going out with Jamie, and I was deeply sorry that I decided to betray her. I was sorry for not being there for her in the last few months, and I was sorry for letting my friends pressure me into situations like these. I wanted to be her best friend again. But she was not as forgiving as I had hoped. "It's not that easy," she said solemnly.

For the next couple of weeks, I did everything I could to win back Michelle's friendship. I sent her a thousand apology notes, I gave her pictures of the two of us, and I called her every night. I even stopped hanging out with my new group of friends who had been so cruel to Michelle. They weren't true friends anyway.

One night, I was sitting on my bed doing homework when I heard the doorbell ring. Unsure of who was at the door, I opened it tentatively, and there stood Michelle. I was shocked. "I forgive you," she said. "I wanted to let you know."

"Really?" I responded excitedly. "So, do you want to come in? Maybe you could sleep over, and we can talk."

"No, I can't. I don't want to," she said.

"Well, maybe we can catch a movie this weekend," I said with a hint of desperation.

"No," she answered.

"I thought you forgave me, Michelle," I said, unable to hide the disappointment in my voice.

"I do forgive you, but what you did changed what we used to be and what we are now. There is still a hole in my heart from what you did; it will never be the same."

She turned away. "I'll see ya around," she said, without looking back.

Every once in a while, Michelle and I run into each other at school, and she waves without saying a word. I always held out hope that our friendship would rekindle. But it hasn't, and things between us will never be the same. I lost my best friend, and it changed my heart forever. I wish I could undo the damage and take back what I have done. Never again will I let the influences of others get in the way of genuine friendships. I owe that to Michelle.

*Celine Geday*

# The Birth of an Adult

*The ultimate measure of a man is not where he stands in moments of comfort and convenience, but where he stands at times of challenge and controversy.*

Martin Luther King, Jr.

The doctors started to rush into the room. The delivery was going smoothly, but to me it felt like hysteria. The walls were a chalky gray like the wall of a jail cell. It wasn't the best setting for Jamie's labor, but it would have to do. Jamie was only a seventeen-year-old junior in high school. And now she was giving birth. She lay back in pain. Her only movements consisted of shaking her head from side to side, in an effort to escape the pain.

I took Jamie's hand, comforting her and trying to soothe her agony. Her eyes opened, and she looked at me. Our eyes met, and suddenly I felt every emotion I have ever known. I always knew Jamie would challenge me to better myself; however, I didn't think it would entail being her sidekick during her pregnancy.

All this began on the afternoon of New Year's Eve, 1997.

I sat in Jamie's basement awaiting the urgent news she had to tell me. She collapsed onto the couch and told me how she had broken up with her boyfriend, Eric, who had left the country to study abroad. This came as something of a relief, although I did my best not to show it. I didn't think Eric, or any other guy she had dated, was good enough for her. Okay, I'll admit it, I was—how should I put it—a little jealous. But I'd convinced myself we were better off as friends, anyway. And now she needed one.

Then the real news came: She was six weeks pregnant. Tears rolled down her face as she told me. I sat in shock and disbelief. The words were not registering in my head. She reached out and gave me a hug, which must have lasted only a few seconds but seemed like hours. My arms were still at my sides. We talked for a little while, and then I left her house and drove around in my car. I was in shock. I was upset about her lack of birth control because this whole ordeal could have been prevented. I was too young to deal with her pregnancy. Being a seventeen-year-old and a junior in high school was confusing enough without dealing with my own real-life afterschool special.

That evening I arrived at a party to drink my worries away. The air was filled with smoke and the partygoers reeked of alcohol. I could not take the atmosphere for long, so I left. I went to Jamie's house and stood on her front porch staring at the front door. *What should I do?* I asked myself. My foot started to turn from the door, but my hand reached out and pushed the doorbell. I wanted to run and go back to the party. I wanted to have fun this New Year's Eve. Suddenly, the door opened and Jamie stood in the doorway with her head down. "You can't spend New Year's Eve by yourself," I blurted out. She smiled, and we hugged in the doorway. This symbolized the beginning of the new journey that lay ahead for us. That night, we sat and laughed like usual while watching

Dick Clark ring in the New Year. After that night, my life would change. I wouldn't be a crazy teenager anymore. I would become a young adult.

Weeks passed and Jamie told her parents about the pregnancy. She and her parents made the decision to go through with the pregnancy, but to give the baby up for adoption. My parents talked with her parents and offered their support, almost like they were discussing our marriage; Jamie and I were growing and maturing together.

During her first trimester, I found myself at Jamie's house every day after school giving her a foot massage while she relaxed and watched her soap opera. She wasn't able to walk very much. I made snacks for her and enough food runs to Taco Bell to last us both a lifetime. My friends were not considerate about what I was going through. While I was busy helping a friend, they were busy making fun of me. They would call Jamie's house wondering what I was doing. They already knew, but they just wanted to poke fun. At school, the jokes surfaced like, "Gonna be a good daddy?" and "What are you doing this weekend . . . Lamaze class?" I shrugged them off and ignored them. I went on with my daily chores and focused on Jamie. I tried to make her life as easy as possible.

Later, one Saturday afternoon as I was catching up on sleep, Jamie called.

"Did you want to do something today?" she asked.

"What did you have in mind?" I replied.

"I want you to help me choose the baby's family," she said.

My ears turned hot, and I felt uneasy. But I told her I would pick her up. As I drove to her house, I thought about how much I had changed. I was more responsible, but I still considered myself a child. I felt I had no business choosing a path for an unborn baby. I groaned and doubted myself. I arrived at her house and helped her into the car.

As we were driving to the adoption agency, Jamie pointed out to me, "You're not speeding."

It occurred to me that I was no longer a crazy driver, thinking about how quickly I could get from one place to the other. I was now responsible for making sure we got there safely.

"I'm driving for three people now," I told her.

We arrived at the agency and were seated in a conference room. Fifty manila folders lay on the table, each containing a couple. One of these folders would be the lucky one. One of these couples would be the parents of Jamie's baby. The counselor and Jamie and I went through each folder discussing their spiritual, psychological, financial, genealogical and emotional backgrounds. I began browsing through one folder, which read "Jennifer and Ben." The folder was more like a booklet chronicling their life with pictures of where they'd been, who they are and who they wanted to become. Their explanation of why they wanted a baby caught my attention. This couple intrigued me. We kept narrowing down the couples, until we were down to two couples: Jennifer and Ben and Jamie's pick. We discussed both couples, finally agreeing on Jennifer and Ben.

As we were getting ready to leave, I took a picture of Jennifer and Ben out of the folder and slipped it into my jacket pocket without Jamie noticing. I wanted to have a record of them before their life was to be changed forever. I put on my jacket, and we left the agency.

It was a miserably cold spring day. After helping Jamie into the car, I walked around the car and a warm breeze struck me. I stood by the trunk of my car feeling the summer draft. I couldn't understand it. It was a cold day, but the wind was warmer than an August breeze. It felt like a sign, an anonymous thank you. We drove away and I thought about the decision we made. I thought about the families we didn't pick. How much longer would it take for them to receive the gift of a child?

A few weeks later we met Jennifer and Ben for the first time. They impressed me. They were a close couple, and I knew they would apply the love they had for each other to their child. Jamie told them that I urged her to pick them, which made this meeting even more overwhelming for me. I tried not to show it, though, as we bonded almost immediately. They urged Jamie to take a childbirth class so she would be ready for all of the upcoming events. She needed a partner for the class, so I agreed. She signed up for a class, and every Tuesday night Jamie and I attended together.

The first class was awkward. I had never felt so out of place in my entire life. Jamie and I sat down together, trying to ignore the seven married couples staring at us. We were too young and too ignorant to be going through a pregnancy and a birthing class. Nevertheless, Jamie had to do it, and I would not let her be alone. After time, we all began to bond and develop a tremendous amount of respect for each other. Everyone realized what a struggle it was for us to get this far.

During the "Mom Time," the dads and I sat outside talking about the babies' futures. The dads talked about pee-wee football, mutual funds and insurance. I talked about Shakespeare and Geometry. I was out of place, for sure, but I realized there is more to giving birth than nine months and a doctor. So much freedom was sacrificed, replaced with a huge amount of responsibility. The dads respected me and praised me for my humanity towards a friend, not to mention my maturity. I still just couldn't believe I was sitting around talking about babies. I wanted to be innocent again. I wanted to drive my car fast and go to parties, but more important responsibilities called me. I was maturing.

I was getting ready for school one morning when Jamie called me from the hospital. "Um, do you want to get over here?" she asked.

"It's only another sonogram. Besides, I can't miss class," I said.

"Well, I think you might want to get over here, 'cause I'm having the baby!" she shouted.

I ran out of the house and darted to the hospital. At the hospital, the nurse handed me scrubs and I entered her room. She lay there as I sat next to her.

"Well this is it," she said. "Nine months, and it's finally here." She grimaced with pain and moved her head back and forth. Doctors were in and out of her room every two seconds with medication. She was about to give birth. After a few hours of getting Jamie settled, she was fully dilated.

"Okay, here we go. When I say 'push,' you push," the doctor said.

She acknowledged him while grabbing my hands and nodding her head quickly several times. Jamie gave three pushes of strength and, with one final push, she breathed life into a new baby. The doctors cut the umbilical cord and cleaned the baby off. I sat in awe. Every possible human emotion struck me like a freight train.

"It's a boy," they exclaimed.

I smiled, and tears of joy ran down my cheek. No more fear, no more chores, just pure happiness. The baby was handed to Jamie, and she spent the first moments of the baby's life holding him in her arms. She looked up at me, and I looked at her.

"You did it, kiddo," I whispered in her ear.

The doctors left with the baby to run tests and weigh him. Jennifer and Ben came in with the birth certificate. "What's his name?" Ben asked. Jamie motioned for him to come closer, and she whispered in his ear. Ben smiled and went into a different room. I walked outside to get a drink.

I came back in a few minutes and saw the completed birth certificate. It read Blake Jonathan.

I smiled and cried. The doctors brought Blake back in. They passed Blake to me, and I held new life in my hands. I thought about the dads in birth class. Then I thought about Blake's future. His first steps, peewee football games, the first day of school and his first broken heart. All the dads' talk finally caught up with me. Jennifer and Ben looked at me and smiled. Tears rolled down their cheeks. I gave Blake to Ben and received a gracious hug from Jennifer. They were his parents now. They were his keepers. Jamie still lay there, crying but filled with delight. I went over to her and gave her a big hug.

"Everything okay?" she asked.

"Fine. Absolutely fine," I whispered, and kissed her softly on her forehead. I would never be the same.

*Jonathan Krasnoff*

# My Star

My head plopped down right in the middle of my open calculus book.

*Maybe the information will just work its way into my brain through osmosis.* I was beginning to think that was my only hope for learning this material. I felt like I was on a different planet. *How could this seem so foreign to me?* Of all the classes that I had taken so far in college, I could not make this one work. I couldn't even lay out a logical study plan. *What now?* I pondered, with my head down on my desk in the middle of class.

When I lifted my head off the page, unbeknownst to me, a Post-it Note had stuck to my bangs. There was a pretty picture. I turned to face the guy next to me; he laughed and reached over to pull the note off my bangs in hopes of retrieving some of my dignity.

That was the beginning of a great friendship. The guy who was willing to pull a sticky note off my hair would soon become my calculus savior. I didn't know it at the time, but Matt Starr was the literal "star" of the class. I was convinced he could teach it. And, as luck would have it, he was willing to help me.

He lived in an apartment just off campus, and I would go over there for tutoring. In exchange for his help, I cleaned his apartment and brought over bribe treats. Cookies, snacks, even dinner sometimes. He was so smart and would get so involved in the material. He would say, "Don't you realize that this is the stuff that the universe is made of?" Not *my* universe. I told him that my universe was made up of child development and psychology classes and an occasional shopping mall, not equations like this. He would just laugh and persevere. He was convinced that he could get me to understand this material, and in a way he was right. He was so crystal clear in his understanding that I began to see it through his eyes.

Matt and I started spending more time together. We would take long walks, go to movies—when he wasn't forcing me to study. I helped him put together a very hip wardrobe, and he taught me how to change the oil in my car—something every girl should know. When I brought home a B in calculus, we celebrated for three days.

Throughout college we stayed as close as a guy and a girl who are friends can be. We dated, only briefly, but the chemistry we shared was more like that of a brother and sister. We did, however, help each other through our other various and odd relationships; and when it looked hopeless, like neither one of us would ever find a mate, we took the next logical step—we got a puppy. Having rescued it from the pound, we called this little shepherd mix Tucker. We had been spending so much time together that when I moved out of my dorm, Tucker, Matt and I became roommates.

The day he came home and told me he was sick, it was raining. It rained that entire week, almost as if the world was mirroring our tears. Matt had AIDS.

Two weeks later, he was in the hospital with pneumocystis. The hows and the whys didn't matter when we were both spending every moment trying to get him better. Between taking final exams, figuring out medications, visiting healers and making Matt drink wheatgrass juice, I was exhausted—but he was getting better.

Matt and I decided that we were going to make the time either one of us had left on this planet count. By the time we arrived at our senior year, I had lived life more fully than I had in all my twenty previous years. When we graduated, we all proudly wore our caps and gowns, Tucker included. Two months later, Matt went home to Minneapolis to live with his family.

Life continued; we e-mailed each other voraciously. I sent him tons of JPEG images of Tucker and his antics, and we went back and forth recounting stories of our lives.

Matt lived only two years more. When I got the news that he had been taken to the hospital, I flew out to be with him. By then, he had fallen into a coma from which he would never awaken. At the funeral, I artfully arranged a yellow Post-it Note in my hair and put one of Tucker's favorite chew toys in the casket.

One night, about a year after Matt's funeral, Tucker and I were driving in the hills of Mulholland. Suddenly, I smelled something so very familiar to me, and yet I couldn't place it. It was a lovely cologne-like fragrance. Then Tucker began acting peculiar.

"What's the matter, boy, did you smell it, too? What is that smell? I just can't place it."

Stopped at a red light, I looked up at the night sky and Tucker barked. What I saw next amazed me. It was a shooting star. A star! Of course, Matt Starr! It was his cologne I smelled.

"Is our friend trying to say hello and tell us he's okay?" Tucker started wagging his tail furiously. Whether it was a sign or not, I felt the warmest and most secure feeling I've felt while thinking about Matt since his death. The giant gaping void that was created when he left was suddenly filled with that warm love the two of us always shared. He wasn't gone, he was right here with me, as he always would be.

Suddenly and quite clearly, I understood how it all fit together. The universe, my friend and his beloved calculus.

*Zan Gaudioso*

# 3

# ON LOVE AND KINDNESS

*Kindness in words creates confidence.*
*Kindness in thinking creates profoundness.*
*Kindness in giving creates love.*

*Lao-tzu*

# Bright Heart

*The greatest gift is a portion of thyself.*

Ralph Waldo Emerson

Last year around Halloween, I was invited to participate in a carnival for Tuesday's Child, an organization that helps children with the AIDS virus. I was asked to attend because I'm on a television show; I went because I care. I don't think that most of the kids recognized me as a celebrity. They just thought of me as a big kid who came to play with them for the day. I think I liked it better that way.

At the carnival they had all kinds of booths. I was drawn to one in particular because of all the children that had gathered there. At this booth, anyone who wanted to could paint a square. Later that square was going to be sewn together with the others, to make a quilt. The quilt would be presented to a man who had dedicated much of his life to this organization and would soon be retiring.

They gave everyone fabric paints in bright, beautiful colors and asked the kids to paint something that would make the quilt beautiful. As I looked around at all the squares, I saw pink hearts and bright blue clouds, beautiful orange sunrises and green and purple flowers. The pictures were all bright, positive and uplifting. All except for one.

The boy sitting next to me was painting a heart, but it was dark, empty, lifeless. It lacked the bright, vibrant colors that his fellow artists had used.

At first I thought maybe he took the only paint that was left and it just happened to be dark. But when I asked him about it, he said his heart was that color because his own heart felt dark. I asked him why and he told me that he was very sick. Not only was he very sick, but his mom was very sick also. He said that his sickness was not ever going to get better and neither was his mom's. He looked straight into my eyes and said, "There is nothing anyone can do that will help."

I told him I was sorry that he was sick and I could certainly understand why he was so sad. I could even understand why he had made his heart a dark color. But . . . I told him that it isn't true that there is nothing anyone can do to help. Other people may not be able to make him or his mom better . . . but we can do things like give bear hugs, which in my experience can really help when you are feeling sad. I told him that if he would like, I would be happy to give him one so he could see what I meant. He instantly crawled into my lap and I thought my own heart would burst with the love I felt for this sweet little boy.

He sat there for a long time and when he had had enough, he jumped down to finish his coloring. I asked him if he felt any better and he said that he did, but he was still sick and nothing would change that. I told him I understood. I walked away feeling sad, but recommitted to this cause. I would do whatever I could to help.

As the day was coming to an end and I was getting ready to head home, I felt a tug on my jacket. I turned around and standing there with a smile on his face was the little boy. He said, "My heart is changing colors. It is getting brighter . . . I think those bear hugs really do work."

On my way home I felt my own heart and realized it, too, had changed to a brighter color.

*Jennifer Love Hewitt*
*actress,* Party of Five

# Smile

She smiled at a sorrowful stranger.
The smile seemed to make him feel better.
He remembered past kindnesses of a friend
and wrote him a thank-you letter.
The friend was so pleased with the thank-you
that he left a large tip after lunch.
The waitress, surprised by the size of the tip,
bet the whole thing on a hunch.
The next day she picked up her winnings,
and gave part to a man on the street.
The man on the street was grateful;
for two days he'd had nothing to eat.
After he finished his dinner,
he left for his small dingy room.
(He didn't know at that moment
that he might be facing his doom.)
On the way he picked up a shivering puppy
and took him home to get warm.
The puppy was very grateful
to be in out of the storm.
That night the house caught on fire.

The puppy barked the alarm.
He barked 'til he woke the whole household
and saved everybody from harm.
One of the boys that he rescued
grew up to be President.
All this because of a simple smile
that hadn't cost a cent.

*Barbara Hauck*

# Tell the World for Me

Some fourteen years ago, I stood watching my university students file into the classroom for our opening session in the theology of faith. That was the day I first saw Tommy. He was combing his hair, which hung six inches below his shoulders. My quick judgment wrote him off as strange—very strange.

Tommy turned out to be my biggest challenge. He constantly objected to or smirked at the possibility of an unconditionally loving God. When he turned in his final exam at the end of the course, he asked in a slightly cynical tone, "Do you think I'll ever find God?"

"No," I said emphatically.

"Oh," he responded. "I thought that was the product you were pushing."

I let him get five steps from the door and then called out. "I don't think you'll ever find him, but I am certain he will find you." Tommy shrugged and left. I felt slightly disappointed that he had missed my clever line.

Later I heard that Tommy had graduated, and I was grateful for that. Then came a sad report: Tommy had terminal cancer. Before I could search him out, he came to me. When he walked into my office, his body was badly wasted, and his long hair had fallen out because of chemotherapy. But his eyes were bright and his voice, for the first time, was firm.

"Tommy! I've thought about you so often. I heard you were very sick," I blurted out.

"Oh, yes, very sick. I have cancer. It's a matter of weeks."

"Can you talk about it?"

"Sure. What would you like to know?"

"What's it like to be only twenty-four and know that you're dying?"

"It could be worse," he told me, "like being fifty and thinking that drinking booze, seducing women and making money are the real 'biggies' in life." Then he told me why he had come.

"It was something you said to me on the last day of class. I asked if you thought I would ever find God and you said no, which surprised me. Then you said, 'But he will find you.' I thought about that a lot, even though my search for God was hardly intense at that time.

"But when the doctors removed a lump from my groin and told me that it was malignant, I got serious about locating God. And when the malignancy spread into my vital organs, I really began banging against the bronze doors of heaven. But nothing happened. Well, one day I woke up, and instead of my desperate attempts to get some kind of message, I just quit. I decided I didn't really care about God, an afterlife, or anything like that.

"I decided to spend what time I had left doing something more important. I thought about you and something else you had said: 'The essential sadness is to go through life without loving. But it would be almost equally sad to leave this world without ever telling those you loved that you loved them.' So I began with the hardest one: my dad."

Tommy's father had been reading the newspaper when his son approached him.

"Dad, I would like to talk with you."

"Well, talk."

"I mean, it's really important."

The newspaper came down three slow inches. "What is it?"

"Dad, I love you. I just wanted you to know that."

Tommy smiled at me as he recounted the moment. "The newspaper fluttered to the floor. Then my father did two things I couldn't remember him doing before. He cried and he hugged me. And we talked all night, even though he had to go to work the next morning.

"It was easier with my mother and little brother," Tommy continued. "They cried with me, and we hugged one another, and shared the things we had been keeping secret for so many years. I was only sorry that I had waited so long. Here I was, in the shadow of death, and I was just beginning to open up to all the people I had actually been close to.

"Then one day I turned around and God was there. He didn't come to me when I pleaded with him. Apparently he does things in his own way and at his own hour. The important thing is that you were right. He found me even after I stopped looking for him."

"Tommy," I practically gasped, "I think you are saying something much more universal than you realize. You are saying that the surest way to find God is not by making him a private possession or an instant consolation in time of need, but rather by opening to love.

"Tommy," I added, "could I ask you a favor? Would you come to my theology-of-faith course and tell my students what you just told me?"

Though we scheduled a date, he never made it. Of course, his life was not really ended by his death, only changed. He made the great step from faith into vision. He found a life far more beautiful than the eye of humanity has ever seen or the mind ever imagined.

Before he died, we talked one last time. "I'm not going to make it to your class," he said.

"I know, Tommy."

"Will you tell them for me? Will you . . . tell the whole world for me?"

"I will, Tommy. I'll tell them."

*John Powell, S.J.*

# Like People First

*The more we know the better we forgive.*
*Whoever feels deeply, feels for all who live.*

Madame de Staël

Craig, a close friend of mine in graduate school, brought energy and life into any room he entered. He focused his entire attention on you while you were talking, and you felt incredibly important. People loved him.

One sunny autumn day, Craig and I were sitting in our usual study area. I was staring out the window when I noticed one of my professors crossing the parking lot.

"I don't want to run into him," I said.

"Why not?" Craig asked.

I explained that the previous spring semester, the professor and I had parted on bad terms. I had taken offense at some suggestion he had made and had, in turn, given offense in my answer. "Besides," I added, "the guy just doesn't like me."

Craig looked down at the passing figure. "Maybe you've got it wrong," he said. "Maybe you're the one who's turning away—and you're just doing that because you're afraid. He probably thinks you don't like him, so he's not friendly. People like people who like them. If you show an interest in him, he'll be interested in you. Go talk to him."

Craig's words smarted. I walked tentatively down the stairs into the parking lot. I greeted my professor warmly and asked how his summer had been. He looked at me, genuinely surprised. We walked off together talking, and I could imagine Craig watching from the window, smiling broadly.

Craig had explained to me a simple concept, so simple I couldn't believe I'd never known it. Like most young people, I felt unsure of myself and came to all my encounters fearing that others would judge me—when, in fact, they were worrying about how I would judge *them*. From that day on, instead of seeing judgment in the eyes of others, I recognized the need people have to make a connection and to share something about themselves. I discovered a world of people I never would have known otherwise.

Once, for example, on a train going across Canada, I began talking to a man everyone was avoiding because he was weaving and slurring his speech as if drunk. It turned out that he was recovering from a stroke. He had been an engineer on the same line we were riding, and long into the night he revealed to me the history beneath every mile of track: Pile O'Bones Creek, named for the thousands of buffalo skeletons left there by Indian hunters; the legend of Big Jack, a Swedish track-layer who could lift 500-pound steel rails; a conductor named McDonald who kept a rabbit as his traveling companion.

As the morning sun began to tint the horizon, he grabbed my hand and looked into my eyes. "Thanks for listening. Most people wouldn't bother." He didn't have to thank me. The pleasure had been all mine.

On a noisy street corner in Oakland, California, a family

who stopped me for directions turned out to be visiting from Australia's isolated northwest coast. I asked them about their life back home. Soon, over coffee, they regaled me with stories of huge saltwater crocodiles "with backs as wide as car hoods."

Each encounter became an adventure, each person a lesson in life. The wealthy, the poor, the powerful and the lonely; all were as full of dreams and doubts as I. And each had a unique story to tell, if only I were willing to hear.

An old, stubble-bearded hobo told me how he'd fed his family during the Depression by firing his shotgun into a pond and gathering up the stunned fish that floated to the surface. A traffic patrolman confided how he'd learned his hand gestures by watching bullfighters and symphony conductors. And a young beautician shared the joy of watching residents in a nursing home smile after receiving a new hairstyle.

How often we allow such opportunities to pass us by. The girl who everyone thinks is homely, the boy with the odd clothes—those people have stories to tell, as surely as you do. And like you, they dream that someone is willing to hear.

This is what Craig knew. Like people first, ask questions later. See if the light you shine on others isn't reflected back on you a hundredfold.

*Kent Nerburn*

# Bobby, I'm Smiling

*Little deeds of kindness, little words of love, help
to make Earth happy.*

Julia Carney

When I was ten years old, my grade school closed, and
I was transferred to a school in a nearby town. In each
classroom, the teachers would seat my classmates and me
alphabetically, thus seating me beside the same boy, time
and time again. His name was Bobby, and he was as outgoing as I was shy. I didn't make friends easily, but Bobby
managed to reach beyond my shyness, and eventually,
we became friends.

As the years passed, Bobby and I shared all the normal
school experiences—first loves, double dating, Friday
night football games, parties and dances. He was my
friend. My confidant. My devil's advocate. It didn't matter
that we were so different—he the popular, handsome,
self-assured football star who had a beautiful girlfriend;
me the overweight, inhibited and insecure teenage girl.
We were friends, regardless.

One morning during the spring of our senior year, I

opened my locker and, to my surprise, there was a beautiful flower. I looked around to see who might have left it for me, but no one stood by waiting to take credit.

I knew that Gerry, a guy in my history class, had a crush on me. *Had he left it?* As I stood wondering, my friend Tami walked by.

"Nice flower," she said.

"Yes, it is. It was left in my locker without a note, but I think I know who gave it to me," I said. "I'm just not interested in dating him, but how do I tell him without hurting his feelings?"

Tami said, "Well, if you're not interested in going out with him, tell him *I* will. He's awesome!"

"But Tami," I said, "you know that Gerry and I aren't anything alike. It would never work out."

At that, Tami laughed and said, "Gerry didn't give you that flower. Bobby did."

"Bobby? Bobby Matthews?"

Then Tami explained.

Earlier that morning, she had passed Bobby in the school's parking lot. Noticing the flower and unable to resist, she had asked him who it was for. His only reply had been that it was for someone special and meant to brighten their day.

I was touched by Tami's story but was certain that the flower had been intended to be given anonymously.

Later that morning, I carried the flower to class and set it on my desk. Bobby noticed it and said nonchalantly, "Nice flower."

I smiled and said, "Yes, it's beautiful."

Minutes later, while we stood to recite the Pledge of Allegiance, I leaned over to Bobby and whispered "Thank you," then proceeded to finish the pledge.

As we were retaking our seats, Bobby said, "For what?"

I smiled. "The flower."

At first, Bobby feigned ignorance, but then he realized I had discovered his secret. "But how did you know?"

I simply smiled and asked why he had given it to me.

He hesitated only briefly before answering. "I gave it to you, because I wanted you to know you're special."

In retrospect, as I look back over seventeen years of friendship, I don't believe that I ever loved Bobby more than I did at that moment. The flower itself paled in comparison with his unexpected and purely giving act of kindness. That kindness meant the world to me then—and still does.

As Bobby had hoped, I did feel special—not only on that day, but for many days to follow. To paraphrase Mark Twain, a person can live a month off a compliment. It's true. I've done it.

When my lovely flower finally wilted and died, I pressed it in a book.

In the years that followed, Bobby and I remained good friends, and although our lives took different paths, we kept in touch.

When Bobby was twenty-five, he was diagnosed with terminal cancer. Shortly before his twenty-seventh birthday, he died.

Since then, I've lost track of the times I have recalled that spring day so long ago. I still treasure my pretty pressed flower, and when I hear the old cliché, "Remember with a smile," I'm certain that it was coined by someone who understood the meaning of a friend's love, and the lasting impression of a kind gesture.

Bobby, I'm smiling.

*E. Keenan*

# An A for Mrs. B

I was sitting next to Missy in my ninth-grade world history class when Mrs. Bartlett announced a new project. In groups, we were to create a newspaper around the culture we were studying.

On a piece of paper, we wrote the names of three friends we wanted in our group. After collecting all the requests, Mrs. B. informed us that she would take into consideration the names we chose and would let us know the results the next day. I had no doubt I would get the group of my choice. There were only a handful of sociably decent people in the class, and Missy was one of them. I knew we had chosen each other.

The next day, I anxiously awaited the class. After the bell rang, Missy and I stopped talking as Mrs. B called for our attention. She started to call out names. When she reached group three, Missy's name was called. *So I'm in group three,* I thought. The second, third and fourth members of the group were called. My name was not included. There had to be some mistake!

Then I heard it. The last group: "Mauro, Juliette, Rachel, Karina." I could feel the tears well in my eyes. How could

I face being in that group—the boy who barely spoke English, the one girl who was always covered by skirts that went down to her ankles, and the other girl who wore weird clothes. Oh, how badly I wanted to be with my friends.

I fought back tears as I walked up to Mrs. B. She looked at me and knew what I was there for. I was determined to convince her I should be in the "good" group. "Why. . . ?" I started.

She gently placed a hand on my shoulder. "I know what you want, Karina," she said, "but your group needs you. I need you to help them get a passing grade on this assignment. Only you can help them."

I was stunned. I was humbled. I was amazed. She had seen something in me I hadn't seen.

"Will you help them?" she asked.

I stood straighter. "Yes," I replied. I couldn't believe it came out of my mouth, but it did. I had committed.

As I bravely walked to where the others in my group sat, I could hear the laughter from my friends. I sat down and we started. Different newspaper columns were assigned according to interests. We did research. Halfway through the week, I felt myself enjoying the company of these three misfits. There was no need for pretending—I grew sincerely interested in learning something about them.

Mauro, I found out, was struggling with the English language and his lack of friends. Juliette was also alone, because people didn't understand that she was only allowed to wear long skirts or dresses because of her religion. Rachel, who had requested to do the fashion column, wanted to be a fashion designer. She had a whole barrel of unique ideas. What a walk in another person's shoes did for me! They weren't misfits, just people that no one cared enough about to try to understand—except

Mrs. B. Her insight, vision and thoughtfulness brought out the potential in four of her students.

I don't recall what the newspaper's headline was or even the culture we wrote about, but I did learn something that week. I was given a chance to see other people in a new light. I was given the opportunity to see in myself a potential that inspired my actions in later years. I learned that who we are is more important than what we are or seem to be.

After that semester ended, I always received a friendly hello from my group. And I was always genuinely happy to see them.

Mrs. B gave us an A on that assignment. We should have handed it right back, for she was the one who truly deserved it.

*Karina Snow*

# A Simple Hello

I have always felt sympathy and compassion for the kids I see at school walking all alone, for the ones that sit in the back of the room while everyone snickers and makes fun of them. But I never did anything about it. I guess I figured that someone else would. I did not take the time to really think about the depth of their pain. Then one day I thought, what if I did take a moment out of my busy schedule to simply say hello to someone without a friend or stop and chat with someone eating by herself? And I did. It felt good to brighten up someone else's life. How did I know I did? Because I remembered the day a simple kind hello changed my life forever.

*Katie E. Houston*

# Change for a Dollar

*Make yourself a blessing to someone. Your kind smile or pat on the back just might pull someone back from the edge.*

Carmelia Elliot

All he wanted was some juice. As tables full of high school students sat in Cafeteria B2 on that cloudy afternoon, he was thirsty. We sat near yet away from him, fixing our hair and worrying about the test next period we hadn't studied for. He was far away from our world, yet forced to be a part of it.

He stood at the drink machine with purpose, fumbling through his fake leather wallet for some change. He came up with a wrinkled dollar bill, and nervously glanced back at his table where other students in his special needs class were sitting. With the coordination of a six-year-old, he tried to make the machine accept his money. After a few unsuccessful attempts, the snickers and comments began. People were laughing. Some were even throwing things at him. He began to quiver, and his eyes misted with tears. I saw him turn to sit down, defeated. But for some reason, he decided against it. He wasn't leaving until he got a drink.

With a determined expression, he continued to aimlessly thrust the dollar bill in the machine. Then something terrific happened. A popular senior rose from her seat, and with a look of genuine compassion, went over to the boy. She explained how the machine had a hard time accepting dollars, then gave him some change and showed him where to place it. The boy gave her his dollar and chose a flavor of fruit juice. Then the two walked off in different directions.

Although it was clear that they were from very different worlds, for one moment, they'd shared a real understanding. As I walked away from my lunch table that day, I looked at the boy. I remember thinking how he and the dollar were very much alike. They both weren't accepted where the world said they were supposed to be. But just as the dollar had found a place in a caring girl's pocket, I was sure the boy would eventually find his, too.

*Bonnie Maloney*

# So How Do You Boost an Ego?

*If you treat an individual as he is, he will remain as he is. But if you treat him as if he were what he ought to be and could be, he will become what he ought to be and could be.*

Goethe

Mr. Rickman, our psych teacher, doesn't give the kind of assignments other teachers do, such as read a thousand pages; answer the questions at the end of the chapter; work problems 47 through 856. He's more creative than that.

Mr. Rickman led up to last Thursday's assignment by saying that behavior is a means of communicating. "'Actions speak louder than words' isn't just an empty phrase," he told us. "What people do tells you something about what they are feeling."

He paused a minute for that to sink in before he gave the assignment. "Now see if you can build up somebody, boost his or her ego enough that you notice a change in the way the person acts. We'll report the results in class next week."

When I got home from school that afternoon, my mom was really feeling sorry for herself. I could tell the minute I came in. Her hair was straggling around her face, her voice was whiny and she kept sighing while she got dinner. She didn't even speak to me when I came in. Since she didn't speak, I didn't either.

Dinner was pretty dreary. Dad wasn't any more talkative than Mom and I were. I decided to try out my assignment. "Hey, Mom, you know that play the university drama club is putting on? Why don't you and Dad go tonight? I've heard it's really good."

"Can't make it tonight," Dad said. "Important meeting."

"Naturally," Mom said. Then I knew what was bugging her.

"Well then, how about going with me?" I asked. Right away, I wished I could take back the invitation. Imagine a high school kid being seen out in the evening with his mother!

Anyway, the invitation was hanging there in the air, and Mom said in an excited voice, "Really, Kirk?"

I swallowed a couple of times. "Sure. Why not?"

"But guys don't take their mothers out." Her voice was getting more pleasant all the time, and she pushed the straggles of hair up on top of her head.

"There's no law that says they can't," I told her. "You just go get ready. We're going out."

Mom started toward the sink with some dishes. Her steps were perky now instead of draggy.

"Kirk and I will take care of the dishes," Dad offered, and Mom even smiled at him.

"That was a nice thing for you to do," my dad said, after Mom left the kitchen. "You're a thoughtful son."

Thanks to psychology class, I thought gloomily.

Mom came back to the kitchen looking about five years younger than she had an hour earlier. "You're sure you don't have a date?" she asked, as if she still couldn't believe what was happening.

"I do now," I said. "C'mon, let's go."

That evening didn't turn out so badly after all. Most of my friends had more exciting things to do than watch a play. The ones who were there weren't at all startled to see me with my mom. By the end of the evening, she was genuinely happy, and I was feeling pretty good myself. Not only had I aced a psych assignment, I had also learned a lot about boosting an ego.

*Kirk Hill*

# Coffee-Shop Kindness

*If you can't return a favor, pass it on.*

Louise Brown

My senior year of high school was an extremely hectic one, to say the least. If I wasn't studying and worrying about my grades, I was juggling multiple extracurricular activities or attempting to make sense of my plans for college. It seemed as if my life had turned into one crazy cloud of confusion, and I was stumbling around blindly, hoping to find some sort of direction.

Finally, as senior year began to wind down, I got a part-time job working at the local coffee shop. I had figured that the job would be easy and, for the most part, stress-free. I pictured myself pouring the best gourmet coffees, making delicious doughnuts and becoming close friends with the regular customers.

What I hadn't counted on were the people with enormous orders who chose to use the drive-thru window, or the women who felt that the coffee was much too creamy, or the men who wanted their iced coffees remade again and again until they reached a certain level of perfection. There were moments when I was exasperated with the human race as a whole, simply because I couldn't seem to please anyone. There was always too much sugar, too little ice and not enough skim milk. Nevertheless, I kept at it.

One miserable rainy day, one of my regular customers came in looking depressed and defeated. My coworker and I asked what the problem was and if we could help, but the customer wouldn't reveal any details. He just said he felt like crawling into bed, pulling the sheets up over his head and staying there for a few years. I knew exactly how he felt.

Before he left, I handed him a bag along with his iced coffee. He looked at me questioningly because he hadn't ordered anything but the coffee. He opened the bag and saw that I had given him his favorite type of doughnut.

"It's on me," I told him. "Have a nice day."

He smiled and thanked me before turning around and heading back out into the rain.

The next day was miserable as well, rain spilling from the sky. Everyone in town seemed to be using the drive-thru window because no one wanted to brave the black skies or the thunder and lightning.

I spent my afternoon hanging out the window, handing people their orders and waiting as they slowly counted their pennies. I tried to smile as the customers complained about the weather, but it was difficult to smile as they sat in their temperature-controlled cars with the windows rolled up, while I dealt with huge droplets of water hanging from my visor, a shirt that was thoroughly soaked around the collar and an air conditioner that blasted out cold air despite sixty-seven-degree weather. On top of that, no one was tipping. Every time I looked into our nearly empty tip jar, I grew more depressed.

Around seven o'clock that evening, I was in the middle of making another pot of vanilla hazelnut decaf when the customer from the day before drove up to the window. But instead of ordering anything, he handed me a single pink rose and a little note. He said that not too many people take the time to care about others, and he was glad there were still people like me in the world. I was speechless and very touched; I nearly forgot yesterday's deed. After a moment, I happily thanked him. He told me I was welcome and, with a friendly wave, drove away.

I waited until I saw his Jeep exit the parking lot, then I ran to the back of the shop and read the note. It read:

*Christine,*

> *Thanks for being so sweet, kind and thoughtful yesterday. I was sincerely touched by you. It is so nice to meet someone who's genuinely nice, warm, and sensitive and unselfish. Please don't change your ways because I truly believe that you will excel. Have a great day!*

*Hank*

As the day passed, I had plenty of complaining customers, but anytime I felt depressed or frustrated, I thought of Hank and his kindness. I would smile, hold my head up high, clear my throat and politely ask, "How can I help you?"

*Christine Walsh*

# Mary Lou

It was my first day as newcomer to Miss Hargrove's seventh-grade class. Past "newcomer" experiences had been difficult, so I was very anxious to fit in. After being introduced to the class, I bravely put on a smile and took my seat, expecting to be shunned.

Lunchtime was a pleasant surprise when the girls all crowded around my table. Their chatter was friendly, so I began to relax. My new classmates filled me in on the school, the teachers and the other kids. It wasn't long before the class nerd was pointed out to me: Mary Lou English. Actually she called herself Mary Louise. A prim, prissy young girl with a stern visage and old-fashioned clothes. She wasn't ugly—not even funny looking. I thought she was quite pretty, but I had sense enough not to say so. Dark-eyed and olive-skinned, she had long, silky black hair, but—she had pipe curls! Practical shoes, long wool skirt and a starched, frilly blouse completed the image of a total dork. The girls' whispers and giggles got louder and louder. Mary Lou made eye contact with no one as she strode past our table, chin held high with iron determination. She ate alone.

After school, the girls invited me to join them in front of the school. I was thrilled to be a member of the club, however tentative. We waited. For what, I didn't yet know. Oh, how I wish I had gone home, but I had a lesson to learn.

Arms wrapped around her backpack, Mary Lou came down the school steps. The taunting began—rude, biting comments and jeering from the girls. I paused, then joined right in. My momentum began to pick up as I approached her. Nasty, mean remarks fell unabated from my lips. No one could tell I'd never done this before. The other girls stepped back and became my cheerleaders. Emboldened, I yanked the strap of her backpack and then pushed her. The strap broke, Mary Lou fell, and I backed off. Everyone was laughing and patting me. I fit in. I was a leader.

I was not proud. Something inside me hurt. If you've ever picked a wing off a butterfly, you know how I felt.

Mary Lou got up, gathered her books and—without a tear shed or retort given—off she went. She held her head high as a small trickle of blood ran down from her bruised knee. I watched her limp away down the street.

I turned to leave with my laughing friends and noticed a man standing beside his car. His olive skin, dark hair and handsome features told me this was her father. Respectful of Mary Lou's proud spirit, he remained still and watched the lonely girl walk toward him. Only his eyes—shining with both grief and pride—followed. As I passed, he looked at me in silence with burning tears that spoke to my shame and scalded my heart. He didn't speak a word.

No scolding from a teacher or preaching from a parent could linger as much as that hurt in my heart from the day a father's eyes taught me kindness and strength and dignity. I never again joined the cruel herds. I never again hurt someone for my own gain.

*Lynne Zielinski*

# Healing with Love

On a bitterly cold and cloudy winter's day in upstate New York, I saw my brother again for the first time in a year. As my father and I pulled up to the reform school after four hours of driving, his attempts at cheerful commentary did nothing to ameliorate the dismal apprehension that I felt. I had little hope that my brother would be changed and, furthermore, I had convinced myself that any appearance of change would not necessarily be genuine.

Being with my brother after so long was like getting to know him all over again. Over the next couple of days, I felt a kind of peace developing between us, and, for the first time, I wasn't tense around him, nor was I scared of what he would do or say next. It seemed as though I would finally find a friend in my brother, and, more than that, I would find a true brother in my brother. While part of me rejoiced in his transformation, another part of me thought it was too good to be true, and so I remained skeptical of his seeming progress. Two days was surely not enough time to erase the hostility that had built up between us over the years. I showed this cynical front to my father and brother, while the hopeful voice remained hidden deep inside of my heart, afraid to appear, lest it should be trampled upon. My brother himself commented several times on my depressed disposition, but I knew he would never understand the complexity of my feelings, so I remained elusive.

I wrapped myself in this same protective silence during, what was for me, the most emotionally trying part of the visit. Meals at the school were more than just meals. They were chaperoned with two teachers at each table, and provided a forum for judging the students' progress and/or continued delinquency. My father had told me that these meals often lasted for an hour or two, as each student was treated separately and with the full attention of the table. As we sat down for lunch, I knew I wouldn't be able to make it through the meal without crying.

Several boys and girls were "brought up" in front of the table for transgressions they had committed, but a boy named Brian touched me the most. A fairly new arrival at the school, he hadn't yet lost the initial anger and bitterness at having been brought there against his will. He was an attractive boy, about sixteen years old and was, my father whispered to me, an exceptional soccer player with a promising future in the sport. As the head teacher at our table conducted a heavy interrogation of him, Brian shifted his weight nervously every two seconds, and I saw in his eyes what I had become so good at reading in my brother's. They darted anxiously about the room, resting upon everything except the man addressing him, and I knew that he was searching for someone or something to blame. He wasn't yet aware that only when he stopped looking for excuses could he truly hear and learn from those trying to help him.

Suddenly, out of the corner of my eye, I became aware of a bearded man standing at the closed door and peering in apprehensively at our solemn gathering, which must have looked more like an AA meeting than a meal. The realization that it was Brian's father trying to catch a glimpse of his son precipitated the first tear I had shed all weekend.

"Why is Brian here?" I whispered softly to my father.

"Oh, you know, the usual, drugs, violence . . . I think the last straw was when he hit his father in the head with one of his soccer trophies. . . . He was chosen for the National All-Star team, you know. . . . Must be quite a player."

As the tears flowed more freely down my face, Brian looked straight ahead at the wall and told us that he had refused to see his father who had driven for many hours to see him.

Then the teacher spoke, "Brian, I talked to your dad, and he says he brought you your puppy because he knows how much you must miss him. He's willing to accept the fact that you don't want to see him, but he wants you to know that you can see your puppy."

I was screaming inside. I wanted to stand up and tell Brian how lucky he was to have a father who obviously loved him so much, and who loved him enough to do the hardest thing a parent ever has to do: send his child away. I was bursting to enlighten him, but I knew it was something he would have to learn on his own, so I remained still and just let the overwhelming sadness spread over me like a dark cloud.

That afternoon, I saw my brother waving good-bye as we pulled up the dirt drive and out of the gates of the school. I couldn't look back, as I was too busy trying to suppress the emotion that I felt creeping up on me with the force of a tidal wave. I was filled with hopelessness and empathy for these kids who had somehow gotten lost along the way. I knew there was a fine line between them and me, a line I had walked like a tightrope at several times in my life. Indeed, part of my sadness lay in the guilt I felt for not having such a heavy load to bear and for never being able to fully comprehend the nature and sheer weight of this load my brother carried.

Several months later I returned to the school, this time in early spring and accompanied by my whole family, including my mother and two sisters. Everything looked brighter and more colorful in the sun. Wildflowers bloomed on the hillside looking out over the valley, and the water in the pond sparkled like jewels. I closed my eyes, held my face up to the sun and smiled. It was my family's first reunion in over a year. As it was family weekend, everywhere I looked I saw proud, attentive parents and beaming kids. This is when the full force of what I was experiencing hit me. For the first time in a while, I didn't feel the despair and hopelessness of these kids' lives, but the tremendous amount of love and support that surrounded each one of them. After a whole year spent doubting that my brother would ever be able to function normally in society, I allowed the seeds of hope to germinate in my mind, as well as in my heart.

Moments later, my new outlook was strengthened and forever cemented by the most beautiful sight I think I have ever seen. At first I couldn't believe my eyes. Brian and his father were walking arm in arm across the grass towards the pond and seemed to be in quiet discussion about one of those everyday, mundane things that is the business of fathers and their sons. A golden retriever, now fully grown, wagged its tail in delight as he trotted after them.

*Cecile Wood*

# The Gift of Time

*What we do for ourselves dies with us. What we do for others and the world remains and is immortal.*

Albert Pine

His name was Bryce. I inherited him when I was nine years old. Actually, he became part of our family when my mother married his uncle.

It was a second marriage for my mother, and while it might have been less than desirable for my two older brothers, for me it was a slice of heaven. We moved to a beautiful neighborhood, into a house three times the size of the one in which I had been born and raised. Not only did this marriage come with a big house, a pool and huge yard, it also came with Bryce. He lived in Northern California with his brother and parents, but he visited frequently, sometimes spending entire summers with us.

Bryce became my good friend. He was six years older than I, but we had an instant rapport that belied the gap in our ages. He taught me how to dive and do flips off the diving board, he helped my stepfather build a tree house for me, and he helped me learn how to expertly negotiate my new bicycle built for two that I had won in a contest. By the time I was thirteen, we had become best friends.

Bryce and I spent many summers together, and as the years passed we still remained close. The activities changed—tennis, hiking, beach trips and computers—but our bond didn't. He was handsome, smart and funny, and even though I was only fourteen years old, I fantasized about marrying him someday. I couldn't conceive of my life without him.

Bryce was the eldest of two boys, and he was his parents' pride and joy. He lived nearly a picture-perfect life. Achieving in school, becoming an award-winning athlete, and having this incredibly huge, compassionate heart, he was a parent's dream. When his mother's brother decided to marry my widowed mother, Bryce helped create a bridge that served to unite the two families. He was charismatic, funny and a great mitigating influence for two teenage boys who didn't want their mother to marry this man. But, his family came with Bryce, and at the very least, Bryce was cool.

One summer, Bryce and I went swimming at a friend's house. They had a pool to envy. Complete with diving boards, a slide, waterfalls and a small island in the center, it was by far the coolest pool in the San Fernando Valley. I was fifteen, Bryce was twenty-one. It was one of those perfect days, and we were having so much fun. At one point, I decided to slide down the slide on my belly. Apparently, given the location of the slide, this was not a good idea. I smacked down hard on the bottom of the pool and was knocked out. By the time anyone figured out that I wasn't just playing around (the blood that began to tint the water was probably a good clue) I was starting to drown. Bryce saved my life. He jumped into the pool, pulled me to safety and helped to clear the water out of my lungs so that I could breathe. When I finally regained consciousness, Bryce was kneeling beside me, with tears in his eyes.

He was now my friend and my savior. I grew up with him; he became the first boy that I really loved. He treated me like I was the only person in his life who really mattered, even though I'm sure he had girlfriends.

By the time I turned sixteen, I was already fairly proficient behind the wheel of a car, thanks to Bryce. He made it very clear to me that it was my turn to drive the seven hours it required for us to visit each other. I was more than happy to oblige.

I would drive up to Redding, and we would go to the river and live in the water. We would jet ski, swim, snorkel and sun on the dock until those long summer days finally claimed the sun. Then we'd go back to his parents' house and barbecue, laugh and hang out.

By the end of my senior year in high school, there was only one person I wanted to take me to my prom, so I was thrilled when he finally asked me. I accepted without reservation. Even though there were other boys who had asked, it was Bryce I wanted to share the occasion with. Besides, grad night at Disneyland required someone with the guts to ride all the coasters several times, and I knew he was up for the task.

During that next year, our lives became busy, and we didn't see each other that often. I was starting college, and he was working. We wrote and talked to each other on the phone, but it seemed that our lives were taking us in two different directions. I missed him dearly, so I was overjoyed when I found out he would be coming down for his birthday. My stepfather had a special gift that he wanted to give him.

We had a little party for Bryce, and my stepfather gave him his gift. It was a gold Hamilton tank-style watch that was given to my stepfather by his mother, Bryce's grand-mother, when he was younger. Engraved on the back were my stepfather's initials and the date, 11/30/48. It was a special memento that my stepfather held very dear, so the gesture of giving it to his nephew meant a great deal to Bryce. He cherished it. He wore it all the time. And when the band broke, he just put it in his pocket and carried it around that way. He was never without it.

One winter night, Bryce and I were on the phone on one of those two-hour-long telephone conversations. It was around eleven o'clock at night, he was at his parents' house having dinner with them and some guests who were visiting from out of town. Bryce said that he had to go. His mother had asked him to take these friends back to the hotel where they were staying. It was at least an hour out of town and he was already tired. We made some vague plans to meet on the dock in the summer. Sometimes it was the only thing that would get me through a tough school year. Then before he hung up he said something that made me smile. He said, "Just remember, no matter what you do in this life, I will always be there for you if you bump your head." I told him that he would always be my hero, and then we hung up.

Bryce's car was found the next day. He had driven off the road when he fell asleep at the wheel. My sweet Bryce was killed instantly. He was twenty-five years old. The pain and upset that spread through our family was profound. I was left with a huge hole in my heart, a hole I was afraid would never mend.

That summer, as agreed, I went to the dock. I sat on the dock, knowing that Bryce would never come. I sat down and started to weep, my tears falling into the river. I found myself getting angry. How could he have done this to me? Why did he have to die? I was questioning God, Bryce and whomever else was listening.

Then, remembering our conversation the night before he died, I started to hit my head.

"I'm hitting my head . . . I'm bumping it, where are you? You lied to me! Do I really need to hurt myself?"

In a moment of emotional frenzy, I picked up an oar that was lying on the pier. Suddenly, underneath where the oar had just been, something shiny caught my eye. There was something wedged between the boards. I set the oar down and bent down to retrieve the shiny object. When I finally pried it free, I immediately recognized it. It was the watch my stepfather had given Bryce on his birthday. I sat down and cried. With the object still cradled in my hand, I held it up close to my heart. I soon realized that this little 1948 old-fashioned watch that needed to be wound every twenty-four hours was still ticking. Goose bumps covered my skin, and the warmest, most loving feeling came over me. I felt as if I were being hugged from the inside out. There he was, still with me.

I'll never know exactly how that little watch happened upon that pier. But I think that Bryce left it behind for me. I bought a new band for the watch, and to this very day I still wear it. It will always be a symbol of unconditional love, something time could never stop.

*Zan Gaudioso*

# The Boy Under the Tree

In the summer recess between freshman and sopho-more years in college, I was invited to be an instructor at a high-school leadership camp hosted by a college in Michigan. I was already highly involved in most campus activities, and I jumped at the opportunity.

About an hour into the first day of camp, amid the frenzy of icebreakers and forced interactions, I first noticed the boy under the tree. He was small and skinny, and his obvi-ous discomfort and shyness made him appear frail and fragile. Only fifty feet away, two hundred eager campers were bumping bodies, playing, joking and meeting each other, but the boy under the tree seemed to want to be anywhere other than where he was. The desperate loneli-ness he radiated almost stopped me from approaching him, but I remembered the instructions from the senior staff to stay alert for campers who might feel left out.

As I walked toward him, I said, "Hi, my name is Kevin, and I'm one of the counselors. It's nice to meet you. How are you?" In a shaky, sheepish voice he reluctantly answered, "Okay, I guess." I calmly asked him if he wanted to join the activities and meet some new people. He quietly replied, "No, this is not really my thing."

I could sense that he was in a new world, that this whole experience was foreign to him. But I somehow knew it wouldn't be right to push him, either. He didn't need a pep talk; he needed a friend. After several silent moments, my first interaction with the boy under the tree was over.

At lunch the next day, I found myself leading camp songs at the top of my lungs for two hundred of my new friends. The campers eagerly participated. My gaze wandered over the mass of noise and movement and was caught by the image of the boy from under the tree, sitting alone, staring out the window. I nearly forgot the words to the song I was supposed to be leading. At my first opportunity, I tried again, with the same questions as before: "How are you doing? Are you okay?" To which he again replied, "Yeah, I'm all right. I just don't really get into this stuff." As I left the cafeteria, I realized this was going to take more time and effort than I had thought—if it was even possible to get through to him at all.

That evening at our nightly staff meeting, I made my concerns about him known. I explained to my fellow staff members my impression of him and asked them to pay special attention and spend time with him when they could.

The days I spend at camp each year fly by faster than any others I have known. Thus, before I knew it, mid-week had dissolved into the final night of camp, and I was chaperoning the "last dance." The students were doing all they could to savor every last moment with their new "best friends"—friends they would probably never see again.

As I watched the campers share their parting moments, I suddenly saw what would be one of the most vivid memories of my life. The boy from under the tree, who had stared blankly out the kitchen window, was now a shirtless dancing wonder. He owned the dance floor as he and two girls proceeded to cut a rug. I watched as he shared meaningful, intimate time with people at whom he couldn't even look just days earlier. I couldn't believe it was the same person.

In October of my sophomore year, a late-night phone call pulled me away from my chemistry book. A soft-spoken, unfamiliar voice asked politely, "Is Kevin there?"

"You're talking to him. Who's this?"

"This is Tom Johnson's mom. Do you remember Tommy from leadership camp?"

The boy under the tree. How could I not remember?

"Yes, I do," I said. "He's a very nice young man. How is he?"

An abnormally long pause followed, then Mrs. Johnson said, "My Tommy was walking home from school this week when he was hit by a car and killed." Shocked, I offered my condolences.

"I just wanted to call you," she said, "because Tommy mentioned you so many times. I wanted you to know that he went back to school this fall with confidence. He made new friends. His grades went up. And he even went out on a few dates. I just wanted to thank you for making a difference for Tom. The last few months were the best few months of his life."

In that instant, I realized how easy it is to give a bit of yourself every day. You may never know how much each gesture may mean to someone else. I tell this story as often as I can, and when I do, I urge others to look out for their own "boy under the tree."

*David Coleman and Kevin Randall*

# A Message for Ben

Coming of age in this dangerous world is a dauntingly,
  difficult thing.
How will you live up to the promise of what the future
  will bring?
You've shown by example that God has a plan
for helping this old boy become a young man.

We encourage you, Ben, to accept every challenge
with strength and conviction, with patience and balance.
Be truthful, be gentle and always forgive.
Through compassion you learn how to live and let live.

Take to adventure with your eyes open wide.
To steady the journey, travel often inside.
Seek poetry, passion, beauty and art.
Keep magic and wonder tucked close to your heart.

Celebrate failure with just one more try.
Be mindful of the riches that money can't buy.
Be grateful for wealth, but know what's at stake.
And give back to the earth, always, more than you take.

Plant gardens, feed pigeons, walk softly through snow.
When you nurture all life, you help yourself grow.
Be childlike, laugh often, and share every joy.
Honor the man, remember the boy.

Cry at sad movies and when you feel grief.
Tears are the heart's way of bringing relief.
Learn from your pain, it will help make you wise.
Above all, remember that love never dies.

Then, at the end, as you walk your last mile,
Looking back on your life with a well-deserved smile,
Recall all the faces that helped light the way.
Give thanks for their love and remember this day.

*Tom Witte*

[EDITORS' NOTE: *Ben's uncle, Tom Witte, wrote this poem for Ben for his thirteenth birthday. Tom passed away from complications from AIDS, shortly after he gave him the poem.*]

# $\overline{\underline{4}}$

# ON FAMILY

*O*ther things may change us, but we start
and end with family.

*Anthony Brandt*

*Reprinted by permission of Dave Carpenter.*

# What My Father Wore

What my father wore embarrassed me as a young man. I wanted him to dress like a doctor or lawyer, but on those muggy mornings when he rose before dawn to fry eggs for my mother and me, he always dressed like my father.

We lived in south Texas, and my father wore tattered jeans with the imprint of his pocketknife on the seat. He liked shirts that snapped more than those that buttoned, and kept his pencils, cigars, glasses, wrenches and screwdrivers in his breast pocket. My father's boots were government-issues with steel toes that made them difficult to pull off his feet, which I sometimes did when he returned from repairing air conditioners, his job that also shamed me.

But, as a child, I'd crept into his closet and modeled his wardrobe in front of the mirror. My imagination transformed his shirts into the robes of kings and his belts into soldiers' holsters. I slept in his undershirts and relied on the scent of his collars to calm my fear of the dark. Within a few years, though, I started wishing my father would trade his denim for khaki and retire his boots for loafers. I stopped sleeping in his clothes and eventually began dreaming of another father.

I blamed the way he dressed for my social failures. When boys bullied me, I thought they'd seen my father wearing his cowboy hat but no shirt while walking our dog. I felt that girls snickered at me because they'd glimpsed him mowing the grass in cut-offs and black boots. The girls' families paid men (and I believed better-dressed ones) to landscape their lawns, while their fathers yachted in the bay wearing lemon-yellow sweaters and expensive sandals.

My father only bought two suits in his life. He preferred clothes that allowed him the freedom to shimmy under cars and squeeze behind broken Maytags, where he felt most content. But the day before my parents' twentieth anniversary, he and I went to Sears, and he tried on suits all afternoon. With each one, he stepped to the mirror, smiled and nodded, then asked about the price and reached for another. He probably tried ten suits before we drove to a discount store and bought one without so much as approaching a fitting room. That night my mother said she'd never seen a more handsome man.

Later, though, he donned the same suit for my eighth-grade awards banquet, and I wished he'd stayed home. After the ceremony (I'd been voted Mr. Citizenship, of all things), he lauded my award and my character while changing into a faded red sweatsuit. He was stepping into the garage to wash a load of laundry when I asked what even at age fourteen struck me as cruel and wrong. "Why," I asked, "don't you dress 'nice,' like my friends' fathers?"

He held me with his sad, shocked eyes and searched for an answer. Then before he disappeared into the garage and closed the door between us, my father said, "I like my clothes." An hour later my mother stormed into my room, slapped me hard across the face and called me an "ungrateful little twerp," a phrase that echoed in my head until they resumed speaking to me.

In time they forgave me, and as I matured I realized that girls avoided me not because of my father but because of his son. I realized that my mother had slapped me because my father could not, and it soon became clear that what he had really said that night was that there are things more important than clothes. He'd said he couldn't spend a nickel on himself because there were things I wanted. That night, without another word, my father had said, "You're my son, and I sacrifice so your life will be better than mine."

For my high-school graduation, my father arrived in a suit he and my mother had purchased earlier that day. Somehow he seemed taller, more handsome and imposing, and when he passed the other fathers they stepped out of his way. It wasn't the suit, of course, but the man. The doctors and lawyers recognized the confidence in his swagger, the pride in his eyes, and when they approached him, they did so with courtesy and respect. After we returned home, my father replaced the suit in the flimsy Sears garment bag, and I didn't see it again until his funeral.

I don't know what he was wearing when he died, but he was working, so he was in clothes he liked, and that comforts me. My mother thought of burying him in the suit from Sears, but I convinced her otherwise and soon delivered a pair of old jeans, a flannel shirt and his boots to the funeral home.

On the morning of the services, I used his pocketknife to carve another hole in his belt so it wouldn't droop around my waist. Then I took the suit from Sears out of his closet and changed into it. Eventually, I mustered the courage to study myself in his mirror where, with the exception of the suit, I appeared small and insignificant. Again, as in childhood, the clothes draped over my scrawny frame. My father's scent wafted up and caressed my face, but it failed to console me. I was uncertain: not about my father's stature—I'd stopped being an ungrateful little twerp years before. No, I was uncertain about myself, my own stature. And I stood there for some time, facing myself in my father's mirror, weeping and trying to imagine—as I will for the rest of my life—the day I'll grow into my father's clothes.

*Bret Anthony Johnston*

# She Didn't Give Up on Me

*She never once gave up. My mom is my hero.*

Kimberly Anne Brand

I lay on the floor, furiously kicking my legs and scream-ing until my throat felt raw—all because my foster mother had asked me to put my toys away.

"I hate you," I shrieked. I was six years old and didn't understand why I felt so angry all the time.

I'd been living in foster care since I was two. My real mom couldn't give my five sisters and me the care we needed. Since we didn't have a dad or anyone else to care for us, we were put in different foster homes. I felt lonely and confused. I didn't know how to tell people that I hurt inside. Throwing a tantrum was the only way I knew to express my feelings.

Because I acted up, eventually my current foster mom sent me back to the adoption agency, just as the mom before had. I thought I was the most unlovable girl in the world.

Then I met Kate McCann. I was seven by that time and living with my third foster family when she came to visit.

When my foster mother told me that Kate was single and wanted to adopt a child, I didn't think she'd choose me. I couldn't imagine anyone would want me to live with them forever.

That day, Kate took me to a pumpkin farm. We had fun, but I didn't think I'd see her again.

A few days later, a social worker came to the house to say that Kate wanted to adopt me. Then she asked me if I'd mind living with one parent instead of two.

"All I want is someone who loves me," I said.

Kate visited the next day. She explained that it would take a year for the adoption to be finalized, but I could move in with her soon. I was excited but afraid, too. Kate and I were total strangers. I wondered if she'd change her mind once she got to know me.

Kate sensed my fear. "I know you've been hurt," she said, hugging me. "I know you're scared. But I promise I'll never send you away. We're a family now."

To my surprise, her eyes were filled with tears. Suddenly I realized that she was as lonely as I was!

"Okay . . . Mom, " I said.

The following week I met my new grandparents, aunt, uncle and cousins. It felt funny—but good—to be with strangers who hugged me as though they already loved me.

When I moved in with Mom, I had my own room for the first time. It had wallpaper and a matching bedspread, an antique dresser and a big closet. I had only a few clothes I'd brought with me in a brown paper bag. "Don't worry," Mom said. "I'll buy you lots of pretty new things."

I went to sleep that night feeling safe. I prayed I wouldn't have to leave.

Mom did lots of nice things for me. She took me to church. She let me have pets and gave me horseback riding and piano lessons. Every day, she told me she loved me. But love wasn't enough to heal the hurt inside me. I kept waiting for her to change her mind. I thought, "If I act bad enough, she'll leave me like the others."

So I tried to hurt her before she could hurt me. I picked fights over little things and threw tantrums when I didn't get my way. I slammed doors. If Mom tried to stop me, I'd hit her. But she never lost patience. She'd hug me and say she loved me anyway. When I got mad, she made me jump on a trampoline.

Because I was failing in school when I came to live with her, Mom was very strict about my homework. One day when I was watching TV, she came in and turned it off. "You can watch it after you finish your homework," she said. I blew up. I picked up my books and threw them across the room. "I hate you and I don't want to live here anymore!" I screamed.

I waited for her to tell me to start packing. When she didn't, I asked, "Aren't you going to send me back?"

"I don't like the way you're behaving," she said, "but I'll never send you back. We're a family, and families don't give up on each other."

Then it hit me. This mom was different; she wasn't going to get rid of me. She really did love me. And I realized I loved her, too. I cried and hugged her.

In 1985, when Mom formally adopted me, our whole family celebrated at a restaurant. It felt good belonging to someone. But I was still scared. Could a mom really love me forever? My tantrums didn't disappear immediately, but as months passed, they happened less often.

Today I'm sixteen. I have a 3.4 grade point average, a horse named Dagger's Point, four cats, a dog, six doves and a bullfrog that lives in our backyard pond. And I have a dream: I want to be a veterinarian.

Mom and I like to do things together, like shopping and horseback riding. We smile when people say how much we look alike. They don't believe she's not my real mom.

I'm happier now than I ever imagined I could be. When I'm older, I'd like to get married and have kids, but if that doesn't work out, I'll adopt like Mom did. I'll pick a scared and lonely kid and then never, ever give up on her. I'm so glad Mom didn't give up on me.

*Sharon Whitley*
*excerpted from* Woman's World Magazine

*Reprinted by permission of Randy Glasbergen.*

# Unconditional Mom

*My mother had a great deal of trouble with me, but I think she enjoyed it.*

Mark Twain

I was a rotten teenager. Not your average spoiled, know-it-all, not-going-to-clean-my-room, getting-an-attitude-because-I'm-fifteen teenager. No, I was a manipulative, lying, acid-tongued monster, who realized early on that I could make things go my way with just a few minor adjustments. The writers for today's hottest soap opera could not have created a worse "villainess." A few nasty comments here, a lie or two there, maybe an evil glare for a finishing touch, and things would be grand. Or so I thought.

For the most part, and on the outside, I was a good kid. A giggly, pug-nose tomboy who liked to play sports and who thrived on competition (a nice way of saying: somewhat pushy and demanding). Which is probably why most people allowed me to squeak by using what I now call "bulldozer behavior tactics," with no regard for anyone I felt to be of value. For a while, anyway.

Since I was perceptive enough to get some people to bend my way, it amazes me how long it took to realize how I was hurting so many others. Not only did I succeed in pushing away many of my closest friends by trying to control them; I also managed to sabotage, time and time again, the most precious relationship in my life: my relationship with my mother.

Even today, almost ten years since the birth of the new me, my former behavior astonishes me each time I reach into my memories. Hurtful comments that cut and stung the people I cared most about. Acts of confusion and anger that seemed to rule my every move—all to make sure that things went my way.

My mother, who gave birth to me at age thirty-eight against her doctor's wishes, would cry to me, "I waited so long for you, please don't push me away. I want to help you!"

I would reply with my best face of stone, "I didn't ask for you! I never wanted you to care about me! Leave me alone and forget I ever lived!"

My mother began to believe I really meant it. My actions proved nothing less.

I was mean and manipulative, trying to get my way at any cost. Like many young girls in high school, the boys whom I knew were off limits were always the first ones I had to date. Sneaking out of the house at all hours of the night just to prove I could do it. Juggling complex lies that were always on the verge of blowing up in my face. Finding any way to draw attention to myself while simultaneously trying to be invisible.

Ironically, I wish I could say I had been heavy into drugs during that period of my life, swallowing mind-altering pills and smoking things that changed my personality, thus accounting for the terrible, razor-sharp words that came flying from my mouth. However, that was not the case. My only addiction was hatred; my only high was inflicting pain.

But then I asked myself why. Why the need to hurt? And why the people I cared about the most? Why the need for all the lies? Why the attacks on my mother? I would drive myself mad with all the why's until one day, it all exploded in a suicidal rage.

Lying awake the following night at the "resort" (my pet name for the hospital), after an unsuccessful, gutless attempt to jump from a vehicle moving at eighty miles per hour, one thing stood out more than my Keds with no shoe laces. I didn't want to die.

And I did not want to inflict any more pain on people to cover up what I was truly trying to hide myself: self-hatred. Self-hatred unleashed on everyone else.

I saw my mother's pained face for the first time in years— warm, tired brown eyes filled with nothing but thanks for her daughter's new lease on life and love for the child she waited thirty-eight years to bear.

My first encounter with unconditional love. What a powerful feeling.

Despite all the lies I had told her, she still loved me. I cried on her lap for hours one afternoon and asked why she still loved me after all the horrible things I did to her. She just looked down at me, brushed the hair out of my face and said frankly, "I don't know."

A kind of smile penetrated her tears as the lines in her tested face told me all that I needed to know. I was her daughter, but more important, she was my mother. Not every rotten child is so lucky. Not every mother can be pushed to the limits I explored time and time again, and venture back with feelings of love.

Unconditional love is the most precious gift we can give. Being forgiven for the past is the most precious gift we can receive. I dare not say we could experience this pure love twice in one lifetime.

I was one of the lucky ones. I know that. I want to extend the gift my mother gave me to all the "rotten teenagers" in the world who are confused.

It's okay to feel pain, to need help, to feel love—just feel it without hiding. Come out from under the protective covers, from behind the rigid walls and the suffocating personas, and take a breath of life.

*Sarah J. Vogt*

# The Home Run

On June 18th, I went to my little brother's baseball game as I always did. Cory was twelve years old at the time and had been playing baseball for a couple of years. When I saw that he was warming up to be next at bat, I decided to head over to the dugout to give him a few pointers. But when I got there, I simply said, "I love you."

In return, he asked, "Does this mean you want me to hit a home run?"

I smiled and said, "Do your best."

As he walked up to the plate, there was a certain aura about him. He looked so confident and so sure about what he was going to do. One swing was all he took and, wouldn't you know, he hit his first home run! He ran around those bases with such pride—his eyes sparkled and his face was lit up. But what touched my heart the most was when he walked back over to the dugout. He looked over at me with the biggest smile I've ever seen and said, "I love you too, Ter."

I don't remember if his team won or lost that game. On that special summer day in June, it simply didn't matter.

*Terri Vandermark*

# A Brother's Voice

Most people have an inspiration in their life. Maybe it's a talk with someone you respect or an experience. Whatever the inspiration, it tends to make you look at life from a different perspective. My inspiration came from my sister Vicki, a kind and caring person. She didn't care about accolades or being written about in newspapers. All she wanted was to share her love with the people she cared about, her family and friends.

The summer before my junior year of college, I received a phone call from my father saying that Vicki was rushed to the hospital. She had collapsed and the right side of her body was paralyzed. The preliminary indications were that she suffered a stroke. However, test results confirmed it was much more serious. There was a malignant brain tumor causing her paralysis. Her doctors didn't give her more than three months to live. I remember wondering how this could happen? The day before Vicki was perfectly fine. Now, her life was coming to an end at such a young age.

After overcoming the initial shock and feeling of emptiness, I decided that Vicki needed hope and encouragement. She needed someone to make her believe that she would overcome this obstacle. I became Vicki's coach. Everyday we would visualize the tumor shrinking and everything that we talked about was positive. I even posted a sign on her hospital room door that read, "If you have any negative thoughts, leave them at the door." I was determined to help Vicki beat the tumor. She and I made a deal that was called 50-50. I would do 50 percent of the fighting and Vicki would do the other 50 percent.

The month of August arrived and it was time to begin my junior year of college three thousand miles away. I was unsure whether I should leave or stay with Vicki. I made the mistake of telling her that I might not leave for school. She became angry and said not to worry because she would be fine. There was Vicki lying ill in a hospital bed telling me not to worry. I realized that if I stayed it might send a message that she was dying and I didn't want her believing that. Vicki needed to believe that she could win against the tumor.

Leaving that night feeling it might be the last time I would ever see Vicki alive was the most difficult thing I have ever done. While at school, I never stopped fighting my 50 percent for her. Every night before falling asleep I would talk to Vicki, hoping that there was some way she could hear me. I would say, "Vicki I'm fighting for you and I will never quit. As long as you never quit fighting we will beat this."

A few months had passed and she was still holding on. I was talking with an elderly friend and she asked about Vicki's situation. I told her that she was getting worse but that she wasn't quitting. My friend asked a question that really made me think. She said, "Do you think the reason she hasn't let go is because she doesn't want to let you down?"

*Maybe she was right? Maybe I was selfish for encouraging Vicki to keep fighting?* That night before falling asleep, I said to her, "Vicki, I understand that you're in a lot of pain and that you might like to let go. If you do, then I want you to. We didn't lose because you never quit fighting. If you want to go on to a better place then I understand. We will be together again. I love you and I'll always be with you wherever you are."

Early the next morning, my mother called to tell me that Vicki had passed away.

*James Malinchak*

# Beautiful, She Said

I never thought that I understood her. She always seemed so far away from me. I loved her, of course. We shared mutual love from the day I was born.

I came into this world with a bashed head and deformed features because of the hard labor my mother had gone through. Family members and friends wrinkled their noses at the disfigured baby I was. They all commented on how much I looked like a beat-up football player. But no, not her. Nana thought I was beautiful. Her eyes twinkled with splendor and happiness at the ugly baby in her arms. Her first granddaughter. Beautiful, she said.

Before final exams in my junior year of high school, she died.

Seven years earlier, her doctors had diagnosed Nana with Alzheimer's disease. Our family became experts on this disease as, slowly, we lost her.

She always spoke in fragmented sentences. As the years passed, the words she spoke became fewer and fewer, until finally she said nothing at all. We were lucky to get one occasional word out of her. It was then that our family knew she was near the end.

About a week or so before she died, her body lost the ability to function at all, and the doctors decided to move her to a hospice. A hospice: where those who enter never come out.

I told my parents I wanted to see her. I had to see her. My uncontrollable curiosity had taken a step above my gut-wrenching fear.

My mother brought me to the hospice two days later. My grandfather and two of my aunts were there as well, but they hung back in the hallway as I entered Nana's room. She was sitting in a big, fluffy chair next to her bed, slouched over, eyes shut, mouth numbly hanging open. The morphine was keeping her asleep. My eyes darted around the room at the windows, the flowers and the way Nana looked. I was struggling very hard to take it all in, knowing that this would be the last time I ever saw her alive.

I slowly sat down across from her. I took her left hand and held it in mine, brushing a stray lock of golden hair away from her face. I just sat and stared, motionless, in front of her, unable to feel anything. I opened my mouth to speak but nothing came out. I could not get over how awful she looked, sitting there helpless.

Then it happened. Her little hand wrapped around mine tighter and tighter. Her voice began what sounded like a soft howl. She seemed to be crying in pain. And then she spoke.

"Jessica." Plain as day. My name. Mine. Out of four children, two sons-in-law, one daughter-in-law and six grandchildren, she knew it was me.

At that moment, it was as though someone were showing a family filmstrip in my head. I saw Nana at my baptizing. I saw her at my fourteen dance recitals. I saw her bringing me roses and beaming with pride. I saw her tap-dancing on our kitchen floor. I saw her pointing at her own wrinkled cheeks and telling me that it was from her that I inherited my big dimples. I saw her playing games with us grandkids while the other adults ate Thanksgiving dinner. I saw her sitting with me in my living room at Christmas time, admiring our brightly decorated tree.

I then looked at her as she was . . . and I cried.

I knew she would never see my final senior dance recital or watch me cheer for another football game. She would never sit with me and admire our Christmas tree again. I knew she would never see me go off to my senior prom, graduate from high school and college, or get married. And I knew she would never be there the day my first child was born. Tear after tear rolled down my face.

But above all, I cried because I finally knew how she had felt the day I had been born. She had looked through what she saw on the outside and looked instead to the inside, and she had seen a life.

I slowly released her hand from mine and brushed away the tears staining her cheeks, and mine. I stood, leaned over, and kissed her and said, *"You look beautiful."*

And with one long last look, I turned and left the hospice.

*Jessica Gardner*

# Steeped with Meaning

My mom and I sat in the small college café with our large mugs of something that smelled like lemon and tasted like home. We were catching up on the past four months of our lives and the hours just weren't long enough. Sure, we had talked on the phone and occasionally written. But the calls were long distance, and it was rare to find a moment when my roommate wasn't waiting for the phone, or my younger brother or sister wasn't waiting for my mom. So while we knew of each other's experiences, we had not yet dissected them. As we discussed her new job, my latest paper, my new love and her latest interview, I leaned back into my cushion and thought: *I always knew when she became my mother, but when had she become my friend?*

As far back as I can remember my mom was always the first person that I came to with every tear and every laugh. When I lost a tooth and when I found a friend, when I fell from my bike and when I got back on it, she was there. She never judged me; she let me set my own expectations. She was proud when I succeeded and supportive when I didn't. She always listened; she seemed to know when I was asking for advice and when I just needed a good cry. She multiplied my excitement with her own and divided my frustrations with her empathy and understanding. When she picked me up from school, she always asked about my day. I remember that one day when I asked about hers. I think I was a little surprised that she had so much to say. We rarely had late-night talks (because she was already asleep), nor early-morning ones (because I was not yet up), but in between the busy hours of our filled days, we found the time to fill each other's ears with stories and hearts with love. She slowly shared more and more of her own life with me, and that made me feel more open with her. We shared experiences and hopes, frustrations and fears. Learning that she still had blocks to build and to tumble made me more comfortable with my own. She made me feel that my opinions were never immature and my thoughts never silly. What surprises me now is not that she always remembered to tell me "sweet dreams," but that she never forgot to tell me that she believed in me. When she started going through some changes in her life, I had the opportunity to tell her that I believed in her, too.

My mother had always been a friend. She had given me her heart in its entirety; but her soul, she divulged in pieces, when she knew that I was ready.

I sat across from the woman who had given me my life and then shared hers with me. Our mugs were empty, but our hearts were full. We both knew that tomorrow she'd return to the bustle of Los Angeles and I'd remain in the hustle of New Haven. I know that we are both growing and learning. Yet, we continue to learn about each other and grow closer. Our relationship was like the tea that we had sipped: the longer it steeped, the better it tasted.

*Daphna Renan*

"I already know about sex, but could you explain
where Beanie Babies come from?"

*Reprinted by permission of Harley Schwadron.*

# A Father's Wish

*It's a wonderful feeling when your father becomes not a god but a man to you—when he comes down from the mountain and you see he's this man with weaknesses. And you love him as this whole being, not as a figurehead.*

Robin Williams

I write this . . . as a father. Until you have a son of your own, you will never know what that means. You will never know the joy beyond joy, the love beyond feeling that resonates in the heart of a father as he looks upon his son. You will never know the sense of honor that makes a man want to be more than he is and to pass on something good and hopeful into the hands of his son. And you will never know the heartbreak of the fathers who are haunted by the personal demons that keep them from being the men they want their sons to see.

You will only see the man that stands before you, or who has left your life, who exerts a power over you—for good or for ill—that will never let go.

It is a great privilege and a great burden to be that man.

There is something that must be passed from father to son, or it is never passed as clearly. It is a sense of manhood, of self-worth, of responsibility to the world around us.

And yet, how to put it in words? We live in a time when it is hard to speak from the heart. Our lives are smothered by a thousand trivialities, and the poetry of our spirits is silenced by the thoughts and cares of daily affairs. The song that lives in our hearts, the song that we have waited to share, the song of being a man, is silent. We find ourselves full of advice but devoid of belief.

And so, I want to speak to you honestly. I do not have answers. But I do understand the questions. I see you struggling and discovering and striving upward, and I see myself reflected in your eyes and in your days. In some deep and fundamental way, I have been there and I want to share.

I, too, have learned to walk, to run, to fall. I have had a first love. I have known fear and anger and sadness. My heart has been broken and I have known moments when the hand of God seemed to be on my shoulder. I have wept tears of sorrow and tears of joy.

There have been times of darkness when I thought I would never again see light, and there have been times when I wanted to dance and sing and hug every person I met.

I have felt myself emptied into the mystery of the universe, and I have had moments when the smallest slight threw me into a rage.

I have carried others when I barely had the strength to walk myself, and I have left others standing by the side of the road with their hands outstretched for help.

Sometimes I feel I have done more than anyone can ask; other times I feel I am a charlatan and a failure. I carry within me the spark of greatness and the darkness of heartless crimes.

In short, I am a man, as are you.

Although you will walk your own earth and move through your own time, the same sun will rise on you that rose on me, and the same seasons will course across your life as moved across mine. We will always be different, but we will always be the same.

This is my attempt to give you the lessons of my life, so that you can use them in yours. They are not meant to make you into me. It is my greatest joy to watch you become yourself. But time reveals truths, and these truths are greater than either of us. If I can give them a voice in a way that allows me to walk beside you during your days, then I will have done well.

To be your father is the greatest honor I have ever received. It allowed me to touch mystery for a moment, and to see my love made flesh. If I could have but one wish, it would be for you to pass that love along. After all, there is not much more to life than that.

*Kent Nerburn*

"Someday, son, you'll finally be
old enough to do anything you want to do . . .
but your son will have the car, so you'll have
to stay home and watch television."

*Reprinted by permission of Randy Glasbergen.*

# The Bridge Between Verses

*Things do not change. We change.*

Henry David Thoreau

My brother is the boy with the big black eyes. He has an aura about him that feels strange and nervous. My brother is different. He doesn't understand when jokes are made. He takes a long time to learn basic things. He often laughs for no reason.

He was pretty average until the first grade. That year, his teacher complained of him laughing in class. As a punishment, she made him sit in the hall. He spent all his time on the fake mosaic tile outside the room. The next year, he took a test that showed he needed to be placed in a special-education class.

As I grew older, I began to resent my brother. When I walked with him, people stared. Not that anything was physically wrong with him; it's just something that radiated from him that attracted attention. I would clench my teeth in anger sometimes, wishing he were like other people, wishing he were normal.

I would glare at him to make him uncomfortable. Every time my eyes met his, stark and too-bright, I would say loudly, "What?" He'd turn his head quickly and mutter, "Nothing." I rarely called him by his name.

My friends would tell me I was being mean to him. I brushed it off, thinking that they were also horrible to their siblings. I did not consider the fact that their brothers and sisters could retaliate. Sometimes I would be nice to my brother just because they were around, but return to being mean the minute they left.

My cruelty and embarrassment continued until one day last summer. It was a holiday, but both my parents were working. I had an orthodontist appointment and was supposed to take my brother with me. The weather was warm, being a July afternoon. As spring was over, there was no fresh scent or taste of moisture in the air, only the empty feeling of summer. As we walked down the sidewalk, on impulse I began to talk to him.

I asked him how his summer was going, what his favorite kind of car was, what he planned to do in the future. His answers were rather boring, but I wasn't bored. It turns out I have a brother who loves Cadillacs, wants to be an engineer or a business person, and loves listening to what he calls "rap" music (the example he gave was Aerosmith). I also have a brother with an innocent grin that can light up a room or an already sunny day. I have a brother who is ambitious, kind, friendly, open and talkative.

The conversation we had that day was special. It was a new beginning for me.

A week later, we were on a family trip to Boston, and I was in the back seat of our van. I was reading a Stephen King novel, *Rage,* while my dad and my brother sat up front talking. A few of their words caught my attention, and I found myself listening to their conversation while pretending to be engrossed in my book. My brother said, "Last week, we were walking to the bus stop. We had a good conversation and she was nice to me."

That's all he said. As simple as his words were, they were heartfelt. He held no dislike toward me. He just accepted that I'd finally become the sister I should have been from the beginning. I closed the book and stared at the back cover. The author's face blurred as I realized I was crying.

I will not pretend everything is fine and dandy now. Like changes in a *Wonder Years* episode, nothing's perfect, and nothing's permanent. What I will say is that I do not glare at my brother any more. I walk with him in public. I help him use the computer. I call him by his name. Best of all, I continue to have conversations with him. Conversations that are boring in the nicest possible way.

*Shashi Bhat*

# The Ones in Front of Me

At some point in my childhood, I realized that my parents were never going to get along; the lines had been drawn and the die had been cast. So when my parents announced that they were filing for a divorce, it wasn't a huge shock. I never thought it was my fault. I also never had the illusion that they would miraculously fall back in love. So, I guess I accepted their decision.

For most of my childhood it didn't bother me that they weren't together. In fact, I had the best of both worlds. I got to live in Hawaii with my mom and travel to Los Angeles to see my dad. Somewhere during the process, however, I began to feel the effects of our "broken home." Although they tried not to make it too obvious, my parents' disdain for each other was becoming apparent.

When I was twelve, I wanted to live with my dad, so I moved to Los Angeles. It's not that I didn't love my mom; it's that I had spent most of my childhood with her and started to feel as if I didn't know much about my dad.

After the move, I started to realize how much my parents' divorce really affected me. My dad would tell me to tell my mom to send me money, and my mom would tell me to tell my dad that she shouldn't have to. I felt caught in the middle. My mom would try to pull information out of me about how it "really" was at my dad's. It was a constant struggle to duck out of the line of fire.

My parents tried to respect each other, for my sake I guess, but it was obvious that a lot of hurt lay underneath their actions. It had been ten years since they divorced, but it felt as if the struggle had just begun. They constantly argued over money and parenting styles. As much as they both promised that it didn't involve me, it always did. I felt they were fighting over me, and that it was somehow my fault—feelings I didn't have when I was five.

Growing up with divorced parents today seems to be a regular occurrence. It's actually rare to find two parents who are still together, but that doesn't make going through it hurt any less. Although I may not have felt it at the time, eventually, it was something that I had to work through—whether I was five or fifteen.

I wish I could say that my parents have worked out all their problems, and that we now work as a perfect team. It is never that simple. But, they try. They love me, and while it took all of us a while to realize it, now we know that their love for me will always keep them together in some way—they have learned to work together in order to raise me.

The other day, the three of us got together to talk about my upcoming trip to visit colleges. I think they are both sad about the idea of me leaving—and that is what keeps them together: the joy and sadness of watching me grow.

As we sat there the thought crossed my mind, *What if my family were still together?* Then, as I watched my parents intently looking through my college brochures, I smiled to myself, *This is my family, and we are "together."*

*Lia Gay*

"You mean Dad started out as a date?"

# Snowdrops

"Are they up yet?" Grandmother asks hopefully.

"No, not yet," Mother answers patiently, as if address-ing an eager child. From her position on the edge of my grandmother's bed, I see her smile silently as she contin-ues knitting. She is smiling because of the familiarity of the question. For the last few weeks of her illness, my grandmother has been living to see the snowdrops bloom in her garden. Sometimes I think the only reason she doesn't succumb to her cancer is so she will live to see the tiny, white flowers she so adores, one last time. I don't understand her strong feelings for the snowdrops, as they are, by far, not the most beautiful flowers growing in Grandmother's garden. I wish to ask why she is so drawn to them but Mother's presence stops me. For some rea-son, I feel the need to ask the question in private. I realize then that Grandmother's eagerness for such a simple thing is almost childlike, and this causes me to reflect. We come into this world as children, and exit in almost the same way.

"Grandmother, why do you like snowdrops so much?" I ask during a visit one day, once Mother has gone downstairs.

She looks so fragile lying in her bed, I almost regret asking the question. Answering may prove to be too much exertion for her weak lungs to handle. However, she takes a breath and begins to talk, slowly and quietly.

"When your grandfather and I were married, around this time of year, the snowdrops were in bloom. I wore them in my hair at our wedding. Your grandfather adored them. Every year we planted them in our garden, and through some bizarre miracle, they always bloomed on our anniversary.

"After your grandfather died, I missed him terribly. All I had to do, though, was look at the snowdrops, and I felt close to him, as if he were with me again. Our snowdrops were what saved me on days I missed him so much I wanted to die." Grandmother finishes her story and stares silently into space, thinking. I don't want to interrupt her thoughts, so when she closes her eyes and drifts off to sleep, I still don't speak.

We visit Grandmother again, but on this day Mother asks me to stay downstairs. Grandmother's condition is worsening and she can't cope with any visitors except Mother. She no longer has the strength to talk, and I remember my most recent talk with Mother. She was in need of someone to confide in, and I was the only ear available; otherwise, I'm sure she wouldn't have burdened me with her pain. She told me of her visits alone with Grandmother, and how she wished Grandmother would just give up and allow herself to go, to end her own suffering. I could see Mother's pain, and how much she longed to cry; but for my sake, she would not. I imagine what my mother is doing upstairs right now—sitting on Grandmother's bed, holding her hand and encouraging her not to fight anymore.

My thoughts are interrupted as I notice a glossy, white album on a shelf across from where I am seated. On the binding there is a date printed in gold ink: April 13, 1937. I pull the large book from the shelf and gingerly open it. I am mesmerized by the black-and-white photo that greets my eyes. I recognize Grandmother and Grandfather, posing together happily, and I know this must be their wedding album. Grandmother's beautiful white gown draws my attention. Then my eye is attracted by the tiny white flowers perched in Grandmother's hair. They are her snowdrops, and for the first time, I can see just how beautiful they really are.

The telephone rings on the most gorgeous day of spring so far. When Mother answers it, I know right away what has happened. My first question is, "What day is it?" Through her tears, Mother answers, confirming my suspicions. She doesn't want me to come with her today, but I insist. There is something I need to see.

When we arrive at Grandmother's house I immediately run to the backyard. While the image of the snowdrops is blurred by my tears, they have bloomed just the same. I am upset that Grandmother didn't get to see them, but then I realize that this year she didn't need to. For the first time in many years, she won't miss Grandfather on their anniversary. Despite my sadness I smile, for I know they are celebrating together in heaven.

*Sarah McCann*

# Kicki

Throughout my childhood, I constantly dreamed of being an only child—having no one around to fight with, to share with, to grab the remote away from me in the middle of a "big game." I would have the biggest bedroom in the house and be able to talk on the phone as long as I wanted, without being asked a million times, "Are you off yet?" But I was not born an only child; I was born with an older sister. I have always called my sister "Kicki," instead of her real name, Christie, because, when I was younger, I had trouble pronouncing the *r* and *s*. To this day, she is still "Kicki."

I started playing basketball when I was eight years old. My dad was the coach of my team, and my mom kept score. So my sister, not old enough to stay home alone, was forced to come to all of my games. I remember looking into the stands for my mother's approval during games and seeing my sister's face, confused. It was obvious that she wasn't thrilled to be there, but she cheered along with the crowd anyway. Her hair was cut short, almost as short as mine, and her teeth stuck out. I teased her often, calling her "bucky beaver." She wasn't a very attractive little girl, and she looked more like my older brother than my sister.

After the games, on the car rides home, my parents and I relived every move I had made on the court. My sister sat in the backseat with me in silence, not knowing how or when to enter the conversation. Most nights she came into my room and said, "Good night, Brad. Good game." I would smile and thank her. I never really took her compliment seriously. I mean, she hardly understood what was going on in the games; she couldn't possibly know whether I had played well or not.

It wasn't until I reached high school that I realized what a truly beautiful person my sister was. Everybody knew her and thought highly of her, and I was referred to as "Christie's little brother." Kicki was on the Homecoming Court her senior year, and she stood tall and beautiful. I was astonished at the person she had become: smart, sweet and beautiful. To me, she was still the ten-year-old little girl with the boyish looks and buckteeth.

I played basketball in high school, and although Christie wasn't forced to attend my games anymore, she still came every week, cheering me on from the stands. I remember one game in particular, the last game of the season. My sister sat in the bleachers with her boyfriend and a large group of friends. Printed on her shirt, in big bright red letters, were the words "BRAD'S SISTER." Suddenly I was embarrassed. But it wasn't her presence that embarrassed me, rather, it was the fact that I had never appreciated her support before. She was never embarrassed to be my sister, even though I had been embarrassed to call her that so many years ago. She didn't care what anyone thought, and she never had.

I am an only child now; my sister left for college a few months after that last game. I finally have the biggest room in the house and the remote control all to myself.

But now that she's gone, I kind of miss having someone to fight with for the phone, and the big bedroom isn't all that great anyway.

I went to visit her at college for a weekend, and as I stood outside her dorm, waiting for her to come out, a friend of hers walked past me and questioned, "Hey, aren't you Christie's brother?" I beamed and said proudly, "Yeah, I am. I'm Christie's brother."

*Brad Dixon*

# Rikki's Hug

I'm walking up the sidewalk to our brown, three-bedroom condo. I've lived here for so many years that I can't even remember the day we moved in. I know that sidewalk, steps and porch so well that I could easily walk them blind. As I pause at the door to search for my key in my purse, I get a whiff of the familiar dryer sheet smell that is flowing from the vent near the porch. It's a comforting smell, one that most people would overlook. But I've always noticed it. I gaze up at the same old gray Connecticut sky. The cool breeze that frequents early spring in the Northeast whips my windbreaker around my shoulders and leaks through the sleeves, causing me to shiver. My day at school was pretty typical, although I didn't do as well in all of my classes as I wanted to. I'm behind in my outlining for history, which is usually the most lacking area of my schoolwork because I dread it so much.

Tonight I am supposed to go out for a mid-week dinner and then to the gym, but play rehearsal ran over. It's getting late, and I have so much work ahead of me this evening. What began as an ordinary day is now anything but ordinary. The breeze feels like a fierce, wintry gust. My head hurts, my liveliness faded to a shade of tired. It's too much. I can't do it anymore. I struggle to turn the key in the door when it swings wide open.

There she stands, her little body clad in Osh-Koshes that have Pooh on them, her long brown curls free and flowing down her back to her waist. She lets me put her hair up very rarely; she prefers it to be let alone to do what it wants. She's wise beyond her years. Her eyes remind me of milk chocolate with a fleck of summer sunshine in them. They retain the gentle radiance of summer long after the leaves have fallen off the trees and have been replaced with frigid snow. But it's her smile that I notice. Her smile never ceases to amaze me. It lights up her face with an innocent and happy luminescence. It's a contagious smile. "Gaga is home!" She's called me that name since she first started talking. She's put behind her all of the other baby names for friends and family, but mine sticks. That's because I'm her favorite sister, her favorite person. Well, that's what she tells me and I choose not to acknowledge that she's only four and doesn't understand yet what the depths of the word "favorite" are. I understand what it means, so I can legitimately say that she's my favorite. Though she may not understand the extremity in this word, she sure understands me.

Her little arms wrap around me as I hug the little girl whom I still call, "Baby." Only when she misbehaves do I use her real name. Though she's at that age when babies no longer are babies and want to be "big girls," she never corrects me. And only when she's upset with me does she ever use my actual name. With that one gesture, everything's okay again. She puts a butterfly kiss on my cheek. Then come the sweetest words you could ever hear, which could easily be mistaken for the sound of an angel: "I missed you." *Isn't it funny how with one simple display of affection, everything turns around?* The world suddenly seems okay and I can no longer find a reason to be tired. And even though when that moment is over, the toils and troubles of life return, it's always waiting for me at my front door. All I have to do is turn the key.

*Kathryn Litzenberger*

# What Siblings Know

When I was twelve and my brother David was seventeen, we were home one Halloween night watching a horror movie we'd rented. It was an entertaining but silly movie about a woman who becomes a witch. The woman who played the witch was young and looked like a model. Every time she cast a spell, her long red hair whipped around her face and her eyes got bright green. Once when this happened, my brother said, "Wow, she looks really hot."

I stared at him. I was astonished at what he'd said. I hadn't noticed it before, but until that night I'd never, ever heard my brother voice an attraction to women, even though he was a teenager and supposedly in the prime of his life.

This is what I remember when people ask me when I first knew my brother was gay. I didn't realize he was different until I heard him saying something that most guys his age would say without a second thought.

My brother tried to like girls. The thought of him trying—even by saying something as trivial as "She looks hot" about an actress on a television screen—breaks my heart. All that time he was trying, through middle school and high school and into college, he couldn't tell me or my parents how hard it was for him. He was all alone.

When I was twelve, David went out of state for college. He came home for holidays and a few weeks in the summer, and he called every week, but every year he seemed to pull farther away from me and my parents. When he was home, he was quiet and distant, and on the phone he was polite but tense, the way people get when they are hiding really big secrets.

My parents were slow, but they weren't stupid. A couple of years after David left for college, when they still hadn't heard mention of any girlfriends or even dates, they became suspicious. My mother started asking me questions, thinking that I must know something she didn't know, because siblings tell each other things they don't tell their parents. But David hadn't told me anything. He never had, not even before he left for college. I always knew he loved me, but he was more independent than the rest of us, and I never felt he needed me.

The next time David came home, I did a terrible thing. I wanted to borrow his leather backpack and I knew he wouldn't let me if I asked him, so I just took it. But before I filled it with my things, I had to take out his things to make room. There were some schoolbooks and a fancy notebook bound with a rubber band. I was curious. I pulled off the rubber band and started reading.

Immediately, I found myself immersed in a world of suppressed anger, self-loathing and tentative romances. I learned more about my brother in those pages than I ever could from him, at least back then. I learned that he'd known he was gay his entire life, but that not until he escaped to college did he admit it to another human being. That human being was his roommate, Rob. I remembered him mentioning how Rob had transferred dorm rooms in the middle of the semester, and when I read my brother's journal I learned that Rob changed rooms because he didn't want to live with someone who was gay.

It was a little while—a few pages into the journal—before my brother told anyone else. He joined a campus group and made some gay friends, and slowly his life forked into two lives. There was the life my parents and I saw—a life with lies and friends who didn't know him, and no one to love—and there was a second life, a life with friends and crushes and dates. A life where he was happy.

I put the backpack—and the little notebook—back in my brother's room, and I never told him what I'd learned. But my parents continued to badger me about David and his lack of love life—they knew he was gay, I'm sure, but denied it even to themselves—and eventually I called him up. "David," I said, "you have to tell them."

He didn't ask me how I knew, and I didn't tell him. But looking back, I understand that reading my brother's journal—a horrible crime I would never commit again— only filled in some of the details. Somehow, I already knew the story. Maybe it is true that siblings know each other better than their parents know them. I like to think so.

The next Thanksgiving, after a pretty typical family meal, my brother suggested we all take a walk. We walked past the end of our street and onto the grounds of the high school, then onto the track. Then my brother stopped. "I have something to tell you," he said. I felt my parents' hearts skip a beat—they wanted so badly, back then, for it not to be true. "I wanted to tell you that I'm gay."

My parents were pretty rational, considering. They told David that he was just experimenting, that eventually he'd find a woman he wanted to marry. He listened to them, then politely but firmly said that this was something that wasn't going to change. They argued but never raised their voices, and eventually we went home and took naps in separate rooms. The following days were very quiet. Then David went back to school, to his happy life.

It was five years before my parents came to truly accept my brother. My brother was fortunate to be out of the house during that time, but I was not so lucky. My parents fought more than ever, my father drank a lot, and I spent time out of the house. But slowly—*very* slowly—my parents got used to the idea. After a year, my mother told one of her friends about David, then my father told one of his. They received love and support—David was a great kid, said my parents' friends. That hadn't changed. Secretly, I'm sure they were relieved that it wasn't their kid who was gay. After my parents learned not to hide it, there was still the matter of being proud of David, of not only tolerating hearing about his romantic life, but wanting to hear about it.

About a week before Christmas one year, my brother called home to ask my parents if he could bring a friend home for the holiday. A boyfriend. My parents told David they'd think about it, then called him back and said absolutely not. My brother felt hurt and rejected, and when he came home, relations between him and my parents were strained. Then he and my father got into a fight on Christmas Eve, and David took an early flight back to school. Christmas Day was sadder and lonelier than it had ever been.

I called David a few days later. "You can't rush them," I said, feeling guilty for defending them.

"It's been three years," said David. He was frustrated, which I understood. So was I. I didn't understand why my parents couldn't just get over it. It seemed simple. Every time my mother asked me how a date had gone or said she liked a boy I'd introduced to her, I thought, *What's so different between me and David? Don't you want him to be happy, too?*

But David's patience paid off. My mother joined a support group for parents of gays and lesbians, and soon she was succeeding in dragging my father with her to the meetings. She was even asked to speak at a conference for high-school teachers about being unbiased toward homosexuality in the classroom. Time passed. My parents eased into not only accepting the fact that David wasn't ever going to be straight, but also that it wasn't a bad thing at all. That for David, it was a very good thing.

Then they did the craziest and most wonderful thing. I still laugh when I think about it. They made a list of all the people they hadn't told about David, including old friends, siblings and their own parents, and they planned a three-week road trip across the country. They had news to deliver, and they wanted to deliver it in person and do some sightseeing in the meantime. They'd gotten this idea in their heads that it wasn't enough for David to come out of the closet. He would never feel they'd truly accepted him until they came out of the closet, too, as the loving parents of a gay son.

David's apartment was the last stop on their journey, and I took an airplane up to meet them when they arrived. We took another family walk, and David told us about his new boyfriend and I told them about mine. Finally, after so much pain and hard work, my brother's two lives started to merge.

*Danielle Collier*

# Relief

I'm not quite sure when the turning point came. But I know that it came after a fight I had with my mother. It was a typical fight for that rebellious summer. You know how it is, you lie once, and then they all start to pile up. And nothing happens evenly—it's always all at once. That summer I drifted apart from my mother, and my two best friends, whom I needed to turn to, were angry with me. That's where I learned my second lesson (the first being not to lie)—never keep your feelings hidden. That's what my friends did, and when I found out, it was too late.

Anyway, my house was a battle zone. I'd sleep till I had to go to work and then sleep after work. In between, I'd cry and feel sorry for myself, well, when I wasn't fighting with my mom. That day it all changed.

She was screaming at me about how I wasn't a part of the family anymore—that no one liked being around me because I was always so hostile. I yelled back, as most sixteen-year-olds would. But my mom doesn't ground me (well, I was already grounded) or take away the phone; she assigns essays. My assignment was to apologize for my behavior.

I cried tears of rage in my room, yelling about what I could possibly write. But then I started to write. And the apology turned into an explanation. I poured out every pain and emotion, ones that I had hidden behind my rage, the ones I cried about at night. I didn't know how to get back to being me, and I hated what I had become. I felt so lost. And, most of all, I felt like everyone that I had depended on had left me. Alone.

I left the letter on her bed and went to sleep, exhausted from sobbing. I wrapped myself up in my warm, flannel blankets to ease the cold. Although it was a warm and humid summer night, I shivered. The next morning I woke up early enough to go to work so that no one was awake yet. I crept into the bathroom and noticed a card with my name written on it in my mother's handwriting taped to the mirror. I opened it. It said that she understood. She understood that I was lost and scared. And she promised that she would help me.

I got into the hot shower, silently sobbing. My salty tears mixed with the water on my face. Except that this time, the tears were of relief, not of despair.

*Kathryn Litzenberger*

# Don't Cry, Dad

During my years in junior high, I developed an after-school routine. Every day I walked in the back door of my home and proceeded up the three flights of stairs to my bedroom. I closed the door, turned my music up loud and lay on my bed for two hours until someone came to get me for dinner. I ate dinner in silence; I tried desperately to avoid talking to my family and even harder not to make eye contact with them. I hurriedly finished my dinner and rushed back to my room for more music. I locked myself in my room until it was time for school the next day.

Once in a while, my parents would ask me if there was anything wrong. I would snap at them, saying that I was just fine and to stop asking so many questions. The truth was, I couldn't answer them because I didn't know what was wrong. Looking back, I was very unhappy. I cried for no reason, and little things made me explode. I didn't eat well, either. It wasn't "cool" at that time to be seen actually eating lunch during school. I wasn't much of a break-fast eater, and if I weren't required to eat dinner with my family every night, I probably wouldn't have eaten at all.

The summer before my freshman year, my dad told me

that he wanted to talk. I was *not* thrilled. In fact, I resented him. I did not want to talk to anyone, especially my dad.

We sat down, and he started the conversation by asking the usual questions: "Are you okay? Is everything all right?" I didn't answer; I refused to make eye contact.

"Every day I come home from work, and you're locked in your room, cut off from the rest of us." He paused a moment, his voice was a little shaky as he began again. "I feel like you're shutting me out of your life." Having said that, my father, a man who I thought was stronger than steel, began to cry. And I don't mean just a few tears rolling down his cheeks. Months of hidden pain flooded from his eyes. I felt like I had been slapped. Never in my fourteen years had I seen my dad cry. Through his tears he went on to tell me that he wanted to be a part of my life and how he ached to be my friend. I loved my dad more than anything in the world, and it killed me to think I had hurt him so deeply. His eyes shifted towards me. They looked tired and full of pain—pain that I had never seen, or maybe that I had ignored. I felt a lump forming in my throat as he continued to cry. Slowly, that lump turned to tears, and they started pouring from my eyes.

"Don't cry, Dad," I said, putting my hand on his shoulder.

"I hope I didn't embarrass you with my tears," he replied.

"Of course not."

We cried together a little more before he left. In the days that followed, I had a hard time breaking the pattern I had become so accustomed to over the last two years. I tried sitting in the living room with my parents while they drank their coffee. I felt lost in their world, while I was desperately trying to adjust to new habits. Still, I made an effort. It took almost another full year before I felt completely comfortable around my family again and included them in my personal life.

Now I'm a sophomore in high school, and almost every day when I come home from school, I sit down and tell my dad about my day while we have our coffee. We talk about my life, and he offers advice sometimes, but mostly, he just listens.

Looking back, I am so glad my father and I had that talk. Not only have I gained a better relationship with my father, I've gained a friend.

*Laura Loken*

"Thanks anyway, Dad, but I'll walk.
I wouldn't be caught dead driving around
with your bumper stickers."

*Reprinted by permission of Dave Carpenter.*

# Dear Diary . . .

*The greatest happiness of life is the conviction that we are loved—loved for ourselves or rather, loved in spite of ourselves.*

Victor Hugo

*Dear Diary,*

Drip. Drip. Drip. *For three hours I've waited in this train station and for three hours I've heard the faint splash of water fall from an old water fountain onto the cold, hardwood floor. The wood is old and worn but somehow doesn't allow any of the water drops to seep through. Funny, how something . . . Suddenly a horn whistles from a departing train, interrupting my thoughts and allowing them to come crashing back to reality.*

*I glance at my watch and realize I've missed my train, and the next one isn't going to leave this town for the next four hours. What am I going to do now? It's a quarter past midnight, and I'm cold and hungry. I have a meeting with the admissions officer in a college at 8:00 A.M., and by the look of*

*things, I'm not going to make it on time. What a way to make
a first impression, huh?*

*I begin to feel the tears burn the back of my eyes, and soon
they are dancing upon my cheek. I am here alone. There isn't
a familiar face around to comfort me. My mother was supposed to be here with me, to say one final good-bye before I
enter adulthood. But with the many fights and unkept
promises we've shared I didn't expect her to want to come here
with me. Maybe I shouldn't have left the house this evening
without saying I'm sorry. Sorry for the many disagreements
and disappointments. Sorry for my hurtful words and
actions. But we've passed the point where "sorry" heals
things and makes them better again. Still, what I wouldn't
give to have her here with me. Maybe she's right. Maybe I'm
not the know-it-all mature adult I think I am. Maybe I am
still just a scared kid who needs the protection of a mother's
love.*

*It's almost 4:00 now, and the morning sun should be ris-
ing soon. I am able to grab a cup of coffee and change my
clothes during the wait. I figure if I catch a 7:00 bus in
Boston I can still make my appointment. . . .*

*Until next time,*
*Me*

Putting away my journal I reach into my bag to get out
my ticket, but instead a plain white envelope emerges in
my hand. I don't need to read the name on the front to
know who it's from. She wants us to have a better relationship and put the past behind us. Have a fresh start.
My mother even admitted she was sorry for all the arguments we've had over the course of the years. The note
also said she would be waiting for me at the train station
in Boston and we would walk into college together.
Enclosed was an upgraded ticket and a "P.S." telling me to
look in the bottom of my bag. There I would find money

for a bite to eat and a sweater in case I got cold in the station. As I make my way to the train I pass the broken water fountain, which no longer drips, and I realize, for the first time in this life, I'm about to see a woman for who she truly is. My mother.

*Liz Correale*

# The Mother Who Matters

I have eyes that are said to be "cow brown," and my long blond hair is my best feature. My nose is a little too big; my face is oval shaped. I am not overweight, but I'm not skinny either. The only way to describe my height is "vertically challenged."

I'm relatively happy with my appearance, but where did I get it? Do I share the same features as some unknown stranger? Oftentimes, while walking down the street, I try to pick out that stranger, imagining that one of the women I pass could possibly be my biological mother.

I never met my birth mother. I was adopted the moment I was born, and I was taken into a wonderful family. For a long time I wondered what life would be like with my birth mother. Would I still be the same? Where would I live? Would I be happier? Who would my friends be?

I was never dissatisfied with my life; I just never stopped wondering what it would be like to have been raised by my biological mother. And then one day, I was baby-sitting with a friend, and I came across a poem on the nursery wall. It compared adoption to a seed that was planted by one person and then taken care of by another.

The second person had watered the seed and made it grow to be tall and beautiful. I found that it compared perfectly to my situation.

I realized that my mom had made me who I am today, no matter what either of us looks like. And I started to notice that we had the same silly personality, the same outlook on life, and the same way of treating people, along with some other things. She curled my hair for my first dance. She was there for my first heartbreak. She held my hand every time I got a shot at the doctors. She'd been smiling in the crowd for my first school play. She'd been there for everything that ever mattered, and what could compare to that? She's my mom.

Sometimes when we're out somewhere, people comment on how much we look alike, and we turn to each other and laugh, forgetting until that moment that it wasn't she who carried me in her womb for nine months.

Though I may not know why I look the way I do, I know why I am who I am. The mom I have now is the best one I ever could have hoped for, not only because she holds a tremendous amount of unconditional love, but because she has shaped who I am today, my qualities and characteristics. She is the one who made me beautiful!

*Kristy White*

# Never Enough

Sometimes I know the words to say,
Give thanks for all you've done,
But then they fly up and away,
As quickly as they come.

How could I possibly thank you enough,
The one who makes me whole,
The one to whom I owe my life,
The forming of my soul.

The one who tucked me in at night,
The one who stopped my crying,
The one who was the expert,
At picking up when I was lying.

The one who saw me off to school,
And spent sad days alone,
Yet magically produced a smile,
As soon as I came home.

The one who makes such sacrifices,
To always put me first,

Who lets me test my broken wings,
In spite of how it hurts.

Who paints the world a rainbow,
When it's filled with broken dreams,
Who explains it all so clearly,
When nothing's what it seems.

Are there really any words for this?
I find this question tough . . .
Anything I want to say,
Just doesn't seem enough.

What way is there to thank you,
For your heart, your sweat, your tears,
For ten thousand little things you've done,
For oh-so-many years.

For changing with me as I changed,
Accepting all my flaws,
Not loving 'cause you had to,
But loving "just because."

For never giving up on me,
When your wits had reached their end,
For always being proud of me,
For being my best friend.

And so I come to realize,
The only way to say,
The only thank you that's enough,
Is clear in just one way.

Look at me before you,
See what I've become,
Do you see yourself in me?
The job that you have done?

All your hopes and all your dreams,
The strength that no one sees,
A transfer over many years,
Your best was passed to me.

Thank you for the gifts you give,
For everything you do,
But thank you, Mommy, most of all,
For making dreams come true.

 Love,
 Your Daughter

*Laurie Kalb*

# 5

# ON LEARNING AND LESSONS

*I am always ready to learn, but I do not always like being taught.*

*Winston Churchill*

# Egg Lessons

*We should be careful to get out of an experience
only the wisdom that is in it.*

Mark Twain

Robby Rogers . . . my first love. What a great guy, too.
He was kind, honest and smart. In fact, the more I think
about him, the more reasons I find for loving him as much
as I did. We had been going out for a whole year. As you
know, in high school that's a very long time.

I don't remember why I was not at Nancy's party that
Saturday night, but Robby and I had agreed we would see
each other afterward. He would come over around 10:30.
Robby always showed up when he said he would, so at
11:00 I started feeling sick. I knew something wasn't right.

On Sunday morning he woke me with a phone call. "We
need to talk. Can I come over?"

I wanted to say, "No, you cannot come over here and
tell me something is wrong." Instead, I said, "Sure," and
hung up with a knot in my stomach.

I had been right. "I got together with Sue Roth last

night," Robby informed me, "and we're going out now." He followed with the usual, "I'm so confused. I would never do anything to hurt you, Kim. I'll always love you."

I must have turned white because I felt the blood leave my face. This wasn't what I expected; my reaction surprised me. I felt such anger that I was unable to complete a sentence. I was so hurt that everything but the pain in my heart seemed to be moving in slow motion.

"Come on, Kim, don't be like this. We can be friends, can't we?"

Those are the cruelest words to utter to someone you're dumping. I had loved him deeply, shared every little weakness and vulnerability with him—not to mention the four hours a day I had spent with him for the last year (not counting the phone time). I wanted to hit him really hard, over and over, until he felt as horrible as I did. Instead, I asked him to leave. I think I said something sarcastic like, "I hear Sue calling you."

As I sat on my bed and cried for hours, I hurt so bad that nothing could make it stop. I even tried eating an entire gallon of ice cream. I played all of our favorite songs again and again, torturing myself with memories of good times and kind words. After making myself ill with shameless self-indulgence, I made a decision.

I would turn to revenge.

My thinking went like this: Sue Roth is—was—one of my closest friends. Good friends do not throw themselves at your boyfriend when you're not around. Obviously, she should pay.

That weekend, I bought a few dozen eggs and headed for Sue's house with a couple of friends. I started out just venting a little anger, but it got worse. So when someone found an open basement window, we threw the remaining eggs inside. But that's not the worst part. The Roths were out of town for three days!

As I lay in my bed that night, I started to think about what we had done. *This is bad, Kim . . . this is really bad.*

Soon it was all over school. Robby and Sue were going out *and* someone had egged her house while she was out of town, *and* it was so bad that her parents had to hire a professional to get rid of the smell.

As soon as I got home from school, my mom was waiting to talk. "Kim, my phone has been ringing all day, and I don't know what to say. Please—you have to tell me. Did you do it?"

"No, Mom, I didn't." It felt really bad to lie to my mom.

My mother was furious when she got on the phone to call Mrs. Roth. "This is Ellen. I want you to stop accusing my daughter of throwing eggs at your house." She was yelling at Sue's mother now, her voice getting louder and louder. "Kim would *never* do such a thing, and I want you to stop telling people that she did!" She was really going now. "And what's more, *I want you to apologize to me and to my daughter!*"

I felt good about the way my mom was sticking up for me, but awful about the reality. The feelings were all sort of twisted inside of me, and I knew that I had to tell her the truth. I signaled for my mom to get off the phone.

She hung up, reached for the table and sat down. She knew. I cried and told her how sorry I was. Then she cried, too. I would have preferred anger, but she'd used all of that up on Mrs. Roth.

I called Mrs. Roth and told her I'd give her every penny of my baby-sitting savings to help pay for the damages. She accepted, but told me not to come over until she was ready to forgive me.

Mom and I stayed up late that night, talking and crying. She told me about the time her boyfriend left her for her sister. I asked her if she'd egged her own house, and she actually laughed. She told me that although I'd done a terrible thing, it made her furious to think about the things Mrs. Roth had said on the phone. "After all," Mom said, "what about the fact that her daughter steals boyfriends?"

Then she told me how hard it is sometimes being a parent because you want to yell at everyone who causes your child pain, but you can't. You have to stand back and watch while your children learn hard lessons on their own.

I told my mom how incredible it had felt to hear her defend me like that. And at the end of the night, I told her how special it was to spend this kind of time with her. She gave me a hug and said, "Good. We can spend next Saturday night together, and the one after that. I did tell you, didn't I, that you're grounded for two weeks?"

*Kimberly Kirberger*

# A Long Walk Home

*Experience: that most brutal of teachers.*
*But you learn, my God do you learn.*

C. S. Lewis

I grew up in the south of Spain in a little community called Estepona. I was sixteen when one morning, my father told me I could drive him into a remote village called Mijas, about eighteen miles away, on the condition that I take the car in to be serviced at a nearby garage. Having just learned to drive, and hardly ever having the opportunity to use the car, I readily accepted. I drove Dad into Mijas and promised to pick him up at 4 P.M., then drove to a nearby garage and dropped off the car. Because I had a few hours to spare, I decided to catch a couple of movies at a theater near the garage. However, I became so immersed in the films that I completely lost track of time. When the last movie had finished, I looked down at my watch. It was six o'clock. I was two hours late!

I knew Dad would be angry if he found out I'd been watching movies. He'd never let me drive again. I decided to tell him that the car needed some repairs and that they had taken longer than had been expected. I drove up to the place where we had planned to meet and saw Dad waiting patiently on the corner. I apologized for being late and told him that I'd come as quickly as I could, but the car had needed some major repairs. I'll never forget the look he gave me.

"I'm disappointed that you feel you have to lie to me, Jason."

"What do you mean? I'm telling the truth."

Dad looked at me again. "When you did not show up, I called the garage to ask if there were any problems, and they told me that you had not yet picked up the car. So you see, I know there were no problems with the car." A rush of guilt ran through me as I feebly confessed to my trip to the movie theater and the real reason for my tardiness. Dad listened intently as a sadness passed through him.

"I'm angry, not with you but with myself. You see, I realize that I have failed as a father if after all these years you feel that you have to lie to me. I have failed because I have brought up a son who cannot even tell the truth to his own father. I'm going to walk home now and contemplate where I have gone wrong all these years."

"But Dad, it's eighteen miles to home. It's dark. You can't walk home."

My protests, my apologies and the rest of my utterances were useless. I had let my father down, and I was about to learn one of the most painful lessons of my life. Dad began walking along the dusty roads. I quickly jumped in the car and followed behind, hoping he would relent. I pleaded all the way, telling him how sorry I was, but he simply ignored me, continuing on silently, thoughtfully and painfully. For eighteen miles I drove behind him, averaging about five miles per hour.

Seeing my father in so much physical and emotional pain was the most distressing and painful experience that

I have ever faced. However, it was also the most successful lesson. I have never lied to him since.

*Jason Bocarro*

# The Purse

My mother always has the Purse with her. The Purse contains a receipt for everything she has purchased that cost more than twenty-five cents since around 1980. The Purse also contains at least one dose of every conceivable over-the-counter medication, all expired.

If you need something, more likely than not, it can be found in the Purse. Tissues? In the Purse. Breath mint? But, of course. Tweezers, nail polish remover, nail clippers, needle and thread, pens, pencils, calendar, calculator, paper clips, tiny stapler—all in the Purse.

The Purse started out a relatively normal size, but over the years it has expanded to what seems like two feet in width. It is hopelessly, permanently open and overflowing. If you need something, virtually everything in the Purse has to be removed and examined in order to locate it, usually onto the nearest park bench or desktop. Many great discoveries are often found during such expeditions into the Purse, like pieces of paper containing long-forgotten locker combinations or telephone messages that should have been returned three or four weeks ago.

My mom just can't bear to not know what I am up to at any given moment. For example, when I get home from school, I have to download everything that happened during the day. Over the years, she has developed expert interrogation techniques that enable her to remove every tiny detail of a day's events from my brain. No detail is too small or too insignificant or too boring for her. And the same applies when she is telling you a story about something that happened to her.

I think my mother's mind is kind of like the Purse inside—all jumbled up with tiny artifacts and useless items. Most of them have to come out and be spread around before you get to something good or what you were looking for, but when she does get to that one valuable thing, it is as if you have just won the lottery.

When I first started hanging out with Heather, it was mostly at school or on the weekends. I don't know why I didn't tell my mom about her. I guess I just wanted to keep something private, or maybe I didn't want her to make a big deal about it, or maybe I was afraid my mom, with the Purse, would want to meet Heather. I think it was mostly that.

And so, every day I would come home from school and proceed to tell my mom what happened in each class, between each class, at lunch and after school. I would be urged to disclose what happened on the way to school and on the way home from school and up until the very second that I walked into the house. But every day I would conveniently leave out all details about Heather.

This went on for a few months and I knew my mom was starting to get suspicious, but I just couldn't tell her about Heather. I didn't want to admit it to myself, but I was ashamed of my mother. It made it worse that she prided herself on the honesty we shared, telling her friends that I could tell her anything and it would be okay.

Since I mostly saw Heather in groups, I would tell my mom that I was going to the movies with Katrina and

Steve and Trevor and Julian, but conveniently leaving out Heather. But one Saturday night I decided I wanted to see Heather alone. I wanted to go out on a real date with her. I had two choices: Either come clean and tell my mom about Heather, or lie. So I told my mom I was going to the movies with "some friends." I don't know why I thought this would work. She wanted to know which friends, what movie, what theater, who was driving, what time, if it was an R-rated movie, where I was going afterward, what time I would be home and whether or not I planned on buying popcorn. She left me no choice. I lied to her, and once I got started, I couldn't stop. I lied about things that didn't matter. I told her I was going to buy Red Vines when I knew I wanted Raisinettes, and I told her the wrong movie at the wrong theater. I told her I was going with Katrina and Trevor. I told her Katrina's mom was driving.

And so I left the house with a pit in my stomach. I wasn't good at this lying thing, and I felt guilty. I walked to Heather's house, and we caught the bus to the movies. I don't even remember what movie we saw, but the whole time I could only think about the fact that I had lied to my mom. We came out of the movie holding hands and, to my complete horror, my mom was standing there with the Purse. She had decided to take my sister to a movie and since she didn't want to intrude on me with my friends, she had chosen a different theater than the one I had told her, which of course was the wrong one because I had lied.

She didn't say anything, but if I had been paying attention, I would have been able to read the look of disappointment on her face. I was too busy worrying about her embarrassing me in front of Heather. All I could see was the Purse. I couldn't lie anymore, so I introduced my mom to Heather. My mom just stood there. She was in shock. I was in shock. And then I saw the look.

I guess I should have been relieved when she smiled at me, and then Heather, and invited us to dinner. It seems she had a coupon for Sizzler, they were having some sort of family dinner special for four, and my mom thought it was just perfect that we had run into each other. A coupon? What were we, homeless? I couldn't believe she suggested a coupon in front of Heather. And just when I thought things couldn't get worse, she started looking for the coupon. Oh no! Not the Purse!

At first I tried to stop her as she started to open the Purse. Then I realized there was no stopping her, so I tried to help. The Purse had to be completely unloaded onto a bench outside the theater. I was shuffling through the papers, trying to find the prized coupon, and I guess I was moving my hands too fast and I knocked the Purse. It flipped up in the air and as it did, I saw my life flash before my eyes, as if in slow motion, each one of those million receipts representing an important event. They ended up on the ground, spread about the theater, just as the movie next door was letting out. Crowds of people were stepping on all those papers.

That's when I lost it. The words came out in torrents, and I was powerless to stop them. "I can't believe you!" I yelled. "You are totally embarrassing me! Why do you have to carry all this crap with you all the time? Who cares about all these stupid receipts?" I picked up a Target receipt from the early 1990s. "Look at this," I said. "You bought T-shirts for Dad, and you got them on sale. Isn't that special?"

Heather looked on in shock. She grabbed me by the arm and pulled me to the side. "It's no big deal," she said.

"Yes, it is. I can't believe she's embarrassing me like that. She's so lame."

"Calm down," Heather replied. "It's okay. She was just trying to take us out to a nice dinner. I like Sizzler."

I couldn't calm down. Heather and I just stared at each other.

My mom and my sister were on their hands and knees picking up all those little pieces of paper and bits of string and lint-covered pills. I got down there and helped them. We left the theater and drove Heather home in silence. Other than hello and good-bye, my mom didn't speak to me for the rest of the weekend. I went to school on Monday, and Heather acted weird. I came home from school and walked in as usual. My mom was there, but she didn't say anything to me. Not even, "How was your day?" She just had that look of disappointment on her face. As long as I live, I will never forget that look.

I went up to my room to do some homework and play around on the computer. It was eerily silent. *Hey, this isn't so bad,* I thought. *I have a lot more time to myself.* But after a few hours, I began thinking about my day. I had gotten an A on an algebra test. It didn't seem to have any value until I could tell my mom about it. And I wanted to go down there and tell her about Heather. I wanted her to know how bad I felt. Worst of all, I had disappointed her. We had a good relationship and an honest one until I blew it. I lied. I was so disappointed in myself.

I finally got up the courage to go down there. She was sitting at the kitchen table with the Purse, sorting through all those receipts. Next to her was a *new* purse. A nice, flat, closable purse. She was transferring things into the new one. Just a few things. I sat there silently for a few minutes watching her sort. I noticed a restaurant receipt from Pizza Hut. I picked it up from the discard pile and noticed the date: August 26. My birthday.

"Hey, remember my birthday party last year?" My mom just looked at me. "You know, when I got the new skateboard?" Silence. More sorting. "I got an A on my algebra test." Silence. It was unbearable. I couldn't take it.

"I'm sorry. I'm really sorry. I didn't mean any of the stuff I said. I . . . I . . . miss you." She looked up from the sorting. There was a long pause. I was waiting for her to yell at me. I expected her to tell me how mad she was. I was ready for the worst, but all she said was, "How was your day?"

It's a few months later now, and that new purse, the one my mom was sorting, has become *the* Purse. And the next time Heather and I run into my mom and the Purse, I hope she has dinner plans in there somewhere.

*Tal Vigderson*

# The Cost of Gratefulness

I was about thirteen. My father frequently took me on short outings on Saturdays. Sometimes we went to a park, or to a marina to look at boats. My favorites were trips to junk stores, where we could admire old electronic stuff. Once in a while we would buy something for fifty cents just to take it apart.

On the way home from these trips, Dad frequently stopped at the Dairy Queen for ten-cent ice cream cones. Not every single time; just often enough. I couldn't expect it, but I could hope and pray from the time we started heading home to that critical corner where we would either go straight for the ice cream or turn and go home empty-handed. That corner meant either mouth-watering excitement or disappointment.

A few times my father teased me by going home the long way. "I'm just going this way for variety," he would say, as we drove by the Dairy Queen without stopping. It was a game, and I was well fed, so we're not talking torture here.

On the best days he would ask, in a tone that made it sound novel and spontaneous, "Would you like an ice cream cone?" and I would say, "That sounds great, Dad!" I'd always have chocolate and he'd have vanilla. He would hand me twenty cents and I would run in to buy the usual. We'd eat them in the car. I loved my dad and I loved ice cream—so that was heaven.

On one fateful day, we were heading home, and I was hoping and praying for the beautiful sound of his offer. It came. "Would you like an ice cream cone today?"

"That sounds great, Dad!"

But then he said, "It sounds good to me too, Son. How would you like to treat today?"

Twenty cents! Twenty cents! My mind reeled. I could afford it. I got twenty-five cents a week allowance, plus some extra for odd jobs. But saving money was important. Dad told me that. And when it was my money, ice cream just wasn't a good use of it.

Why didn't it occur to me that this was a golden opportunity to give something back to my very generous father? Why didn't I think that he had bought me fifty ice cream cones, and I had never bought him one? But all I could think was "twenty cents!"

In a fit of selfish, miserly ingratitude, I said the awful words that have rung in my ears ever since. "Well, in that case, I guess I'll pass."

My father just said, "Okay, Son."

But as we turned to head home, I realized how wrong I was and begged him to turn back. "I'll pay," I pleaded.

But he just said, "That's okay, we don't really need one," and wouldn't hear my pleading. We drove home.

I felt awful for my selfishness and ungratefulness. He didn't rub it in, or even act disappointed. But I don't think he could have done anything to make a deeper impression on me.

I learned that generosity goes two ways and gratefulness sometimes costs a little more than "thank you." On that day gratefulness would have cost twenty cents, and it would have been the best ice cream I'd ever had.

I'll tell you one more thing. We went on another trip the next week, and as we approached the crucial corner, I said, "Dad, would you like an ice cream cone today? My treat."

*Randal Jones*

# Mrs. Virginia DeView, Where Are You?

*There are high spots in all of our lives, and most of them come about through encouragement from someone else.*

George Adams

We were sitting in her classroom, giggling, jabbing each other and talking about the latest information of the day, like the peculiar purple-colored mascara Cindy was wearing. Mrs. Virginia DeView cleared her throat and asked us to hush.

"Now," she said smiling, "we are going to discover our professions." The class seemed to gasp in unison. Our professions? We stared at each other. We were only thirteen and fourteen years old. This teacher was nuts.

That was pretty much how the kids looked at Virginia DeView, her hair swirled back in a bun and her large, buck teeth gaping out of her mouth. Because of her physical appearance, she was always an easy target for snickers and cruel jokes among students.

She also made her students angry because she was demanding. Most of us just overlooked her brilliance.

"Yes; you will all be searching for your future professions," she said with a glow on her face—as though this was the best thing she did in her classroom every year. "You will have to do a research paper on your upcoming career. Each of you will have to interview someone in your field, plus give an oral report."

All of us went home confused. Who knows what they want to do at thirteen? I had narrowed it down, however. I liked art, singing and writing. But I was terrible in art, and when I sang my sisters screamed: "Oh, please shut up." The only thing left was writing.

Every day in her class, Virginia DeView monitored us. Where were we? Who had picked their careers? Finally, most of us had selected something; I picked print journalism. This meant I had to go interview a true-blue newspaper reporter in the flesh, and I was terrified.

I sat down in front of him barely able to speak. He looked at me and said: "Did you bring a pencil or pen?"

I shook my head.

"How about some paper?"

I shook my head again.

Finally, I think he realized I was terrified, and I got my first big tip as a journalist. "Never, never go anywhere without a pen and paper. You never know what you'll run into."

For the next ninety minutes, he filled me with stories of robberies, crime sprees and fires. He would never forget the tragic fire where four family members were killed in the blaze. He could still smell their burning flesh, he said, and he would never forget that horrid story.

A few days later, I gave my oral report totally from memory, I had been so mesmerized. I got an A on the entire project.

As we neared the end of the school year, some very resentful students decided to get Virginia DeView back for the hard work she put us through. As she rounded a corner, they shoved a pie into her face as hard as they could. She was slightly injured physically, but it was emotionally that she was really hurt. She didn't return to school for days. When I heard the story, I felt a deep, ugly pit fill my stomach. I felt shame for myself and my fellow students who had nothing better to do than pick on a woman because of how she looked, rather than appreciate her amazing teaching skills.

Years later, I forgot all about Virginia DeView and the careers we selected. I was in college scouting around for a new career. My father wanted me in business, which seemed to be sound advice at the time, except that I had no sense of business skills whatsoever. Then I remembered Virginia DeView and my desire at thirteen to be a journalist. I called my parents.

"I'm changing my major," I announced.

There was a stunned silence on the end of the phone.

"What to?" my father finally asked.

"Journalism."

I could tell in their voices that my parents were very unhappy, but they didn't stop me. They just reminded me how competitive the field was and how all my life I had shied away from competition.

This was true. But journalism did something to me; it was in my blood. It gave me the freedom to go up to total strangers and ask what was going on. It trained me to ask questions and get answers in both my professional and personal life. It gave me confidence.

For the past twelve years, I've had the most incredible and satisfying reporting career, covering stories from murders to airplane crashes and finally settling in on my forté. I loved to write about the tender and tragic moments of people's lives because somehow I felt it helped them in some way.

When I went to pick up my phone one day, an incredible wave of memories hit me and I realized that had it not been for Virginia DeView, I would not be sitting at that desk.

She'll probably never know that without her help, I would not have become a journalist and a writer. I suspect I would have been floundering in the business world somewhere, with great unhappiness shadowing me each day. I wonder now how many other students in her class benefited from that career project.

I get asked all the time: "How did you pick journalism?"

"Well, you see, there was this teacher . . ." I always start out. I just wish I could thank her.

I believe that when people reflect back over their school days, there will be this faded image of a single teacher—their very own Virginia DeView. Perhaps you can thank her before it's too late.

*Diana L. Chapman*

"I imagine you'll be interested in one of the
more highly visible occupations?"

# If I Knew

You know how you always hear people say, "If I knew then what I know now . . ."?

Have you ever wanted to say . . . yeah . . . well . . . go on . . .

So here we go . . .

> *I would listen more carefully to what my heart says.*
>
> *I would enjoy more . . . worry less.*
>
> *I would know that school would end soon enough . . . and work would . . . well, never mind.*
>
> *I wouldn't worry so much about what other people were thinking.*
>
> *I would appreciate all my vitality and tight skin.*
>
> *I would play more, fret less.*
>
> *I would know that my beauty/handsomeness is in my love of life.*
>
> *I would know how much my parents love me and I would believe that they are doing the best they can.*
>
> *I would enjoy the feeling of "being in love" and not worry so much about how it works out.*
>
> *I would know that it probably won't . . . but that something better will come along.*

*I wouldn't be afraid of acting like a kid.*

*I would be braver.*

*I would look for the good qualities in everyone and enjoy them for those.*

*I would not hang out with people just because they're "popular."*

*I would take dance lessons.*

*I would enjoy my body just the way it is.*

*I would trust my girlfriends.*

*I would be a trustworthy girlfriend.*

*I wouldn't trust my boyfriends. (Just kidding.)*

*I would enjoy kissing. Really enjoy it.*

*I would be more appreciative and grateful, for sure.*

*Kimberly Kirberger*

# Making Sarah Cry

He stood among his friends from school,
He joined their childhood games
Laughing as they played kickball
And when they called poor Sarah names.
Sarah was unlike the rest;
She was slow and not as smart,
And it would seem to all his friends
She was born without a heart.
And so he gladly joined their fun
Of making Sarah cry.
But somewhere deep within his heart,
He never knew just why.
For he could hear his mother's voice,
Her lessons of right and wrong
Playing over and over inside his head
Just like a favorite song.
"Treat others with respect, son,
The way you'd want them treating you.
And remember, when you hurt others,
Someday, someone might hurt you."
He knew his mother wouldn't understand

The purpose of their game
Of teasing Sarah, who made them laugh
As her own tears fell like rain.
The funny faces that she made
And the way she'd stomp her feet
Whenever they mocked the way she walked
Or the stutter when she'd speak.
To him she must deserve it
Because she never tried to hide.
And if she truly wanted to be left alone,
Then she should stay inside.
But every day she'd do the same:
She'd come outside to play,
And stand there, tears upon her face,
Too upset to run away.
The game would soon be over
As tears dropped from her eyes,
For the purpose of their fun
Was making Sarah cry.
It was nearly two whole months
He hadn't seen his friends.
He was certain they all must wonder
What happened and where he'd been
So he felt a little nervous
As he limped his way to class.
He hoped no one would notice,
He prayed no one would ask
About that awful day:
The day his bike met with a car,
Leaving him with a dreadful limp
And a jagged-looking scar.
So he held his breath a little
As he hobbled into the room,
Where inside he saw a "Welcome Back" banner
And lots of red balloons.

He felt a smile cross his face
As his friends all smiled, too
And he couldn't wait to play outside—
His favorite thing to do.
So the second that he stepped outdoors
And saw his friends all waiting there,
He expected a few pats on the back—
Instead, they all stood back and stared.
He felt his face grow hotter
As he limped to join their side
To play a game of kickball
And of making Sarah cry.
An awkward smile crossed his face
When he heard somebody laugh
And heard the words, "Hey freak,
Where'd you get the ugly mask?"
He turned, expecting Sarah,
But Sarah could not be seen.
It was the scar upon his own face
That caused such words so mean.
He joined in their growing laughter,
Trying hard to not give in
To the awful urge inside to cry
Or the quivering of his chin.
*They are only teasing,*
He made himself believe.
*They are still my friends;*
*They'd never think of hurting me.*
But the cruel remarks continued
About the scar and then his limp.
And he knew if he shed a single tear
They'd label him a wimp.
And so the hurtful words went on,
And in his heart he wondered why.
But he knew without a doubt

The game would never end, until they made him cry.
And just when a tear had formed,
He heard a voice speak out from behind.
"Leave him alone you bullies,
Because he's a friend of mine."
He turned to see poor Sarah,
Determination on her face,
Sticking up for one of her own tormentors
And willing to take his place.
And when his friends did just that,
Trying their best to make poor Sarah cry,
This time he didn't join in,
And at last understood exactly why.
"Treat others with respect, son,
The way you'd want them treating you.
And remember, when you hurt others,
Someday, someone might hurt you."
It took a lot of courage
But he knew he must be strong,
For at last he saw the difference
Between what's right and wrong.
And Sarah didn't seem so weird
Through his understanding eyes.
Now he knew he'd never play again
The game of making Sarah cry.
It took several days of teasing
And razzing from his friends,
But when they saw his strength,
They chose to be like him.
And now out on the playground,
A group of kids meets every day
For a game of kickball and laughter
And teaching their new friend, Sarah, how to play.

*Cheryl Costello-Forshey*

# A Lesson for Life

*The turning point in the process of growing up is when you discover the core strength within you that survives all hurt.*

Max Lerner

"Look at fatso!"

Freshmen in high school can be cruel and we certainly were to a young man named Matt who was in my class. We mimicked him, teased him and taunted him about his size. He was at least fifty pounds overweight. He felt the pain of being the last one picked to play basketball, baseball or football. Matt will always remember the endless pranks that were played on him—trashing his hall locker, piling library books on his desk at lunchtime and spraying him with icy streams of water in the shower after gym class.

One day he sat near me in gym class. Someone pushed him and he fell on me and banged my foot quite badly. The kid who pushed him said Matt did it. With the whole class watching, I was put on the spot to either shrug it off or pick a fight with Matt. I chose to fight in order to keep my image intact.

I shouted, "C'mon, Matt, let's fight!" He said he didn't want to. But peer pressure forced him into the conflict whether he liked it or not. He came toward me with his fists in the air. He was no George Foreman. With one punch I bloodied his nose and the class went wild. Just then the gym teacher walked into the room. He saw that we were fighting and he sent us out to the oval running track.

He followed us with a smile on his face and said, "I want you two guys to go out there and run that mile holding each other's hands." The room erupted into a roar of laughter. The two of us were embarrassed beyond belief, but Matt and I went out to the track and ran our mile—hand-in-hand.

At some point during the course of our run, I remember looking over at him, with blood still trickling from his nose and his weight slowing him down. It struck me that here was a person, not all that different from myself. We both looked at each other and began to laugh. In time we became good friends.

Going around that track, hand-in-hand, I no longer saw Matt as fat or dumb. He was a human being who had intrinsic value and worth far beyond any externals. It was amazing what I learned when I was forced to go hand-in-hand with someone for only one mile.

For the rest of my life I have never so much as raised a hand against another person.

*Medard Laz*

# Courage

*Darkness cannot drive out darkness; only light can do that. Hate cannot drive out hate, only love can do that.*

Martin Luther King Jr.

The excited sound of seventh-grade laughter and voices tumbled down the hallway as the students filed into the gym. I scanned the room, searching for my friends, and soon spotted them near the door to the restroom. I weaved my way through the mass of people and sat down next to my best friend, Lauren.

"So, what exactly are we doing here?" she questioned.

"Well, according to Mrs. Marks, we're supposed to be listening to a speaker about bullying, peer pressure and put-downs." I said this somewhat sarcastically, because the entire year our grade had been lectured over and over again on these topics. We were earning the reputation as the worst class in the school, which was not a reputation that my friends nor I were particularly proud of. As our science teacher stood in front of the entire grade level, attempting to get our attention, my friends and I sat back, prepared to sit through another monotonous speech full of harsh remarks about "Kids these days . . ." and "Your maturity level when you put someone down is no greater than that of an eight-year-old."

But as soon as she started talking, I snapped to attention. She had this way about her, as if she knew how to reach into our minds and souls and make us think. And for once, I actually began to think about what it was she was preaching about. I thought about all the kids who came to school every day, despite knowing that they would have to face cruel comments and sneering faces all day long.

One boy, in particular, came to mind. Every day, this boy came to first hour late, and I suspected it was because he needed to get medicine from the nurse. But this didn't stop the kids in the class from making fun of him. They punched him in the shoulder and said, "Hey, man! Where have you been?" And then another would add, "How's that girlfriend of yours? Oh sorry, we forgot. You don't *have* a girlfriend. You only have *boyfriends*." This harassment would continue until the teacher cut in, forcing the boys to stop. But it was too late—it always was. The boy would put his head down on his desk in shame. The worst, though, was when he tried to retaliate. His attackers only laughed and continued the cruelty until the entire room was laughing at his expense.

As I sat in the auditorium, absorbing everything the speaker had to say, thoughts of this poor boy crept into my head. I sighed, thinking how sorry I felt for him, not that there was anything I could do. I tuned back into the speaker and listened intently to her words of wisdom.

"Now, before I leave today, I would like to give everyone here an opportunity to say *anything* he or she wants to on the subject of bullying or peer pressure. You may apologize to a friend, thank someone for his or her kindness, *anything*. And this is the one time I can promise that *no one*, but *no one*, will laugh at you."

The stillness in the room made me believe her. Slowly, I saw a few hands raise tentatively in the air behind me. One girl wanted to apologize to a friend she had been ignoring recently. Another thanked a boy for his kindness when she slipped on the steps the other day. It was then that my moment of courage happened. The speaker called on me, and with shaking hands and clammy palms, I began to talk.

"What you said today really made sense. I know that it's true, because I see it every day in class. There is one person who is always made fun of. It doesn't matter why—it could be the way he looks, talks or even takes notes." My voice shook. "I think that everyone here has made fun of him at one time or another. I know I have. And now I really regret it. To us, it may just be a game, but to him, it must hurt. And I think . . . well, I think we need to stop."

Scared of my classmates' reaction, I felt like the silence that followed lasted forever. But then, soft clapping started in the front of the room, quickly spreading through the entire crowd. By the time I looked up, the soft pitter-patter had turned into a thunderous roar of applause. I had voiced something that everyone was feeling.

Later on that day, the boy whom I had been talking about came up to me privately and said thank you.

I noticed that from that day on, people began to treat him a little better. The teasing stopped, and people greeted him in the halls with a friendly, "Hi!" It was those little, everyday things that I noticed, and I'm sure he noticed them, too.

*Ruth Ann Supica*

# Call Me

"I know it's here somewhere." Cheryl drops her book bag at her feet so she can dig through her coat pockets. When she dumps her purse out onto the table, everyone waiting in line behind her groans.

Cheryl glances up at the lunch room clock. Only three minutes until the bell and this is the last day to order a yearbook, if you want your name imprinted in gold on the front. And Cheryl did, if only she could find her wallet. The line begins to move around her.

"Come on, Cheryl." Darcy might as well stamp her foot, she sounds so impatient. "We'll be late for class."

"Darcy, please!" Cheryl snaps back. Best friends or not, Darcy and Cheryl often frustrate each other. They are just so different. Today is a good example. Darcy had "budgeted" for her yearbook and ordered it the first day of school while Cheryl had almost forgotten . . . again.

"Darcy, my wallet's gone." Cheryl throws her things back into her purse. "My yearbook money was in it." The bell interrupts her search.

"Someone took it!" Darcy, as usual, is quick to point away from the bright side of things.

"Oh, I'm sure I just misplaced it," Cheryl hopes.

They rush into class just before the second bell rings. Darcy takes center stage to Cheryl's problem and happily spreads the news about the theft.

By gym the last hour, Cheryl is tired of being stopped and having to say over and over again, "I'm sure I just left it at home." Rushing into the locker room, she changes quickly and checks the list posted by the field door to see where her group is playing soccer, then hurries out to catch up with them.

The game was a close one, and Cheryl's team is the last one back to the locker room.

Darcy stands waiting for Cheryl by her locker. Cheryl brushes passed Juanita, the new girl. It's the shocked look on Darcy's face and the startled gasps of those around her that stop Cheryl.

There, at her feet, is her wallet.

"It fell out of her locker!" Darcy points at Juanita. "She stole it."

Everyone speaks at once.

"The new girl stole it."

"Darcy caught her red-handed."

"I knew there was something about her."

"Report her."

Cheryl turns and looks at Juanita. She's never really noticed her before, beyond her "new girl" label.

Juanita picks up the wallet and holds it out to Cheryl. Her hands are trembling. "I found it in the parking lot. I was going to give it to you before gym, but you were late."

Darcy's words spit anger. "I'm so sure!"

"Really. It's true." Juanita's voice is high and pleading.

Cheryl hesitates. Juanita's eyes begin to fill with tears.

Cheryl reaches for her wallet.

"I'm so glad you found it." Cheryl smiles. "Thanks, Juanita."

The tension around them breaks. "Good thing she found it." Everyone but Darcy agrees.

Cheryl does another quick change and then bangs her locker closed. "Hurry, Darcy. There's just enough time to order a yearbook."

"*If* there is any money left in your wallet."

"Not now, Darcy!"

"You are so naive!"

It isn't until they are standing in line that Cheryl opens her wallet.

"It's all here." Cheryl can't help feeling relieved. A small piece of paper flutters down from her wallet.

"She just didn't have time to empty it yet." Darcy bends down to pick up the note. "I know her type. I had her pegged the first day she came." She hands the note to Cheryl.

Cheryl reads it and then looks up at Darcy. "You had her pegged, all right. Maybe that's the problem. Maybe you spend too much time pegging people."

Darcy grabs the note, reads it and throws it back at Cheryl. "Whatever!" she says and stomps off.

Cheryl reads the note again.

*Cheryl,*

*I found your wallet in the parking lot. Hope nothing is missing.*

*Juanita*

*P.S. My number is 555-3218. Maybe you could call me.*

And Cheryl did.

*Cynthia Hamond*

# The Player

It was his attitude that got me. That self-assured smile and those cocky mannerisms gave me the irresistible urge to challenge such conceit. I had never met a person so sure of himself. He assumed that when you first met him, you had no choice but to like him. It made me want to prove him wrong. I would show him that I could not only resist his charms, but that I could beat him at his own game.

So our relationship began as a battle, each trying to gain a foothold, trying to pull ahead of the other and prove our dominance. We waged an unrelenting war of mind games, insults and tests.

But somewhere in the middle of our warfare, the teasing became playful and we became friends. We found in each other not just a challenge, but someone to turn to when we didn't feel like fighting anymore. Josh loved to "communicate." He often talked for hours as I listened, covering every topic that affected him and his life. I soon realized that he was more concerned about himself than anything else. But because I didn't always have a lot to say, it didn't seem that it would be a conflict in our relationship.

It was several months after our friendship started that

Josh began a discussion about love. "It takes a lot for me to love someone," he told me, in a tone more serious than I had ever heard from him. "What I need is trust. I could never fall in love with someone who I didn't feel I could tell everything to. Like you. You're my favorite person in the entire world. I could tell you anything," he said, looking straight at me.

I blushed, unsure of what response I should give in return, afraid that whatever I said would betray the new emotions I had begun to feel for Josh over the past few weeks. The look in my eyes must have given me away, because from that moment on, it seemed that he began to do everything in his power to make me fall deeper and deeper into the way I felt about him. Was it love? He seemed to glow in the attention that I paid him. And I enjoyed adoring him. Yet it didn't take me very long to figure out that Josh had no intention of returning my devotion.

When we were alone, he would kiss me and hold me and tell me how special our relationship was to him, and that he didn't know anyone else who made him so happy. But a few weeks into our relationship, I found out that he was involved with another girl and had been for some time. The pain I felt at his betrayal was overwhelming, but I found I couldn't be angry with him. I felt sure inside that he really did care, and that it was his friendship that was important to me.

At school one day, I saw him standing with a group of girls, and by the flirtatious smile on his face, I could tell he had again been working his magic. "Josh!" I yelled down the hallway to him. He looked up at me, then back at the girls, and with a groupie under each arm, he turned and made his way in the opposite direction. I stood completely deflated, not wanting to acknowledge what had just happened. But I couldn't avoid the truth any longer. My "best friend" had ignored me so I wouldn't hurt the reputation he was working on.

After that, I began to watch Josh, not as someone who had a crush on him, but as an outside observer. I began to see the darker side of his personality. It was only when I moved away from him that my cloudy vision cleared. It was as if the shadow my adoration had thrown over the situation grew smaller, and I finally saw what I had not been able to see before.

Josh spent day after day making new acquaintances that he thought might adore him. He flirted with girls, knowing how to make them feel pretty. He knew how to play the game just right—to make sure that everyone felt they had his complete attention. When you were with him, you felt he was interested only in you. He hung out, telling jokes and acting cool, giving off an aura that made people want to be around him. But now I could see that he did it all for himself because he needed to be surrounded by people who thought he was great.

And while he acted as though he really cared about these people, I heard him belittle them behind their backs, saw him ignore them in the process of making new friends. I saw the pain on their faces that I understood only too well.

I talked to Josh once more after that day. Even though I understood his nature and was opposed to everything he stood for, there was still a part of me that wanted him to care, and still wanted things the way they used to be.

"What happened?" I asked him. I cringe when I think how pitiful I must have sounded. "I mean, I thought we were best friends. How can you just give up all the time we spent together? All the things we talked about? The . . . the love that you always told me was there?"

He shrugged and replied coldly, "Hey, these things happen," before he turned and walked away.

I stood, watching him go, with tears running down my

face. I cried not for him, but for the friendship I thought we had, for the love I thought we had felt. I had lost the game in a big way.

Now, even though it was one of the most painful experiences I've ever endured, I am grateful for my "friendship" with Josh because it made me stronger. Now I know the kind of person and the kind of friend I never want to be.

Perhaps I won the game after all.

*Kelly Garnett*

"I want the prime rib with a baked potato.
My boyfriend isn't sure what he wants.
He can't commit to anything."

# Kissing the Bully

I looked down at my skinny body and turned to the side. I was awkward; my knobby knees led down to thin, bony legs. I looked around, enviously watching as the other girls pulled on their bras and hooked the back. I pulled on the bra I barely fit into, the one I had forced my mom to take me to buy, just so you could see the outline through the back of my shirt. I was a late-bloomer; there was no questioning that.

I walked home from school with my equally skinny best friend Laura at my side; she had hidden her embarrassment of her not-yet-developed body with a larger-than-life attitude. It was the normal walk home: She and I were taunted by Ben and a few other boys our age who inevitably found a way to make me cry.

I reached my house, knowing that the phone would ring later that night with some crank call and muffled sounds of prepubescent boy's laughter. I knew that the same pattern would be repeated the next day: They would walk behind us on the way to school, laughing about the "wall," Ben's less-than-endearing reference to my chest.

To ease my despair, I was told, "They only do that because they like you." My dad reassured me that once I blossomed, they'd be begging to go out with me. I hadn't had a boyfriend yet, and it seemed like everyone else was well on his or her way to awkward handholding and spin-the-bottle games. I pined for some sort of attention from the opposite sex. I didn't realize at the time that the torture from Ben and his friends was actually attention.

By the ninth grade, Laura and I were no longer walking to school; we caught the number-three bus on our corner to the local high school. Ben, by this point, had moved on to hitting us with spitballs. So every morning, I had to clean the wads of gross spit-covered paper out of my hair, making sure the evidence was gone. I would yell at him to stop, which only provoked more torture. I had known him for four years at this point, and the funny thing was we considered each other friends. He would talk to me, if the other boys weren't around, and I knew, despite his tough exterior, that he actually enjoyed my company.

Throughout middle school, Ben maintained the ritual of Rollerblading to my house after school, but I'm sure he never told his friends that in the seventh grade he had held my hand down the street, teaching me to use the Rollerblades I had just received for my birthday. It seemed that the nicer he was to me in private, the meaner he had to be to me in public.

I vowed that once I "blossomed," he would want to be my boyfriend, that the group of boys who tortured me in middle school would long for me in high school. I had a cruel fantasy of one of them asking me out and my rejecting him coldly, in front of everyone. I wanted to make them feel the embarrassment I had felt during all those walks home, and on all the bus rides with spitwad-filled hair.

High school finally came along and, better late than

never, I did blossom. I grew out of my awkward, bony body. My wavy red hair grew longer and straightened itself out. Although I didn't transform, I grew up, more in mind than in body. I started to accept the freckles and felt blessed to be naturally thin. I even wore a little makeup. And my dad was right, it did happen. I finally had a boyfriend. He was from a different middle school than I had attended, and he was unaware of my uncomfortable beginnings.

I still saw Ben; we attended the same high school parties and shared the same group of friends. He teased me a bit, but it didn't really bother me as much. I went through a few boyfriends in high school, and it seemed that the awkward years were finally over.

This summer I returned home from my first year of college. Ben and I ran into each other. He stood about a foot taller than I did, and I realized how much he had grown up throughout our eight years of friendship. He lives on his own now and invited me over to see his new apartment. The walls were sparse; it looked like a college boy's room, which struck me as odd. I knew so many college boys, but it was hard for me to picture Ben as one. I still saw the skinny blond boy who sat behind me in eighth grade snapping my bra straps.

We started talking about those years, and we both laughed. A few other old friends filled the apartment, and one of Ben's old partners-in-crime leaned over and said, "You have gotten so pretty." I thanked him, smirking at the same time. It seemed like I had waited eight years for this, for my revenge.

I found myself sitting outside with Ben, and then, it happened. He leaned over, and he kissed me, something that had never happened between us before. For a second, I thought, *This is it, I can finally tell him off and embarrass him for all the times he belittled me.* But I didn't. I no longer needed revenge. I continued to look at him, and I asked, "Did you ever have a crush on me?"

And he responded, "I had a crush on you the whole time. I was just too embarrassed to tell you."

*Lia Gay*

# A Difficult Lesson

*Of all the words of tongue or pen, the saddest are those . . . it might have been.*

John Greenleaf Whittier

It was August 1984, Kalamazoo, Michigan, Western Michigan University. The temperature was in the mid-eighties, the sun was shining and it was my first day of college. And, as if all this weren't enough, it was also the day I met Cindy.

She was stunningly beautiful. The type of beauty that turned heads. Casual attire and sparse amounts of makeup reflected her confident and self-assured persona. No need to flaunt her beauty.

Cindy and I met under precarious terms on this special day. While riding up in the elevator, she gave me a smile, which I returned. We got off on the same floor, which shocked me into insinuating that she must have been mistaken. Boys and girls on the same floor? In college? I shrugged it off, still not believing. As I stood outside my room, waiting for my brother's arrival with a load of my stuff, Cindy walked down the hall directly toward me. As she approached me, the butterflies began to stir in my stomach. Outwardly I tried to be cool, confident and funny. I calmly said with a wide grin, "I am not waiting for you." Cindy shot back with "You're a jerk" and entered her dorm room key into the very next door. I could not believe the most beautiful girl in the whole dorm lived on the other side of my wall. So much for me having a clue.

I was able to overcome my less-than-desirable first impression and we began to date. By mid-November we were an inseparable pair. We were in love. For me, this type of love was a first. We had many things in common. We were both outgoing, fun seeking and shared the same musical tastes. We shared close to a year-and-a-half of wonderful but tumultuous times. Being in love brought forth many different emotions from within me, the majority of which were positive. Some however were negative. Negative emotions I had never dealt with, like jealousy, the most powerful of those emotions.

Cindy and I broke up, for good, in February of 1986. I had allowed jealousy to consume, smother and destroy my first love. When I last saw Cindy, the only emotion I shared with her was anger. My anger compelled me to present to her a full envelope of pictures of good times we shared together. Pictures that, in anger, I had torn into thousands of little pieces. I did not keep one single picture. Cindy opened the envelope and saw the pictures. The last words she spoke to me were the same as the first: "You're a jerk." This time she was right. The last words I spoke to her I will live with forever. I looked her in the eyes, with passion no longer of the loving kind, and said, "I don't care if I ever see you or hear from you again." And I walked away.

Unfortunately for me the story doesn't end with just another jealous young man messing up. Within that year, I began to grow up. I regretted the way I dealt with my jealousy and anger. I regretted the things I said and did that stemmed from those emotions. I wanted desperately to apologize, to make things right and tell her I didn't mean those hurtful things. I wanted to let her know that she was right, that I was a jerk and if she didn't forgive me I would understand. I wanted to tell her she was really special to me and I would always love her.

I finally got the nerve to call her one night in December however there was no answer. I found out two weeks later that my first love had died. She died the very night I had attempted to say I'm sorry, in a car accident involving a drunk driver. She died not knowing that I was sorry for my actions. She died too soon.

*Rick Reed*

# Myself

*A human being's first responsibility is to shake hands with himself.*

Henry Winkler

I have to live with myself, and so
I want to be fit for myself to know
I want to be able as days go by
Always to look myself straight in the eye;
I don't want to stand, with the setting sun,
And hate myself for things I have done.
I don't want to keep on a closet shelf
A lot of secrets about myself,
And fool myself, as I come and go,
Into thinking that nobody else will know
The kind of man I really am;
I don't want to dress myself up in sham.
I want to go out with my head erect,
I want to deserve all man's respect;
And here in the struggle for fame and wealth,
I want to be able to like myself.
I don't want to look at myself and know

That I am a bluffer, an empty show.
I can never hide myself from me:
I see what others may never see,
I know what others may never know;
I never can fool myself, and so,
Whatever happens, I want to be
Self-respecting and guilt-free.

*Peer Counsellor Workbook*

# Love and Belonging

Walking down the steps of the psychology building, I spot my buddy Walter and his girlfriend, Anna. Walt and I have known each other almost all our lives. We grew up next door to each other, and fought and played our way through elementary school, adolescence, junior high and high school. Our parents had been best friends, and life even as recently as a year ago seemed so simple, so secure.

But now, while I'm struggling with my parents' divorce, Walter's world is intact—his parents are still together and living in the same house where he grew up. My mom is alone now in our house, while Dad is living the life of a newlywed with his second wife, in an apartment across town. I feel my stomach churn as I think of that, and mild irritation as Walter puts his arm around Anna.

"Hey, Jesse," he says as he sees me. I notice a sudden, self-conscious grin wash over his face. "How was the exam?"

"Oh, okay, I guess." I wish Anna would disappear. Walter's apparent happiness irritates me, and I suddenly feel very tired. "What are you up to?" I don't care if I seem rude in ignoring Anna.

"Well," Walter begins, and his grip around Anna's shoulder tightens, "we're on our way to check out some CDs at that new sound shop down the street. Want to come along?"

"Nah, I think I'll take a nap before my next class."

Anna speaks up. "How are you doing these days, Jesse?" I can see the sympathy in her eyes, and I hate her.

"I'm fine—just great. Life couldn't be better."

"Well . . ." she struggles with what to say next. I find myself enjoying her obvious discomfort. "Sorry you can't go with us." But I hear relief in her voice even as she says it. Walter takes Anna's hand, and together they cross the street.

Why should they seem so happy and look so secure? They don't have a clue as to what's going on in the real world.

I turn and walk down the sidewalk and across the Commons. Maybe it's true, what my Coach Carter said, that I have my antennae out these days. It seems as if every couple reminds me of the failure in my family.

"How can this have happened to my family, Carter? Why didn't I realize what was happening? Maybe I could have done something!"

Just then Carter picked up a crystal paperweight from his desk and tossed it to me. I caught it purely from reflex.

"Why did you do that?" I asked, half mad–half serious.

Looking around the room, he said, "You knew you had to be careful with that paperweight, didn't you, Jesse?"

"Sure. It might break." I put it back on his desk.

"People take care of things that seem obviously fragile. Think about it. When you buy a house, you don't expect it to maintain itself. Or a car; you make sure you do things like change the oil every few thousand miles and buy tires when they are worn.

"With so many things in life, Jesse, you expect to have to care for them, keep a close eye on them, nurture them.

We're more careful with an insignificant paperweight than we are with our closest relationships."

"You're telling me that my mom and dad were careless with their marriage?" I heard my voice rise unnaturally, my fingers clenched in my palms.

"Not necessarily careless, Jesse. Perhaps they just expected it to flourish on its own. But marriage, like anything else, won't flourish in an environment of neglect. No one should take a good relationship for granted."

"But what do I do? You're telling me to accept all this— Mom and Dad splitting up; Dad marrying someone I don't even know. She can't take Mom's place. No way!"

"I'm suggesting that you try to accept it," Carter said gently, "because for you, that's all you can do. You can't change your parents, and you can't change what happened. You don't have to love your stepmother as you do your mother, and probably no one expects you to. But to get beyond this and to be able to handle your parents' new, more complex relationships—and your future relationships with women—then you do need to learn to accept what has happened."

"Well, I just don't see how you can ask me to do that. I can't stand seeing them apart!"

As I stood up to leave his study he said, "I know you're feeling pretty alone right now. But believe me, you'd be surprised at how many young people have sat in this office and asked me why divorce had to happen in their family. Maybe it will help if you remember that there are a lot of people who are hurting just like you. And remember—this divorce is not your fault. Don't ever forget that."

Walking down the street, I see a city bus slow down and then stop at the corner. On impulse, I get on.

I pay the driver and begin to look for a seat.

An elderly couple is seated at the back of the bus. I sit beside them.

We ride in silence toward town. I glance over at the couple and notice that they are holding hands. The wedding ring on the old woman's finger is a dull gold, and there is a tiny diamond in the center of the band.

I watch as the old man rests his left hand on top of hers, and I see that his wedding ring matches hers. His, too, is scratched and dull with age.

As they sit in companionable silence, I notice the resemblance of their features. Both wear glasses, and both have short, pure white, wiry hair. They even wear the same style of shirt—simple white cotton, short-sleeved.

Occasionally the woman points at something as we pass by, and the man nods in agreement. I am mystified, and yet I feel a sense of peace sitting next to them.

Before too long we reach their stop. A row of neat, white frame houses lines the quiet side street.

The old man gets up slowly and pulls his walking stick from the seat next to him. He waits patiently for his wife to get up before he starts to walk to the front of the bus. The woman rises just as slowly and pulls a blue cardigan over her thin arms. He takes her hand, and as they turn to walk to the front of the bus, I catch his eye. I can't let them leave without asking, "How long have you two been married?"

He looks inquisitively at her. She smiles and gently shrugs her shoulders. It doesn't matter. It hasn't mattered for some time.

Finally he says in a raspy voice, "I don't know exactly— many years." Then he adds, "Most of our lives."

They walk down the aisle of the bus and are gone.

I lean back in my seat. It takes me a few moments to realize that the cold, hard knot in my stomach doesn't seem so tight now. And the face reflected back at me from the glass of the bus window looks a little less tense.

Watching the colors of the trees slide by, my mind wanders back to the old couple and finally comes to rest on my parents. The realization quietly dawns on me that I have been looking for answers when maybe I don't have to know at all. I don't have to hurt for them and me, too. I don't have to have all the answers about love and life and why things work out the way they do sometimes. Maybe no one has the answers.

"Hey, buddy," the bus driver says to me. I look up and realize I'm alone on the bus. We're downtown at the square. "This is the end of the line. You can get off here or go back."

I think for a minute. "Do you go by that new sound shop close to campus?"

"Yeah, sure."

"Well, drop me off there," I say. "There's someone there. A friend. And I need to talk to him."

*T. J. Lacey*

# Forever Changed

*The great use of life is to spend it for something that will outlast it.*

William James

Every morning when I wake up, I peel back the blankets that keep my body warmth hostage and look around my room. I see cherished family photos, my favorite mahogany dresser and of course my love beads that hang from the windows. I can't imagine my life without a loving family surrounding me or a roof shielding me from the night.

This past July, I went on a mission trip to Monterrey, Mexico, with my youth group. I sat on a bus for two days, not knowing what to expect. My friends on the bus described all the bugs that had infested the orphanages we were to work at for the next week. They told me how dirty everything would be and how dangerous the streets were. Secretly, I was hoping the bus would turn around somehow. But it did not. The first night we arrived, a man said, "We have come here to change Mexico, but instead, Mexico will change us."

Each morning during the hour-and-a-half bus ride to the orphanage, I would think of how little I had slept the night before, how tired I was, and how there was no air conditioning on the bus. But, as soon as the orphanage came into view, all those feelings melted away. The children would run up to the gates, scream, and jump up and down because we had finally arrived. The first day I walked cautiously inside the metal gates. I saw one girl with a huge smile on her face. When I walked over to her, she gave me a hug. I looked around at all the other children. All were smiling. All were laughing. They were not upset, nor complaining about their lives and living conditions.

I met a little girl at the orphanage named Erica. She had short black hair and a big scar beneath her nose. I picked her up and swung her around. She squealed with laughter. Every day when we arrived, she always ran up to me, gave me a hug and kissed my cheeks. I began looking forward to this.

The whole time, I was thinking, *Who would give such a wonderful child up?* I saw other children in the orphanage. They did not fight over the toys we brought them. Instead, they shared them because they wanted everyone to experience the joy of the new toys.

On the last day, the kids were singing songs to us. Rose, the lady in charge, told us that one of the children wanted to share her story with us. To my amazement, Erica went up to speak. She smiled at me and began her story: "I am so happy to be here in the orphanage." *Happy,* I thought. *Who would be happy to be in an orphanage?* "When I was in my house," she continued, "my parents used to beat me. They threw me against the wall and hurt me."

When she was done, I ran over to tell her how proud I was of her. I looked down and saw the scar near her nose. Now I knew how she got it.

The day we left is a day I'll never forget. Everyone was crying. I held Erica for fifteen minutes, too scared to put her down. I kissed her scar, hoping, once more, to erase her memories. I told her I loved her. She stopped crying and smiled. When our time with the children was done, they waved once again through the gates. This time it was good-bye.

When I came home, I looked in my room while unpacking. I looked at all my clothes hanging in my closet on multicolored hangers. The visions of Erica's closet with two shirts in it flashed before my eyes. She tried to give me one of her stuffed animals in return for my friendship. I told her I did not need one. She said she didn't either because she had two. Erica is only seven. It will take me a long time to learn what she already knows.

*JoLynn Shopteese*

# 6

# TOUGH STUFF

*The soul would have no rainbow had the eyes no tears.*

*John Vance Cheney*

# I'll Always Be with You

On a quiet September night our seventeen-year-old son, Mike, got into his cherished yellow '68 Mustang, his heart broken after the sudden ending of his first romance. His girlfriend had told him she was going to get engaged to someone else. Sitting in the car he had so lovingly restored and treasured, Mike shot and killed himself. In the note he left, he wrote: "I wish I could have learned how to hate. . . . Don't blame yourselves, Mom and Dad. I love you." His note ended "Love, Mike, 11:45 P.M." At 11:52 P.M. that night, we and Mike's older brother, Vic, pulled into the driveway alongside Mike's car—seven minutes too late!

It wasn't long before stories about Mike started coming in from all sides. We heard many of them for the first time. His oldest friend, Danny, told us about the time he was frightened to have his picture taken in kindergarten. "It's easy. Just go like this," Mike assured him as he grinned from ear to ear, displaying the bright smile that became his trademark. Years later, when a classmate became a single parent, Mike helped her care for her baby. One of Mike's friends was shot in a drive-by shooting but recovered, with Mike's support. When his high school band went to Florida to march in the Orange Bowl parade, Mike assisted a fellow band member who was blind.

A young mother phoned to tell the story of how Mike had helped her when her car broke down. She and her children were stranded on the roadside when Mike came by. He stopped, showed her his driver's license to assure her he wouldn't hurt her and her children, and got her car started. He followed them home to make sure they arrived safely.

One of Mike's friends revealed the truth about why Mike never got the new transmission we thought he planned to install in his Mustang in preparation for the local drag race. Mike canceled his order for the transmission and instead bought two transmissions from a salvage yard—so his friend could get his car running, too. Mike had told us the reason he didn't buy the brand-new transmission was that it just wasn't right for the way he wanted his car to perform.

Mike's niece was born with cerebral palsy. He learned how to replace her tracheotomy tube and how to perform CPR, should the need arise. He learned sign language with her (the tracheotomy tube made it impossible for her to speak), and they would "sing" together in sign language.

In the days following Mike's death, many teenagers came to comfort us and asked if they could do anything to help. Our response to their question was: "Don't ever do this. Don't commit suicide. Reach out to someone and ask for help!" Before Mike's memorial service, Mike's close friends met with us to share their grief, tell their stories about their friendship with him and discuss the tragedy of teen suicide. We talked about ways to prevent teen suicide. This was how the Yellow Ribbon Project came to life.

We decided to establish a foundation dedicated to eliminating suicide, a leading cause of death among teens.

Within days after Mike's death, we began printing pocket-sized cards that read:

*YELLOW RIBBON PROJECT*
*In loving memory of Michael Emme*

*THIS RIBBON CARD IS A LIFELINE! It carries the message that there are those who care and will help. If you are in need and don't know how to ask for help, take this card to a counselor, teacher, clergy, parent or friend and say:*

*"I NEED TO USE MY YELLOW RIBBON!"*

Someone, remembering Mike's beloved yellow Mustang, had the idea of attaching yellow ribbons to the cards, which we did. At Mike's memorial service we set out a basket containing five hundred of these yellow-ribbon cards. By the end of the service, the basket was empty (and Mike's Mustang was covered with one hundred yellow miniature roses, put there by his friends).

Mike's tragic death made us decide to help others, just as Mike did during his life. In the time since Mike's death, the Yellow Ribbon Project has touched—and saved—the lives of teens around the world. We receive many letters from teenagers about the Yellow Ribbon Project with comments such as:

"Your Web site has helped me recover from my depression."

"I've tried to commit suicide several times. This time I found the Yellow Ribbon card in my pocket and held onto it until a friend came by and I was able to give them the card. They recognized that I was suicidal and got me help."

"Thank you for being there to let those without hope know that there is always someone who cares."

Mike's final letter to us contained another important message. In that letter he told us, "I'll always be with you." Every time we speak to a group of teenagers or receive a letter from a teen or child who needs help, we know Mike's words are true.

*Dale and Dar Emme*

[EDITORS' NOTE: *This story, which was first printed in* A 3rd Serving of Chicken Soup for the Soul *in April 1996, has resulted in an even greater distribution of The Yellow Ribbon Project. The following are excerpts from some of the letters the Emmes received.*]

*My name is Jessica and I am a senior in high school. I was very deeply touched by your story. I am a survivor of depression and suicidal impulses. I've struggled with this for the past five years and if I hadn't had someone who reached out to help me, I would not be here.*

*Last week a senior in high school shot himself. What if someone had stopped him and asked him how he was and really meant it? I think that would have made the difference between life and death.*

*So if you could please send information, suggestions and ribbons, I would greatly appreciate it. I've wanted to get the message out about teen suicide but never knew how. Thank you for helping me.*

*Jessica Magers*

*I found out about The Yellow Ribbon Project in* A 3rd Serving of Chicken Soup for the Soul. *Your story really made me think about how much my friends and family mean to me, and if an occasion should arise when they do use their ribbon then I will be ever more grateful for your idea of creating The Yellow Ribbon Project. Thank you,*

*Nicole Nero*

*Two months ago I broke up with my boyfriend who I loved very much. I could not deal with the pain and emptiness so I attempted suicide. I spent the night in I.C.U., the pills I took caused me to stop breathing. Because I am only sixteen, a straight-A student with everything going for me, this event shocked me and I realized I have a lot to live for and also my parents could not bear it if I were dead. So I am writing to ask if I could get two of your yellow ribbons. One for me and for my best friend. Thank you very much,*

*Jen Vetter*

# My Story

*The journey in between what you once were and who you are now becoming is where the dance of life really takes place.*

Barbara De Angelis

I never thought about killing myself; it just became a condition. Kind of like catching a cold. One minute you are fine, and the next minute you are sick. Whenever people would talk about suicide, I would think to myself, "I would never do that." Why would someone want to do something so final, so stupid?

For me, I just wanted the pain to stop. And it got to the point where I was willing to do whatever it took to make that happen. It started with the usual stuff . . .

I am sixteen. I spend the summer with my mom and during the school year I live with my dad. I feel like an inconvenience to both of them. At my mom's I have no room. My mom isn't there for me when I need her because she always has something more important to do. At least, that is how it feels.

I was having trouble with my friends. The ones I had

not lost already to "different lifestyles" were unable to help me. In their own words, my problems were "too much" for them. The intensity of my pain scared them, like it did me.

Oh, yeah . . . did I mention my boyfriend, John, had dumped me that day? My first boyfriend had left me, too. He said I had become impossible to love and now John was gone, too. And it wasn't that I would be without him that mattered . . . it was me. What was wrong with me? Why is it so hard to love me and why is it that when it gets hard, everyone bails?

I was alone. All I had were the voices in my head telling me I blew it, I was too needy, I was never going to be loved once someone really got to know me. I felt that I wasn't even good enough to be loved by my own parents.

You know how, when you are really hurting, you feel like you can just call the person (the boyfriend, the friend) and tell him or her how much it hurts and they'll say, "Oh, I am so sorry; I didn't mean to hurt you; hang on, I will be right there"? Well, I called and I was crying, and I said it hurts too much, please come talk to me. He said he couldn't help me . . . and he hung up.

I went into my mom's bathroom and took a bottle of Tylenol PM, some tranquilizers and a couple pain pills I had left from an injury. Soon the pain would be over.

I will spare you the gruesome details of what followed. It was a whole new kind of pain. Physically, I puked until I couldn't move. Emotionally, I was more scared than I have ever been. I did not want to die. (Statistics show that immediately after "attempting" suicide, the person desperately wants to live . . . not die, which makes it even sadder to think about those who do succeed.) Luckily for me, I did not die. But I hurt my body (my stomach still aches). And I scared and hurt a lot of people. I scared myself, but I didn't die and I can't even begin to tell you how happy I am about that.

I cringe every time someone else finds out. I did not want to write this story, but I did want to help anyone else who might be thinking about it or who is in a lot of pain.

It has been a month since that night. I have laughed at least five hundred times, many of those real "pee your pants" kind of laughing. I have a therapist who really cares about me, and we are making real progress in building up my confidence. She is also helping my mom and dad be "better parents." I have realized that they really do care and that they are doing the best that they can. I have a new friend who has gone through some hard stuff herself. My intense feelings do not scare her, and we know what it means to "be there" for someone you care about. I have worked things out with some of my old friends and we are closer than ever. I have earned $500 and spent it all on myself . . . without guilt (well, maybe a little). And I am starting to forgive myself.

Oh, yeah . . . I met a guy. He is really sweet and he knows "my story." We have agreed to take things really slow.

These are only a few of the things I would have missed. Life gets really hard sometimes and really painful. For me, I couldn't feel everyone else's love because I had forgotten how to love myself. I'm learning now—learning how to accept, forgive and love myself. And I'm learning that things change. Pain *does* go away, and happiness is the other side. Although the pain comes back, so does the happiness. It is like waves in the ocean coming and going . . . coming and going . . . breathing in and breathing out.

*Lia Gay*

# Just One Drink

There's a small cross by the side of Highway 128, near the town of Boonville. If this cross could talk, it would tell you this sad story:

Seven years ago my brother, Michael, was at a friend's ranch. They decided to go out for dinner. Joe arrived and volunteered to drive—after just one drink.

Lightheartedly, the four friends traveled the winding road. They didn't know where it would end—nobody did. Suddenly, they swerved into the opposite lane, colliding with an oncoming car.

Back home we were watching *E.T.* on video in front of a warm fire. Then we went to bed. At 2:00 A.M. a police officer woke my mom with the devastating news. Michael had been killed.

In the morning, I found my mother and sister crying. I stood there bewildered. "What's wrong?" I asked, rubbing my sleepy eyes.

Mom took a deep breath. "Come here . . ."

Thus began a grueling journey through grief, where all roads lead to nowhere. It still hurts to remember that day.

The only thing that helps is telling my story, hoping

you will remember it if you are tempted to get into a car with someone who has had a drink—even just one drink.

Joe chose the road to nowhere. He was convicted of manslaughter and served time. However, the real punishment is living with the consequences of his actions. He left us with an ache in our hearts that will never go away, a nightmare that will haunt him—and us—for the rest of our lives. And a small cross by the side of Highway 128.

*Chris Laddish*
*Dedicated with love to the memory of Michael Laddish*

# Dead at 17

Agony claws my mind. I am a statistic. When I first got here, I felt very much alone. I was overwhelmed by grief, and I expected to find sympathy.

I found no sympathy. I saw only thousands of others whose bodies were as badly mangled as mine. I was given a number and placed in a category. The category was called "traffic fatalities."

The day I died was an ordinary school day. How I wish I had taken the bus! But I was too cool for the bus. I remember how I wheedled the car out of Mom. "Special favor," I pleaded. "All the kids drive." When the 2:50 P.M. bell rang, I threw my books in the locker. Free until tomorrow morning! I ran to the parking lot, excited at the thought of driving a car and being my own boss.

It doesn't matter how the accident happened, I was goofing off—going too fast, taking crazy chances. But I was enjoying my freedom and having fun. The last thing I remember was passing an old lady who seemed to be going awfully slow. I heard a crash and felt a terrific jolt. Glass and steel flew everywhere. My whole body seemed to be turning inside out. I heard myself scream.

Suddenly, I awakened. It was very quiet. A police officer was standing over me. I saw a doctor. My body was mangled. I was saturated with blood. Pieces of jagged glass were sticking out all over. Strange that I couldn't feel anything. Hey, don't pull that sheet over my head. I can't be dead. I'm only seventeen. I've got a date tonight. I'm supposed to have a wonderful life ahead of me. I haven't lived yet. I can't be dead!

Later I was placed in a drawer. My folks came to identify me. Why did they have to see me like this? Why did I have to look at Mom's eyes when she faced the most terrible ordeal of her life? Dad suddenly looked very old. He told the man in charge, "Yes—he is our son."

The funeral was weird. I saw all my relatives and friends walk toward the casket. They looked at me with the saddest eyes I've ever seen. Some of my buddies were crying. A few of the girls touched my hand and sobbed as they walked by.

Please—somebody—wake me up! Get me out of here. I can't bear to see Mom and Dad in such pain. My grandparents are so weak from grief they can barely walk. My brother and sister are like zombies. They move like robots. In a daze. Everybody. No one can believe this. I can't believe it, either.

Please don't bury me! I'm not dead! I have a lot of living to do! I want to laugh and run again. I want to sing and dance. Please don't put me in the ground! I promise if you give me just one more chance, God, I'll be the most careful driver in the whole world. All I want is one more chance. Please, God, I'm only seventeen.

*John Berrio*

# "Gabby, You're Sooo Skinny"

I am a straight-A student. I am very involved in school activities and considered a "very together" teenager. Or at least, I was.

It all started innocently enough. I weighed about 125 pounds. I was not fat, but felt I could stand to lose a few pounds. A friend of mine had gone on a health kick and was getting great results from it—she was losing weight, she felt better and her friends were telling her how great she looked. I wanted to feel that way, too.

I began exercising and eating healthy snacks instead of the usual Coke-and-chips marathon watching the boob tube. Within a couple of weeks I had lost weight, I was feeling good, I cared more about what I wore and started feeling attractive in a way I had not experienced before. I would go to school and it seemed like everyone noticed. "Gabby, you look great," "Gabby, you look so beautiful," and "Gabby, you're so skinny." I don't think anything ever felt as good as those comments.

I was raised with the message that there is always room for improvement, so I figured if five pounds gets this much notice, just think what ten will do! If cutting back to

1,000 calories works, imagine 500! I figure that was the moment I took off down the road to anorexia.

My previous successes didn't feel as good to me as the success of this weight thing. I think it had something to do with the control I felt I had. I lost weight at a fast rate, and every time I lost a pound I was elated. It was a euphoria that, now in looking back, I realize I became addicted to. I lived for that feeling.

I remember the first day I went the whole day without eating. When I got into bed that night I felt this emptiness in my stomach. But I also felt thinness: a feeling I had come to connect with achievement and success. I remember thinking, *If I can go a whole day without eating, then why not two?*

There were many days I did just that. In fact, I could go three days without eating.

I don't remember exactly when it happened, but it was sudden and total: No one said nice things to me and no one was complimenting me. Instead of seeing the logical conclusion, which was that I was taking this too far, I started feeling that I was failing and needed to try harder. I needed to lose more weight; I would have to get serious now!

I had days where all I ate was an apple, and then I went to bed at night feeling like a failure, feeling fat. It got to the point that any food in my stomach felt like too much. It felt dirty and disgusting. I belittled myself for being so weak. My life was becoming a hell. I felt that if I could just control myself a little more, it would get better. The truth is, all happiness had long ago slipped away, and my whole being was devoted to the moments of success that I felt when I lost another pound.

A part of me knew this was probably wrong, but that part of me was out of reach. It was there, just not able to talk louder than my illness. I needed help, and yet there was no way I could ask for it. I could not even admit it to the people who tried so desperately to give it to me.

Teachers, school nurses, friends—they all suspected I had a problem. My concern was only to put them off and convince them I was fine. I wonder if they really believed me, or if they just knew they couldn't help until I was ready.

I remember one night my dad brought home steak and announced to me that I was going to eat it and he was going to watch me. He would not take no for an answer. I cried and begged him not to make me do this. This thing sitting on my plate had become my worst enemy. It was pure fat; one bite would ruin everything. I had to make him understand I could not eat this, and that if he really loved me, he would not make me. I was crying, begging him to let go of this crazy idea, but he wouldn't. He said he would sit there all night. I had no choice, NO CHOICE! But this was supposed to be my choice. The one thing I had control over. Those words pushed a button in me and I no longer cared about him or his feelings. All I felt were anger and hate. I hated him for making me do this, for making me feel my pain and face how distorted my reality had become. I hated him for making me eat that disgusting, evil food.

All my life I had done things for everyone else. The grades, the manners, the awards—everything for them, nothing for me. This eating thing, this losing weight had become *mine*. It represented me and *my* choices, and now my dad was trying to take that away from me, too!

As I lay in bed that night crying and feeling fat, I knew I needed help. I knew I was hurting people I loved.

After staying up all night, I came to the conclusion that it wasn't my dad I hated. I hated ME! I realized that I wasn't in control. For the first time in my life, I understood that this was *my* problem. I needed to take control of my life—not let the disease control it.

Things didn't change overnight. In fact, it was one long road to recovery. But slowly, with the help of friends and family, I began to heal. Now that I'm at my ideal weight, I have stopped weighing myself altogether. I no longer peruse fashion magazines, either—I may not be "in style," but I feel just right!

*Gabriella Tortes*
*As told to Kimberly Kirberger*

# Already Perfect

*Other people may be there to help us, teach us, guide us along our path. But the lesson to be learned is always ours.*

Melody Beattie

Everyone can identify with the need to fit in. Each one of us struggles with self-esteem and self-worth to some degree. I spent much of my time striving to achieve perfection in every aspect of my life. What I did not realize was that in my desperate need to be perfect, I sacrificed the very body and mind that allowed me to live.

I was a happy kid with lots of friends and a supportive family. But growing up was really hard and even scary sometimes.

During my childhood, I was constantly involved in something that included an audience viewing my achievements or my failures. I was into acting by age seven, and progressed to training for and competing in gymnastics, horseback riding and dance—all of which required major commitment, discipline and strength. My personality thrived on the high energy required to keep up. I wanted everyone's praise and acceptance, but I was my own toughest critic.

After I graduated from high school and moved out on my own, my struggles with self-esteem and happiness increased. I began to put pressure on myself to succeed in the adult world. Meanwhile, I was feeling very inadequate and unsuccessful. I started to believe that my difficulties and what I perceived to be my "failures" in life were caused by my weight. I had always been a thin-to-average sized person. Suddenly, I was convinced that I was overweight. In my mind, I was FAT!

Slowly, my inability to be "thin" began to torture me. I found myself involved in competition again. But this time, I was competing against myself. I began to control my food by trying to diet, but nothing seemed to work. My mind became obsessed with beating my body at this game. I slowly cut back on what I ate each day. With every portion I didn't finish or meal I skipped, I told myself that I was succeeding, and in turn, I felt good about myself.

Thus began a downward spiral of my becoming what is known as anorexic. The dictionary defines it as "suppressing or causing loss of appetite, resulting in a state of anorexia." When taken to an extreme, anorexia can cause malnutrition and deprive the body of the important vitamins and minerals that it needs to be healthy.

In the beginning, I felt great—attractive, strong, successful, almost super-human. I could do something others couldn't: I could go without food. It made me feel special, and that I was better than everyone else. What I didn't see was that I was slowly killing myself.

People around me began to notice my weight loss. At first they weren't alarmed; maybe some were even envious. But then the comments held a tone of concern. "You're losing too much weight." "Elisa, you're so thin." "You look sick." "You'll die if you keep this up." All their words only reassured me that I was on the right path, getting closer to "perfection."

Sadly, I made my physical appearance the top priority in my life, believing that it was the way to become successful and accepted. As an actress, I am constantly being judged by my appearance. The camera automatically makes people appear heavier than they are. So I was getting mixed messages like, "Elisa, you are so skinny, but you look great on camera."

I cut back on my food more and more, until a typical day consisted of half a teaspoon of nonfat yogurt and coffee in the morning, and a cup of grapes at night. If I ate even a bite more than my allotted "crumbs" for the day, I hated myself and took laxatives to rid my body of whatever I had eaten.

It got to the point where I no longer went out with my friends. I couldn't—if I went to dinner, what would I eat? I avoided their phone calls. If they wanted to go to the movies or just hang out at home, I couldn't be there— what if food was around? I had to be home alone to eat my little cup of grapes. Otherwise, I thought I was failing. Everything revolved around my strict schedule of eating. I was embarrassed to eat in front of anyone, believing that they would think I was gluttonous and ugly.

My poor nutrition began to cause me to lose sleep. I found it hard to concentrate on my work or to focus on anything for any length of time. I was pushing myself harder and harder at the gym, struggling to burn the calories that I hadn't even eaten. My friends tried to help me but I denied that I had a problem. None of my clothes fit, and it was hard to buy any, since I had shrunk to smaller than a size zero!

Then one night, like so many nights before, I couldn't sleep, and my heart felt as though it might beat its way out of my chest. I tried to relax, but I couldn't.

The beating became so rapid and so strong that I could no longer breathe. The combination of starving myself and taking pills to get rid of anything that I did eat caused me to nearly have a heart attack. I stood up, and immediately fell down. I was really scared, and I knew I needed help. My roommate rushed me to the hospital, beginning the long road to my recovery. It took doctors, nurses, nutritionists, therapists, medications, food supplements . . . and most important, a new sense of what was really true about myself to get back on track with reality.

Recovering from what I did to my body and reprogramming the way I think about myself has been a very slow and extremely painful process. I still struggle with the effects of anorexia every day. Although it has been a couple of years since that hospital visit, it is by no means over for me. I must be honest with myself and stay committed to being healthy.

I had used my anorexia as a means of expression and control. I used it as my gauge for self-esteem and self-worth. It was my identity. Now I realize that the way to success lies in my heart, mind and soul, rather than in my physical appearance.

I now use my intelligence, my talents and acts of kindness to express myself. This is true beauty, and it has nothing to do with the size of my body. With my experience of trying to be "perfect" on the outside, I had sacrificed who I was on the inside. What I know now is, we are—each and every one of us—already perfect.

*Elisa Donovan*

# No-Hair Day

*Whatever you are doing, love yourself for doing it.*
*Whatever you are feeling, love yourself for feeling it.*

Thadeus Golas

If you are turning sixteen, you stand in front of the mirror scrutinizing every inch of your face. You agonize that your nose is too big and you're getting another pimple—on top of which you are feeling dumb, your hair isn't blonde, and that boy in your English class has not noticed you yet.

Alison never had those problems. Two years ago, she was a beautiful, popular and smart eleventh-grader, not to mention a varsity lacrosse goalie and an ocean lifeguard. With her tall, slender body, pool-blue eyes and thick blonde hair, she looked more like a swimsuit model than a high school student. But during that summer, something changed.

After a day of life-guarding, Alison couldn't wait to get home, rinse the saltwater out of her hair and comb through the tangles. She flipped her sun-bleached mane forward. "Ali!" her mother cried, "what did you do?" She discovered a bare patch of skin on the top of her daughter's scalp. "Did you shave it? Could someone else have done it while you were sleeping?" Quickly, they solved the mystery—Alison must have wrapped the elastic band too tightly around her pony tail. The incident was soon forgotten.

Three months later, another bald spot was found, then another. Soon, Alison's scalp was dotted with peculiar quarter-sized bare patches. After diagnoses of "it's just stress" with remedies of topical ointments, a specialist began to administer injections of cortisone, fifty to each spot, every two weeks. To mask her scalp, bloody from the shots, Alison was granted permission to wear a baseball hat to school, normally a violation of the strict uniform code. Little strands of hair would push through the scabs, only to fall out two weeks later. She was suffering from a condition of hair loss known as alopecia, and nothing would stop it.

Alison's sunny spirit and supportive friends kept her going, but there were some low points. Like the time when her little sister came into her bedroom with a towel wrapped around her head to have her hair combed. When her mother untwisted the towel, Alison watched the tousled thick hair bounce around her sister's shoulders. Gripping all of her limp hair between two fingers, she burst into tears. It was the first time she had cried since the whole experience began.

As time went on a bandanna replaced the hat, which could no longer conceal her balding scalp. With only a handful of wispy strands left, the time had come to buy a wig. Instead of trying to resurrect her once-long blonde hair, pretending as though nothing had been lost, Alison opted for a shoulder-length auburn one. Why not? People cut and dyed their hair all the time. With her new look,

Alison's confidence strengthened. Even when the wig blew off from an open window of her friend's car, they all shared in the humor.

But as the summer approached, Alison worried. If she couldn't wear a wig in the water, how could she lifeguard again? "Why—did you forget how to swim?" her father asked. She got the message.

After wearing an uncomfortable bathing cap for only one day, she mustered up the courage to go completely bald. Despite the stares and occasional comments from less-than-polite beachcombers—"Why do you crazy punk kids shave your heads?"—Alison adjusted to her new look.

She arrived back at school that fall with no hair, no eyebrows, no eyelashes, and with her wig tucked away somewhere in the back of her closet. As she had always planned, she would run for school president, changing her campaign speech only slightly. Presenting a slide show on famous bald leaders from Gandhi to Mr. Clean, Alison had the students and faculty rolling in the aisles.

In her first speech as the elected president, Alison addressed her condition, quite comfortable answering questions. Dressed in a T-shirt with the words "Bad Hair Day" printed across the front, she pointed to her shirt and said, "When most of you wake up in the morning and don't like how you look, you may put on this T-shirt." Putting on another T-shirt over the other, she continued. "When I wake up in the morning, I put on this one." It read, "No-Hair Day." Everybody cheered and applauded. And Alison, beautiful, popular and smart—not to mention varsity goalie, ocean lifeguard and now, school president with the pool-blue eyes—smiled back from the podium.

*Jennifer Rosenfeld and Alison Lambert*

# Losing Hope

*Wherever you go, there you are.*

Buckaroo Bonzai

"Hope is the hat rack upon which I hang my dreams . . .'"? Oh, please! I crumple up the paper and fling it across my bedroom. I can't believe I kept my hopeless seventh-grade attempts at poetry. I thought I was a poet that year. Obviously I wasn't, and never will be.

"Here they are," I mutter, pulling a stack of yearbooks from the depths of the drawer. They go all the way back to elementary school. *Lauren will like these. Best friends since first grade, she's not talking to me now, but I'm sure she'll want these . . . after . . .*

"You're hopeless, Carrie," she yelled at me over the phone Friday night. Because I don't see everything exactly her way, because I tell her things she doesn't want to hear. The way I think best friends should. Now I don't even have a best friend. And I can't stand losing her friendship.

I peer into the drawer, empty of yearbooks but still

containing the debris of my life. Now what would Josh want from me? According to him, nothing. "There's no hope, Carrie," he told me that night two weekends ago. The night he broke up with me, practically pushing me away as I begged him for another chance. No, he shook his head at me. No, it's over. No hope for us. He hasn't spoken to me since. I can't stand losing him, either.

I slip my hand into the pocket of my robe and finger the little container of pills. My stepfather takes these for his back, and I've heard his repeated warnings to my little brothers never to touch them, how dangerous pills like these can be. He never warned me, knowing that I'm old enough, knowing that I understand about things like dangerous pills.

A knock on my door makes my hand fly from the pocket. Of course, my mother barges right in before I can respond.

"Carrie," she says in her exasperated tone, "we're all waiting for you out by the tree. You know we can't open the presents until we're all together." The faint melody of a Christmas carol and the scent of hot cocoa waft into my room through the open door.

"Honestly, Carrie, can't you dress up a little for Christmas Eve? Or at least get that hair out of your eyes," she continues. "Sometimes I think you're hopeless." She sighs—loudly, dramatically, as if otherwise I wouldn't understand the depths of my hopelessness. "Well, hurry up."

With that, she closes the door and leaves me screaming silently after her: *Yes, Mom, I know I'm hopeless, like you always tell me. Every time I forget to empty the dishwasher, fold the laundry, get the hair out of my eyes, whatever.*

So they're all waiting for me. Mom, my stepfather, Dave, and Aaron and Mark. Waiting for me to join in the singing of carols and unwrapping of gifts. Sure, I'll go. I'll unwrap a few presents. Not that they'll mean a thing to me. But it's Christmas. I'm supposed to be happy. I can pretend. After all, I took drama class last semester.

Ah, school. Another one of the victorious arenas of my life.

"I'm sorry, Carrie, but it's hopeless," Ms. Boggio told me the last day before winter break. "You'd have to get an A on every test for the rest of the year to raise that D to a C." Then she left me alone in the biology lab, staring at my latest test, the latest record of my failures.

I tossed the test away. *I won't even have to show Mom,* I thought. *I won't have to hear that lecture again. The one about how I'm ruining my chances for college. That there will be no hope for my future if I keep going on this way. In fact, I'll never have to hear another lecture again. The problem will be solved before school starts in January.*

How about a note? Would they want one? I used to think I was some great writer. I'd spend hours filling note-book after notebook with my stories and poems, some-times just my thoughts and ideas. That's when I felt most alive—writing and dreaming of being good at it, of having other people read my words. And having my words mean something to them. But that was before the hopelessness of being Carrie Brock swallowed me up.

"Just a lousy note," I remind myself. That's all I have to write now. Or ever. I've lost everything: my best friend and my boyfriend. Or I've messed it up: my grades, even my hair. I can't do anything right, and I can't stand facing the reminders of my failures anymore.

"Come on, Carrie," Aaron's voice cries through the door. "I want to open my presents."

*Oh, all right. I'll do the note later.* I drag myself up and tighten the belt on my robe. As I walk down the hall, the pills make a satisfying clicking noise in my pocket.

I sink into the couch and watch as Mark, my youngest brother, tears open his gifts, flinging wrapping paper everywhere. Then it's Aaron's turn. That's the tradition in our family. Youngest to oldest. Everyone oohs and aahs over Aaron's gifts.

"Your turn, Carrie," Mark informs me.

"Can you bring them?" I ask. "I'm tired."

Mark carries over a rectangular box. Clothes, of course. From Mom. I mumble the appropriate thanks. My gifts are few this year. Nothing from Lauren or Josh, of course. Trinkets from Aaron and Mark.

"Okay, I'm done," I say.

"No, wait, here's another one," Mark says, handing me a small package.

"Who's it from?"

"Me." My stepfather speaks up. Dave, the man who resides in the background of my life. A good guy, he treats me well. I've never regretted my mom marrying him.

I tear off the paper, revealing a book. But opening it, I find there are no words inside.

"It's blank," I say, looking up at Dave.

"Well, not quite. There's an inscription up front. But it's a journal, Carrie. For your words."

I flip to the front and find Dave's handwriting in one corner. I read the inscription silently.

> *To Carrie:*
>
> *Go for your dreams. I believe in you.*
>
> *Dave*

I look up at Dave again. He shrugs slightly, as if embarrassed. "Well, I know you want to be a writer, Carrie," he explains. "And I know you can do it."

His last words are almost lost in the noise my brothers are making, digging under the tree and coming up with my mother's presents. But Dave's words are not lost on me.

Somebody believes in me and in my dreams, even

when I've stopped believing in them myself. When I thought I was beyond all hope. I clutch the journal to my chest and a feeling I haven't felt for a long time returns. I do want to be a writer. But most of all, I want to just be.

I watch the rest of the presents being opened, thinking there's something I need to do, but I can't quite figure out what. I can slip the pills back into the cabinet later, so that's not it. Then I know.

I grab a pen from the coffee table and open my journal. On that first blank page I write my words: "Hope is the hat rack I hang my dreams upon."

*H'mm*, I think. *Kind of sounds like a country song. Maybe it's not that bad after all.* I look up and smile at Dave, even though he's not looking my way. He's just given me the best Christmas present ever. I've gotten my dreams back. Maybe there's hope for me, after all.

*Heather Klassen*
*Submitted by Jordan Breal*

# I Never Knew

*The difference between holding on to a hurt or
releasing it with forgiveness is like the difference
between laying your head down at night on a
pillow filled with thorns or a pillow filled with
rose petals.*

Loren Fischer

She was my best friend, and I loved her. She was the
coolest girl in junior high and everyone wanted to be like
her . . . and she chose me to be her best friend. Her name
was Cindy. She was beautiful with her black hair and tall,
thin body. While the rest of us in eighth and ninth grade
were still looking amorphous, trying to take shape, Cindy
was already beautifully poised in her adult body.

Her mother had died when she was a little girl. She was
an only child, and she lived alone with her father. By the
time we would get home from school every day, he would
already be at work. He wouldn't come home until two or
three in the morning, so we had free reign of the house.
No parental supervision was the greatest thing we could
ask for as teenagers. Her house was a big, two-story that

was concealed by a large grove of orange trees. You couldn't see the house from the street, and we liked it that way. It added to the mystique and allure that we were always trying to create.

At school she was pretty much the center of attention. One whole corner of the quad was dedicated to Cindy and her "followers." If there was new music, clothes, hairstyles or even new ways to take notes or study, you could be fairly sure that it came out of that corner of the quad. Even the school faculty caught on to the power this girl held and convinced her to run for class president. Cindy and I were voted in as class president and vice president by a landslide.

By day, we were the acting liaison between students and faculty; by night, we hosted social activities at Cindy's house. If we weren't having a party, people would come just to hang out. Kids would be there for all kinds of reasons—to talk about relationships, their parents, to do their homework, or just because they knew someone they liked would be showing up.

After everyone left, I would usually spend the night. My mom wouldn't like it very much if it was a school night. Sometimes Cindy would come back to my house to spend the night, but my mom didn't like that much either because we would stay up all night laughing and talking. Cindy didn't like to be home alone.

That following summer, after I came home from vacation with my family, things were starting to change. Cindy looked thinner than usual with dark circles under her eyes, and she had started to smoke. The strikingly beautiful girl looked pale and gaunt. She said she missed me a lot. While it was a boost to my ego, I couldn't believe it could be entirely true. After all, there were always people trying to be close to her and get into her circle of friends.

My solution: two weeks at the beach. Our parents pitched in to rent a beach house for two weeks. My mom would be the only supervision. In Cindy's inimitable style, we collected a group of beach friends within a couple of days. We'd all hang out at this local café during the day, when we were not in the water or on the sand, and at night we'd hang out around this fire pit on the beach.

Cindy started to look like her old self, but better. She was tan. She looked great in a bikini, and all the guys on the beach wanted to be around her. But she was still smoking. She told me it calmed her nerves.

One night, Cindy came back to the beach house very late. She was all disoriented and noticeably excited. She told me she and this one guy had been drinking and smoking marijuana, and they had gotten together. She said that I had to try marijuana because it made everything better, clearer, in fact. She said she really liked this guy and wanted to run away with him. I knew she was just high, and she'd feel differently in the morning.

When school started that next year, things weren't the same, and I missed the old routine. Cindy wanted to get into different things than I wanted, and she started hanging around guys more and more. We would still hang out from time to time, but it wasn't as fun as it used to be. Cindy would get really serious and tell me that I just didn't understand how things were. I just thought that she was maturing faster emotionally than the rest of us, like she had physically.

One morning when I arrived at school, there were police cars all around and a lot of nervous activity in the halls. When I proceeded toward my locker, my counselor and another woman stopped me. I was asked to follow them to the office. My heart was pounding so fast and hard that I could hardly catch my breath. My head was racing with the different scenarios that might have caused this odd behavior.

When we all sat down in my counselor's office, the principal came in and took a seat. Was I in some kind of trouble? The principal began by talking about life and maturity and circumstances. Now my head was really spinning. (What was he trying to say?) And then my world froze in time with the words, ". . . and Cindy took her own life last night using her father's gun." I couldn't talk; I couldn't move. Tears started streaming from my eyes before my heart could even comprehend the pain. She was only fifteen years old.

As the suicide note explained, her father had repeatedly sexually abused her and she knew no other way out. Months after he was arrested, he finally confessed. The note also said something else. It said that the only family she ever knew and cared about was me. She left me a ring that her mother had left to her.

I cried for weeks. How is it that I never knew? We were closer than anyone and talked about everything; how come she never told me that? I was certain that I could have helped her, and I began to blame myself.

After weeks of grief counseling, I came to understand that the burden of Cindy's sexual abuse was too much for her to bear, especially when she started to become intimate with boys. The counselor explained to me that her shame was too great to talk about, even to her best friend. It dawned on me how alone she must have felt, and it suddenly became clear to me why she never wanted to spend the night alone in her own house.

My own suffering—weeks of pain and confusion—was eased greatly with all the help and support I received. Teachers, counselors, friends and family members all nurtured me. It was clear to everyone that this situation was going to change my life forever, but because I let help in, it subsequently add to my life an aspect of wisdom and compassion. I wish that Cindy could have known the relief that comes from letting others help you with your pain.

Cindy's suicide note also requested that she be cremated. The note said that I should spread her ashes wherever I wanted to. I chose the ocean off the beach where we had spent two weeks that summer.

On the day of the memorial, we rented a boat to take us out to sea. The boat was packed with friends and teachers, even though it was a rainy, overcast day. We stood on the bow and took turns sharing our experiences and love for our friend. When it came time for me to free her ashes, I hesitated. I didn't want to turn them loose in a sea that looked dark and menacing. I thought she had had enough of that in her own life.

My hesitancy gained attention, and both my mother and my counselor stepped up on the platform and put their arms around me. With their support I opened the lid and set my friend free. As some of the ashes hit the surface of the water, the sun broke through for a moment and sent beautiful rays of light that sparkled on the surface of the water. The clouds parted some more and soon the whole boat was bathed in warm sunlight. At that moment, I felt calmer than I had in weeks. Somehow I knew that the angels had come for my friend and that she would be all right—and so would I.

*Rosanne Martorella*

[EDITORS' NOTE: *Some of the critical signs to watch for if you think someone you know may be suicidal are:*

• *A sudden change in behavior (especially calmness after a period of anxiety or a lift in mood after a period of deep depression, which would indicate that the person now has the energy to act on suicidal thoughts).*

• *Preoccupation with death.*

• *Giving away belongings.*

• *Direct or indirect threats to commit suicide. (It is particularly important to pay attention and take seriously any talk of suicide even if it seems like the person is "joking.")*

*If you or someone you know is feeling suicidal or is showing any of the critical warning signs above, reach out to a professional you can trust (such as a school counselor) or call one of the hotlines listed below.]*

**800-SUICIDE: 800-784-2433**

**Yellow Ribbon Project: 303-429-3530, 3531, 3532**
*www.yellowribbon.org*
*Helps prevent teen suicide.*

**Youth Crisis Line: 800-843-5200, 24 hours**
*www.befrienders.org*
*Can refer you to a crisis hotline in your area.*

# A Call for Help

My dear friend Lindsay: She had been part of my life
since kindergarten. We met over her ninety-six-pack of
Crayolas, a big thing to a five-year-old. She was a constant
fixture in my life. She was a born comedian, with more talent, creativity, laughter, love and curly red hair than she
knew what to do with. The greatest thing about our friendship was that we completely understood each other. We
always had a smile, a joke, a shoulder or an ear to lend one
another. In fact, our favorite thing to do was to have our
parents drop us off at a restaurant, where we would have
these outrageously long talks over Mountain Dews, Diet
Cokes and the most expensive dessert our baby sitting
money would allow.

It was over one such talk in seventh grade where the subject of suicide came up. Little did I know that this would be
a conversation that would forever change our relationship.
We talked about how weird it would be if one of our friends
ever committed suicide. We wondered how families could
ever get over such a tragedy. We talked about what we
thought our funerals would be like. This conversation was
definitely the most morbid one we had ever had, but I did
not think about it too much. I assumed that, at one time or

another, everyone wonders who will cry and what will be said at their funeral. It never entered my mind that this talk was a cry for help from my beloved friend. Whenever this topic came up, I had the same frame of mind as my mother—we could never understand how one's life could get so desperate that the only alternative was death. However, we ended our talk with a laugh about how we were too "together" to ever do something so drastic, and we parted with a hug and a "Call me if you need anything."

I didn't think about our conversation until three weeks later, when I received a phone call from Lindsay. I immediately knew something was wrong when she did not begin the conversation with a bouncy hello and a good story. Today she came right out and asked me if she was important to my life and if she meant anything to this world. I answered with an energetic "Of course! I don't know what I'd do without you!" Lindsay then told me something that sent chills up my spine and neck. She told me that she felt lost, confused, worthless, and that she had a bottle of pills in her hand. She said that she was fully prepared to take them all, to end her life. *Was this the girl who sat next to me in English class and with whom I loved to get in trouble? Was this the girl who loved bright colors, laughing, and striking up conversations with anyone in the world? Was this my wonderful, funny friend who was so bubbly and light that she practically floated through life?*

My reality then came into check and I realized that this was my friend, and for that reason, I had to keep her on the phone. I then started the longest phone conversation in my life. Over the next three-and-a-half hours, Lindsay told me her troubles. And for three-and-a-half hours, I listened. She spoke of how she got lost in her large family (fifteen children, and she was the baby), how her self-confidence was low from her appearance (which I thought was beautiful and unique), how she was anorexic the summer before (I was too busy playing softball to notice), how she was confused about her future—whether or not she would follow her dreams or her parents' wishes, and how she felt completely alone. I kept telling her over and over how original, beautiful and important her dreams and personality were to our lives. By this time, we were both crying: she was frustrated, I was pleading for her life.

My mind then reached out at what I assumed was my final chance at helping Lindsay; I told her three simple things. I first told her that everyone has problems. It's a part of life. That overcoming these problems and moving onto greater heights is what life is all about. The second thing I told her was that if life was as bad as she said, then things couldn't possibly get worse. There wasn't room for any more failure—things had to improve. The final simple thing I told her was that I, or someone else close to her, would always be there, no matter what trials may come into her life. I told her that the fact that we were having this conversation, that she wanted me to know what was going on, proved my theory that she really wanted to live. If she wanted to end her life, she would have just done it. But, since she took time to call, her mind was saying "Help! I want to keep my life!" After I finished that last statement, I heard the best sound in the world—Lindsay flushing the pills down the toilet.

I then went to her house, and we talked about how she could start putting her life back together. We got her some help, and eventually, Lindsay overcame her issues. I am proud to say that Lindsay and I will be starting the eleventh grade together in the fall, she is getting excellent grades, and is a happy teenager. The road there wasn't easy, and we both slipped a few times. But, the important thing is that we raised ourselves up and arrived.

*Jill Maxbauer*

# Nintendo Master

When I first saw you, I thought—*Nintendo Master*. There was this intensity about you. Your piercing blue eyes and the way your hands moved rapidly along the control buttons were subtle hints of your expert skill.

You didn't appear too different from all of the other video-crazed teens out there, but you were. I guess the fact that it was summer, and we were both stuck in the oncology ward of the hospital cruelly betrayed the normality with which you tried to present yourself. Or maybe it was the fact that we were prematurely robbed of the innocence of childhood, and it comforted me to know that there was someone else out there just like me. I can only speculate, but all I know for sure is that I was drawn to your energy and zest for life.

That was the summer of my first post-cancer surgeries. The doctors were trying to fix my left hip joint, which had shattered under the intense bombardments of chemotherapy treatments. It wasn't the only thing that had shattered. I had misplaced my usual optimistic attitude about life and was surprised at how nasty I could be. This did not help to endear me to anyone in my presence.

My surgery had gone "well," the doctors said, but I was in excruciating pain.

I saw you again in physical therapy, realizing only then the extent of what cancer had done to you. I wanted to scream, "Let him go back upstairs and play his video games, you idiots!" But I just sat there in stunned silence. I watched you get up and start walking with the aid of the parallel bars. Prior to your entrance into the room, I had been sitting in my wheelchair, wallowing in self-pity—"Wasn't the cancer enough? Now my hip is screwed up, and I really don't care anymore. If I get up, it is going to kill."

You will never know me, but you are my hero, Nintendo Master. With such courage and poise, you got up on your one remaining leg. Some might have the audacity to call you disabled or even crippled, but you are more complete than many can ever wish to be. After you had your walk for the day, a walk that was perfectly executed on your part, and you were safely tucked into your bed and were enjoying your video games once again, I decided that it was about time that I get up and take a walk myself. You see, Nintendo Master, it dawned on me then that you had innately known what it takes most of us a lifetime to grasp—life is like a game, you can't win them all and yet the game goes on, forcing all to play it. Nintendo Master, you play it better than most!

*Katie Gill*

# Owning the World

*Character cannot be developed in ease and
quiet. Only through experience of trial and suffering can the soul be strengthened, ambition
inspired, and success achieved.*

Helen Keller

I slowly came to understand what had been said.
Instead of the expected dismissal of my illness and being
told to choke down a series of medications, I was told I
had leukemia. It was June 27, 1997. The weather was
pleasant, and I was calm. From the smaller hospital in
Kitchener, my mom and I proceeded directly to London
to begin my own personal hell.

As my mom, dad and I sat listening in a vague stupor,
what we could come to expect was explained to us in the
simplest and nicest way possible. That information was
repeated a lot during the next little while. It was a great
deal to take in while under such shock. However, I
decided right away that my case would be different. I
would not lose all my hair, I would not puff up from

steroids, I would not get mouth sores, and the chemotherapy would not be so hard on me as it is on other
people. I was wrong.

The next couple of days were the most difficult I had
faced in my life. To that point, most of my life had been no
problem. I could dismiss whatever was wrong within a
couple of days and never face very severe or life-changing
consequences. But leukemia was a big deal that I would
have to live with for an indeterminate length of time. I
decided to complete this temporary obstacle with grace,
maturity and an understanding of how much people were
helping me, and how much I had to be grateful for.

Meanwhile, back at home people were slowly hearing
the news. I started getting lots of cards and gifts. I knew
they were meant to cheer me up, but they made me sad. I
didn't want to be the center of bad attention. I didn't
want people to know I was even sick. I wanted to get the
chemotherapy, go home and be happy without everybody knowing. But the gifts and cards piled up, each one
a painful reminder of what a difficult and daunting task
lay before me.

When it was around time for it to fall out, I cut my
shoulder-length black curly hair short. I didn't really care
that much; I was too weak from the leukemia and the first
strong dose of chemotherapy. My hair fell out about a
week later. For the first little while I wore a wig or a hat all
the time because I was so ashamed. Eventually, I came
not to care if the nurses or my parents saw me without
hair. It took quite a while longer for me to show a select
group of my friends. I kept in contact with two of my best
friends. I didn't have the energy or the strength to reassure them all firsthand.

I spent most of July in the hospital, waiting for my
blood counts to come back high enough that I could
return home. I completed a number of paintings, finding

that painting helped to keep my spirits high and my mood cool, calm and collected. It was amazing therapy. I went home for a week in early August. I needed a break. I had to stay out of the sun, didn't have as much stamina as usual and wore a wig, but other than that it was the closest I would feel to normal for quite a while.

The following cycle of chemotherapy was the worst I have ever experienced. I had no idea what was in store for me. Up until then, I had handled all the chemotherapy with flying colors. At the end of August I was back in the hospital, only this time in pain. It was the worst pain I had ever felt. I wasn't allowed to have pain relievers because the doctors had to know if the pain changed in any way. An endless bombardment of seemingly unimportant questions, which in reality were quite significant, drove me insane. They put a tube down my nose to drain the stomach acid, and I suffered severe nausea and stomach pain for the next month. I finally went home feeling better. My bone marrow transplant was scheduled for October, earlier than anticipated. I went shopping, had my friends over, and had a great time. It was a very well-deserved break.

I was very fortunate to have two donors to choose from. Both my brother and my sister were perfect matches. The doctors chose my brother. We went to Toronto's special bone-marrow transplant unit confident and full of hope that this was finally coming to a close. The round of chemotherapy was strong enough to kill me if I hadn't had my brother's marrow to back me up. I did quite well in isolation. Except for the nausea. It just never went away. Everything I ate just came back up again. I went home promising to eat and drink as much as I could or a minimum of one-and-a-half liters a day. That proved to be extremely difficult.

Within a couple of days I was back in the hospital to get

hydrated and for treatment for shingles. The nausea still hadn't gone away. I was angry with myself for letting everybody down. We all had such high expectations for me after the bone-marrow transplant, and I wasn't meeting them. No matter how hard I tried, I could not bring myself to eat. On top of it, I had to take a great number of pills, which just made me more sick.

Even though the nausea continued, I was able to return home. It was torture. I got bronchitis and sinusitis and had no idea how it could possibly get worse. After a CT scan and routine clinic visit, I found out I had relapsed. The chemotherapy and bone-marrow transplant didn't work. The leukemia was back. All I had just been through was for nothing. This bad news came ten times harder than it had the first time. I had already been through all this, suffered the consequences, and lived through the trials and tribulations.

When a patient with AML relapses, the chances of long-term remission, or cure, with conventional treatments is about 20 percent. That news just never left my mind. However, I was able to remain secure in knowing that I was getting the newest and latest treatment. I was the eighth pediatric patient to try this new treatment through Sick Kids' Hospital, and so far it had worked quite well in adults. So I told myself it would be all right and started it along with another program my dad had heard about.

The medication my dad found was an experimental organic medicine that is injected into the lymph nodes. I had to do that every day for three months. It was up to me when to stop. It was as if a great weight had been taken off my shoulders when I finally felt confident enough to stop.

The hospital treatment was quite different. I had to endure a round of chemotherapy, followed by a dose of my brother's white blood cells, hoping that they would identify the leukemia as foreign "bad stuff" and destroy it. The first chemotherapy and batch of my brother's white blood cells proved inadequate. When I got my bone marrow checked there were still signs of leukemia. I went through the chemotherapy once more, knowing that if it didn't work this time I was as good as gone. They gave me the remaining batch of white blood cells, this time many more of them. My brother and I are such a close match that the blood cells hadn't attacked me enough, so, with the second and final round, they gave me the entire batch.

I am proud to say that I no longer show signs of any leukemia.

Slowly, day by day, I approach summer, regain my strength and remind myself of how valuable and fragile *everybody* is. It has been a long, hard fight, but I would not trade the lessons I have learned in those ten months for the world. I have learned to be brave. I have learned to be strong. And, most important, I have learned to persevere.

*Liz Alarie*

[EDITORS' NOTE: *We received the following from the author's parents:*

*Two months later, Lizzie relapsed for the last time. Shortly after, she died at home. Lizzie lived her fifteen months of illness with radiant grace, maturity and ever-present gratitude. She accomplished her greatness here on Earth as a teacher. "Her world" witnessed her valiant actions, kind deeds and motivating stories such as this one. Lizzie's wish for mankind was simple: Begin now to live your life to the fullest—it is possible!*

*Ray and Mary Pat Alarie*]

# My Toughest Decision

Mistakes, mistakes, mistakes. Everyone makes them. No one saw mine coming.

Overall, I was a really good kid. At fifteen, I was a sophomore at a Catholic high school and a member of the National Honor Society. I played softball and ran cross-country. I had, and still have, aspirations of becoming a doctor. If someone would have told me that at the age of fifteen I would become pregnant, I would have said they were crazy. Why would anyone do something so foolish? It's still hard for me to believe, but it happened.

October 11, 1997, was the day my daughter was born. I took one look at her, and it was love at first sight. It was so overwhelming—a flood of emotions that I have never experienced. I loved her in a way that could only be described as unconditional. I looked at her, and in my heart I knew that I could not give her all the things that she needed and deserved to have, no matter how badly I wanted to. Physically, emotionally and in every other way, I was not capable of being a mother. I knew what had to be done. Putting all my emotions aside and doing what I felt was best for my daughter, I decided to give her up for adoption.

Placing my baby in the arms of her mother was the hardest thing I've ever had to do. My very soul ached. Even though I still get to see my daughter because I am blessed with having an open adoption, the pain is still there. I can feel it burning inside me every day, when I think about Katelyn. I only hope that when she gets older, she realizes how much I love her. I love her more than anything in the world.

Today is my daughter's first Christmas. I won't be there to share with her the joy of this season, or to play Santa and open her presents for her (she's only two months old). In fact, I won't be there to see her first step, or hear her first word. I won't be there to take pictures on her first day of kindergarten. When she cries for her mommy, it won't be me that she wants. I know in my heart that I made the right choice. I just wish with all my heart that it was a choice I never had to make.

*Kristina Dulcey*

# It's Tough to Be a Teenager

It's tough to be a teenager, no one really knows
What the pressure is like in school, this is how it goes.

I wake up every morning, and stare into this face
I wanna be good lookin', but I feel like a disgrace.

My friends they seem to like me, if I follow through with
    their dare,
But when I try to be myself, they never seem to care.

My mom, well she keeps saying, I gotta make the grade
While both my parents love me, it slowly seems to fade.

It seems like everyone I know is trying to be so cool
And every time I try, I end up just a fool.

I've thought about taking drugs, I really don't want to
    you know
But I just don't fit in, and it's really startin' to show.

Maybe if I could make the team, I'll stand out in the crowd
If they could see how hard I try, I know they would be
  proud.

You see I'm still a virgin, my friends they can't find out
'Cause if they really knew the truth, I know they'd laugh
  and shout.

Sometimes I really get so low, I want to cash it in
My problems really aren't so bad, if I think of how life's
  been.

Sometimes I'm really lost, and wonder what to do
I wonder where to go, who can I talk to.

It's tough to be a teenager, sometimes life's not fair
I wish I had somewhere to go, and someone to CARE.

*Tony Overman*

# Four Kisses

I am thirteen and going to a baseball game with my father. I bring binoculars, a little Dutch-boy haircut, my glasses, insecurity, a love for the game and a lack of serotonin in my brain. The fog is twisting around Candlestick Park, leaving the feeling of dampness, dirty water on my jacket and wetness on my glasses, making my perspective skewed like a funhouse mirror. My father wants more than anything else to teach me to keep score, but I am desperately trying to never learn anything new again, because the things I have learned in the last year have been all-around destructive: that I am clinically depressed, that a school day is too long, that I have obsessive-compulsive disorder, and that I am losing even more weight, and am down to eighty-five pounds.

My father grabs my hand. "Did you see that pitch? Right on the money, right on the money. Whoever says they're not going to take it all the way . . ." Asleep in the car on the way home, I can only vaguely hear the music he has on softly so as not to wake me. Something about going home, going home, going home. Mom is asleep in their bed with her red-and-gray quilt that smells just like she does.

My father stops in my room on his way to his. "Good night, Kater." He is standing in the one spot in my doorway where everything echoes. "Good night, Daddy. I love you. Can I have four kisses?" I need four of everything, because obsessive-compulsive disorder has me believing in plastic number power, power I can't have in other arenas. So I make my bed sixteen times and wash my hands until I have slammed the door to the cabinet under the sink just so, so that nobody dies or gets in a car wreck.

My father notes that I have been sleeping wildly. I am usually a still sleeper, the biggest moves I make are a shift from one side to the other, so that I go to sleep staring at the green light from my clock, and wake up with my face towards the wall. But starting last year, I have been waking up having kicked my quilt off, with my stuffed animals relegated unconsciously to the coldness of the floor.

The next day my father says, "Maybe you're getting better." He tries.

"I just want it to end."

"I know you do."

"But I really, really need it to end. Dad, I can't deal with it."

"You know how when you're cleaning out your desk or your room, you have to empty everything out, spread it all over the floor?"

"I guess." I wipe the tears from my face. I hate not being able to see.

"Well, you're there right now."

I hadn't noticed until now how foggy it is. We are walking across the street from a mortuary on the way back from my therapist. It is a Tuesday.

"What?" I asked, not understanding his point.

"Katie, you have everything spread out all over the floor. You have to wait, to pick it all up." This only makes me cry harder, because I am frustrated by the reality of the metaphor blown up, enlarged, unreachable.

My father and my mother are constant reminders to me of what I leave when I go to school for abbreviated days. They are what I stand to lose.

Graduation day. My father and my mother sit in the white plastic chairs; I am on an elevated platform. It is wood painted brown, and parts of it have chipped off so that the chairs that my eighth-grade class sits on are tipping and making plastic-to-wood noises through hollow speeches. Somewhere in the middle, I start to cry. For once it's okay, nobody jeers. I am leaving a part of my life on an uneven platform with my above-the-ears-but-growing-out haircut, bangs clipped back with golden barrettes, a white dress and wonderful parents.

My father drives me to my first day at high school. I haven't been to the therapist in three months. I am walking on legs and feet and ankles that I trust. A senior tells my older sister that I am strutting around school. I keep my bangs pulled away from my face. I hate not being able to see.

My father and I have begun to fight. He does not want me staying out too late. He is upset that my grades are lower than he expected. He always wants to know when I'll be home. When I argue with him, and he leaves, I almost don't know what to do with myself. My obsessive-compulsive power is gone. I am empty so that I can start over.

"Fall came today," my dad says, his first words to me that morning. Since the recent death of my friend's brother, I think of first words and last words more carefully than I should. There have been other first words on other mornings, mostly about the weather or the Giants and how they blew it in the seventh with two runners on, one of them in scoring position. I nod. I'm ineffectual with him that way, letting him bounce off me, because if I let him in, I would be admitting to something. I have thoughts now. And they are mine. My insides and my breaths and my friends and my words, they are all mine. I cling to them more and more.

When my father and I fight, it is loud and articulate. There's something cleansing about it, and it makes me shake. He tells me that he's proud of how well I can argue, that I can always get my point across. My father blames me when my mother gets sick, because it's the stress that I cause, manifesting itself in her.

I am finally sixteen. I have a best friend and contact lenses, a father, a mother and a past. I have beaten something. And that is what I have inside me: strength. I realize, midway through the first quarter of my junior year, that I don't know who bats cleanup for the Giants. I realize that the mortuary across from my old therapist was torn down to build a parking lot. I realize that I haven't talked to my father, sat down and talked to him, since I went away this summer by myself and came back with crisp white inspiration.

I finally have enough serotonin in my brain. I know what I need. I have respect for myself and what I went through. It used to be inexplicable. My father, my mother, a dry bedspread, a song about going home and the National League champion Giants went through it with me. I had built a fresh new me, but I had lost my father. And I wasn't willing to give him up.

I hear his sweaty-feet footsteps coming up the stairs in the house. I lie in my bed tonight, a sixteen-year-old at 110 pounds with long hair, a daughter, home by curfew. Warm and whole, stubborn, stronger, older, and I ask my father for one solitary kiss.

*Kate Reder*

# No Matter What Happens

I remember a time when each day was long,
When the world was a playground and my life a song,
And I fluttered through years with barely a care,
Ignoring the future and what waited there.

School was intriguing and filled with delights.
I played away daytimes and dreamed away nights.
My parents assured me I had nothing to fear,
And that no matter what happened, they'd always be there.

Little I knew of a world outside home,
Where tragedy, sorrow and murder could roam.
All I saw were blue skies, rainbows and stars.
I looked past destruction of buildings and cars.

As a child, my biggest concern was just me;
I had to be happy, I had to be free.
And if I was content, I would not shed a tear,
And no matter what happened, I still would be here.

But as I grow up, darkness starts to set in;
My bright world has turned into concrete and tin.
I now see the violence I looked past before;
My friends start to die and my heart hits the floor.

Deadly diseases claim people I love,
There are landfills below me, pollution above.
I often think back to when life was a game.
But no matter what happens, it can't be the same.

There are days when I just want to break down and howl,
To give up completely, to throw in the towel,
But I hold my head high and I push my way through.
I have too much to give and so much to do.

And I make a vow that, though it'll be hard,
I'll go on with a smile and play every card.
I'll give all I can, help others and love.
No matter what happens, life will bloom again,
And the strength I don't have will come from above.

So come, take my hand, and through darkness we will
    sail—
If we all join together, we never can fail.
We'll remember to care, remember to feel,
And no matter what happens, our world we will heal.

*Alison Mary Forbes*
*Submitted by Barry Weber*

# Hero of the 'Hood

*When you have to cope with a lot of problems,
you're either going to sink or you're going to
swim.*

Tom Cruise

By all odds, Mike Powell should never have survived.
Addiction, drug pushing, prison or early death are the
most likely cards dealt to street kids growing up in the
"jungle" of South-Central Los Angeles—a violent combat
zone of drug wars, gang slayings, prostitution and crime.
But Mike's young life had a special purpose. For eight
years, he braved terror and brutalization to keep his
family of seven kids together. Incredibly, during that time,
no one ever discovered that the only real parent the
family had was just another kid.

When Mike was born, his father, Fonso, was in prison
for drug dealing. Mike's fifteen-year-old-mother, Cheryl,
dropped out of school to support the baby. "Without you,
my life could have been different," she later told Mike
over and over. It was the guilty glue that would make
Mike stick with her through the coming years of horror.

Fonso was released from prison when Mike was four, but instead of security, the six-foot-five, 300-pound Vietnam vet brought a new kind of fear into Mike's life. Fonso had severe psychological problems, and his discipline was harrowing. For minor infractions, such as slamming a door, he forced Mike to do pushups for hours. If the little boy collapsed, his father beat him. So fanatical was Fonso's insistence on school attendance that Cheryl had to hide Mike in a closet when he was sick.

Perhaps it was some dark premonition that drove Fonso to toughen up his young son and teach him self-reliance far beyond his years. Mike was barely eight when his father was murdered in a run-in with drug dealers.

Overnight, the protection and income Fonso had provided were gone. It was back to the streets for twenty-four-year-old Cheryl, who now had three kids: Mike; Raf, age four; and Amber, one year. Life was bitterly hard, and another baby was on the way.

It wasn't long before Cheryl brought home Marcel, a cocaine addict who terrorized the family even more than Fonso had. When Mike innocently questioned what Marcel had done with Cheryl's wages as a transit worker, Marcel broke the little boy's jaw so badly it had to be wired in place.

Marcel soon got Cheryl hooked on cocaine, and the two would disappear on drug binges, at first leaving the children locked in a closet but eventually just leaving them alone for weeks at a time. Cheryl had convinced Mike that if anyone found out what was happening, the children would be separated and sent to foster homes. Remembering his father's fierce admonitions to "be a man," the eight-year-old became consumed by the need to keep his family together, no matter what.

To make sure no one suspected anything, Mike began cleaning the apartment himself, doing laundry by hand

and keeping his sisters fed, diapered and immaculate. He scavenged junk shops for hairbrushes, bottles and clothes, whatever they could afford, and covered up for his mother's absences with an endless litany of excuses. Cheryl and Marcel were soon burning through everything the family had in order to buy crack—even money for rent and the children's food. When their money situation became desperate, Mike quietly quit elementary school at nine to support the family himself. He cleaned yards, unloaded trucks and stocked liquor stores, always working before dawn or late at night so the smaller children wouldn't be alone while awake.

As Cheryl and Marcel's drug binges and absences became longer and more frequent, their brief returns became more violent. Sinking deeper into addiction, Cheryl would simply abandon Marcel when his drugs ran out and hook up with someone who was better supplied. A crazed Marcel would then rampage through the slum apartment, torturing and terrorizing the children for information about where more money was hidden or where he could find their mother.

One night, Marcel put Mike's two-year-old sister in a plastic bag and held it closed. Without air, the toddler's eyes were bulging and she was turning blue. "Where's your mother?" the addict screamed. Sobbing, Mike and little five-year-old Raf threw themselves at Marcel again and again, beating on his back with small, ineffectual fists. In desperation, Mike finally sank his teeth into Marcel's neck, praying the savage tormentor would drop the plastic bag and pick on him instead. It worked. Marcel wheeled and threw Mike through the window, cutting him with shattered glass and breaking his arm.

Cheryl's parents, Mabel and Otis Bradley, loved their grandchildren deeply, but they worked long hours and lived a difficult multiple-bus commute away, and could see them only rarely. Sensing the family was struggling, Mabel sent toys, clothes and diapers, never dreaming that even the diapers were being sold by Cheryl for drug money. Although Mabel's constant phone calls and unconditional love became Mike's only anchor of support, he didn't dare tell her that anything was wrong. He feared his gentle grandmother would have a heart attack if she learned the truth—or worse, a violent confrontation with Marcel.

The family was forced to move constantly, sleeping in movie theaters, abandoned cars and even fresh crime scenes at times. Mike washed their clothes in public restrooms and cooked on a single-burner hot plate. Eventually, Cheryl and Marcel always caught up with them.

Despite the moves, Mike insisted the younger kids attend school, get good grades and be model citizens. To classmates, teachers and even their grandmother, the children always seemed normal, well-groomed and happy. No one could have imagined how they lived or that they were being raised by another child. Somehow Mike had managed to sort through the good intentions but brutal methods of his father, and blend them with the loving example of his grandmother, to form a unique value system. He loved his family deeply, and in return, the children loved, trusted and believed in him. "You don't have to end up on the street," he told them. "See what Mamma is like? Stay off drugs!" Secretly he was terrified that his mother would one day O.D. in front of them.

Over the next few years, Cheryl was jailed repeatedly for possession and sale of narcotics and other crimes, and was sometimes gone for up to a year at a time. Out of jail, she continued to have more children, making the family's financial situation increasingly critical. Hard as Mike tried, it was becoming impossible for him to care for three new babies and support a family of seven kids at the same time. One Christmas there was only a can of corn and a box of macaroni and cheese for all of them to share. Their only toys for the past year had been a single McDonald's Happy Meal figurine for each child. For presents, Mike had the children wrap the figurines in newspaper and exchange them. It was one of their better Christmases.

The young teenager now lived in constant anxiety, but still refused to fall into the easier world of drug dealing and crime. Instead, he braved the dangerous streets late at night selling doctored macadamia nuts, which, to half-crazed addicts, looked like thirty-dollar crack-cocaine "rocks." He knew he risked his life every time he took such chances, but he felt he had few choices. In the nightly siege of gang and drug warfare, the odds were against him, though. By age fifteen, Mike had been shot eight times.

Worse, his reserves of strength and hope were running dangerously low. For as long as he could remember, he had lived with relentless daily fears: *Will we be able to eat today? Will we all be on the street tonight? Will Marcel show up tomorrow?*

And after more than forty moves, it seemed they had finally hit rock bottom. "Home" was now the Frontier Hotel, a filthy dive on Skid Row where pimps and prostitutes stalked the halls and drug deals went down on the stairways. The kids had watched a murder in the lobby, and Mike was now afraid to leave them alone or to sleep. For the few nights they had been there, he had stayed up with a baseball bat to kill rats as they crawled under the door.

Sleep-deprived and overwhelmed by stress, Mike felt crushed by the responsibilities of his life. It was 2:00 A.M. His brother and sisters were huddled under a single blanket on the floor. Michelle, the youngest baby, was crying, but he had no food for her. The boy who had shouldered his secret burden for so many years suddenly lost hope.

Stumbling to the window in despair, Mike stood at the edge, steeling himself to jump. Silently asking his family to forgive him, he closed his eyes and took a last deep breath. Just then, a woman across the street spotted him and began screaming. Mike reeled back from the edge and fell into a corner, sobbing. For the rest of the night, he rocked the hungry baby and prayed for help.

It came a few days later on the eve of Thanksgiving 1993, shortly before Mike's sixteenth birthday. A church outreach group had set up a sidewalk kitchen nearby to feed the hungry, and Mike took the children there for free sandwiches. So impressed were the volunteers with him and the polite youngsters that they began asking gentle questions. A dam deep inside Mike finally broke, and his story spilled out.

Within days, the church group was at work trying to find the family permanent shelter, but no single foster home could take all seven children. Advised that the family would have to be separated "for their own good," Mike adamantly refused, threatening to disappear back into the jungle with the kids. The only person he trusted to keep the family together was his grandmother. Reluctantly, he finally told her of their life for the past eight years.

Stunned and horrified, Mabel Bradley immediately agreed to take the children, but the Los Angeles County social welfare system balked. Mabel was sixty-six, retired, and the children's grandfather was diabetic. How could the Bradleys possibly cope with seven youngsters? But Mike knew better. He hid the children and refused to negotiate any alternative except his grandparents. Finally the social workers and courts agreed, and an ecstatic Mabel and Otis Bradley were granted permanent legal custody of the children. Somehow every child had survived unscathed. Nothing short of miracles, it

seemed—and Mike's unfathomable strength and love—
had kept them together.

Mabel has since returned to work and now willingly
commutes more than one hundred miles a day, while Otis
cares for the children. Mike works as many jobs as he can
to help support the family, but smart, willing and honest
as he is, only minimum-wage jobs are available. More
than anyone, he realizes the value of an education and is
working on his GED.

His dream is to someday start a small company that
can simultaneously employ and counsel street kids like
himself who are without the traditional education and
skills to make it in the normal work world, but who don't
want to be forced back to street life because they can't
find work.

Mike is also dedicated to reaching other inner-city kids
through his music. A talented singer and songwriter, he
writes inspirational rap with his own unique message of
hope. Having seen so many kids die in his young life, he
wants desperately to reach those who might live.
"Surviving is against the odds, but it happens, and we
have to get that message out. If a thousand people hear
me and two kids don't get shot, don't deal, don't die, then
we've done something."

There is little time to sing right now, though, for Mike
and his family are still struggling themselves. But Raf,
Amber and Chloe are now stepping proudly into Mike's
big shoes to do their part at home. They are the three oldest street babies he raised—and taught to live with
courage and hope.

They remember well all of Mike's words, whispered
fiercely to them over and over during the bad times, during the many moves when, each time, they had to leave
everything behind: "Whatever you have, be grateful for
it! Even if you have nothing, be grateful you're alive!

Believe in yourself. Nobody is stopping you. Have a goal. Survive!"

Mike Powell will have his company for street kids some day. And there will be time, later, for the rest of his dreams, too. Mike is, after all, only nineteen.

*Paula McDonald*

# Good Night, Dad

"You afraid of heights?" my dad asked, as I climbed up the seemingly unstable ladder to the second-story rooftop. I was up there to help him fix our TV antenna.

"Not yet," I replied, as he climbed up after me with tools in hand.

I didn't have much to do up there on the roof—mostly I just held the antenna still and handed my dad tools—so I began to talk to him as he worked. I could always talk to my dad. He was more like a big kid than an actual adult. In fact, he looked much younger than his forty-one years. He had straight black hair and a mustache, with no signs of graying or balding. He stood at a strong six feet and had dark green eyes that seemed to always be laughing at some secret joke. Even my friends, whom he'd make fun of without mercy, loved him. Most of my peers would be embarrassed to have their dad hang around with them, but not me; in fact, I took great pride in him. No one else had a dad as cool as mine.

After he finished working on the antenna, we went inside, and I began to get ready for bed. As I entered my room, I looked over and saw my dad working intently at his computer in his office, which was adjacent to my bedroom. As I watched him, I had the most incredible urge to just poke my head in and tell him that I loved him. I quickly brushed that urge away and continued on into my room. I couldn't possibly say to him "I love you"; I hadn't said that to him or anyone else since I was seven, when my mom and dad would come and tuck me in and kiss me good night. It just wasn't something a man said to another man. Still, as I walked in and closed my bedroom door behind me, the feeling continued to grow inside of me. I turned around, opened my door and poked my head into my dad's office.

"Dad," I said softly.

"Yes?"

"Um . . ." I could feel my heartbeat rising. "Uh . . . I just wanted to say . . . good night."

"Good night," he said, and I went back to my room and shut the door.

*Why didn't I say it? What was I afraid of?* I consoled myself by saying that maybe I'd have the courage to say it later; but even as I told myself that, I knew it might never happen. For some reason I felt that was going to be the closest I'd ever come to telling my dad I loved him, and it made me frustrated and angry with myself. Deep within me, I began to hope he'd know that when I said "Good night," I really meant to say "I love you."

The next day seemed like any other. After school, I began to walk with my best friend to his house, as I frequently do; however, his mom surprised us by picking us up in the parking lot. She asked me whose house I was going to, and when I said "Yours," she paused and said, "No, I have this feeling that your mom probably wants you home right now." I didn't suspect anything; I figured she had something she wanted to do with her own family, and so I shouldn't butt in.

As we pulled up to my house, I noticed a lot of cars in front and quite a few people I knew walking up our front steps.

My mom greeted me at the front door. Her face was streaming with tears. She then told me, in the calmest voice she could manage, the worst news of my life. "Dad's dead."

At first, I just stood there as she hugged me, unable to move or react. In my mind, I kept repeating *Oh God, no; this can't be true! Please*... But I knew I wasn't being lied to. I felt the tears begin to run down my face as I quickly hugged some of the people who had come over, and then I went upstairs to my bedroom.

As I got to my bedroom, I looked over into my dad's office. *Why didn't I say it?!* That was when I heard my little three-year-old brother ask, "Mommy, why is my brother crying?"

"He's just feeling a bit tired, honey," I heard my mom tell him as I closed my bedroom door behind me. She hadn't told him yet that Daddy wouldn't be coming home from work again.

Once in my room, I hurt so badly that my body went numb and I collapsed on the floor, sobbing. A few moments later, I heard a scream from downstairs and then my baby brother's voice crying out, "Why, Mommy?!" My mom had just told him what had happened. A few seconds later, she came into my room and handed my crying baby brother to me. She told me to answer his questions while she stayed downstairs to greet people who came over. For the next half hour I tried to explain to him why Heavenly Father wanted our dad back with him, while I simultaneously tried to pull myself back together.

I was told that my father had died in an accident at work. He worked in construction and somehow, he had been knocked off the crane he was inspecting. Some workers nearby said they didn't hear him shout or anything, but had run over to him when they heard him land. He was pronounced dead on arrival around eleven o'clock that morning, April 21, 1993.

I never really told my dad I loved him. I wish I had. I miss him very much. When I see him again after this life, I know that the first thing I'm going to say to him is "I love you." Until then, "Good night, Dad."

*Luken Grace*

# A Name in the Sand

I sit on the rocky edge of a boulder, letting my feet dangle in the stillness of the water, and gaze out at the rippling waves crawling into shore like an ancient sea turtle. A salty mist hangs above the water, and I can feel it gently kissing my face. I lick my lips and can taste the familiar presence of salt from the ocean water. Above my head seagulls circle, searching the shallow, clear water for food and calling out to one another. And in my hand rests. . . .

The sound of a hospital bed being rolled down the hallway outside my mother's hospital room brought me out of my daydreams. The ocean was gone and all that was left was a bare hospital room, its only decorations consisting of flowers, cards and seashells carefully arranged on a table next to my mother's bed.

My mother was diagnosed with cancer about a year ago, a year full of months spent in various hospitals, radiation therapy, doses of chemotherapy and other methods to try to kill the cancer eating away at her life. But the tumors keep growing and spreading, and all the treatments have done is weaken her already frail body. The disease is now in its final course and, although nobody has told me, I know my mother won't be coming home this time.

I tried to change my thoughts, and they once again returned to my daydreams. Everything seemed so clear and so real, the sound of the waves, the taste of salt, the seagulls, and the . . . what was in my hand? I glanced down at my hands and realized I was holding my mother's favorite shell. I placed it against my ear, and the sound of the ocean sent cherished memories crashing into my mind.

Every year, my mother, my father and I would spend our summer vacations in a little cabin down by the ocean. As a little girl, I would explore this stretch of sand with my parents. Walking hand-in-hand, they would swing me high into the air as we ran to meet the incoming surf. And it was there, in those gentle waves, where my parents first taught me how to swim. I would wear my favorite navy blue-and-white striped swimsuit, and my father's strong arms would support me, while my mother's gentle hands would guide me through the water. After many mouthfuls of swallowed salty ocean water I could swim by myself, while my parents stood close by, proudly and anxiously watching over me. And it was in those grains of sand, not on a piece of paper that could be saved and displayed on a refrigerator, that I first painstakingly wrote my name.

My family's fondest memories weren't captured on film and put in a photo album, but were captured in the sand, wind and water of the ocean. Last summer was the final time my family would ever go to the ocean all together. This summer was nearly over and had been filled with memories of various hospitals, failed treatments, false hopes, despair, sorrow and tears.

I glanced over at my mother lying in her hospital bed, peacefully asleep after the doctor had given her some medicine for her pain. I wanted to cry out to God, "Why, why my mother? How can I live without her to help me through my life? Don't take her away from my father and me!" My tears and sobs began to fade away, as the dripping of my mother's IV hypnotized me into a restless sleep.

*  *  *  *

"Ashes to ashes, and dust to dust," droned the pastor, while my father and I spread my mother's ashes over the ocean water. Some of them fell into the water and dissolved, while others were caught in the wind and carried away. This was my mother's final wish—to be in the place she loved the most, where all her favorite memories live on.

As the funeral concluded and people began to drift away saying words of comfort to my father and me, I stayed behind to say my final farewell to Mother. I carried her favorite shell that brought her so much comfort while she was in the hospital and unable to hear the sounds of the ocean. I put it to my ear and the sound of the ocean seemed almost muted. I looked into the shell and was surprised to find a piece of paper stuck inside of it. I pulled the paper out and read its words:

*To my daughter, I will always love you and be with you.*

*A name in the sand will never last,*
*The waves come rolling into shore high and fast.*
*And wash the lines away,*
*But not the memories we shared that day*
*Where we have trod this sandy shore,*
*Our traces we left there will be no more.*
*But, wherever we are,*
*The memories will never be far.*

*Although I may not be with you,*
*Know that my love for you will always be true.*
*Those memories will last forever,*
*And in them we shall always be together.*
*Hold them close to your heart,*
*And know that from your side I will never part.*

As I crossed the beach, I stooped and wrote my mother's name in the sand. I continued onward, turning only to cast one last lingering look behind, and the waves had already begun to wash my lines away.

*Elizabeth Stumbo*

# Tears

I did not cry for Michigan.
It seemed before my time.
I did not cry for Jonesboro,
too far away to mind.
I did not cry for Palisades
even though it may be mine.
I did not cry for Conyers, Georgia
By then it all seemed fine.
But I poured my heart right through my eyes
The day they shot up Columbine.

The tears they fell for children lost
And children on the line.
My head fell quick into my hands
for parents who must pine.
My eyes stayed glossy to a screen
Watching kids of my own climb.

But,
What shook my body up the most,
What made it hard to breathe,

What bolted all my stomach down
And wouldn't let me leave.
What made me think about those boys
And try to empathize
Was the fright, the fear, the look of death
In one scared victim's eyes.

She described a scene so horror filled
So wrapped with movie cuts.
I thought about these kids and film,
what put them in their ruts.
I ruled out only media—
we all watch similar things
But combined with loneliness and fear
Who knows what games can bring?

One lesson to be learned from this,
The only one for which I'm sure,
Is that a gun manufacturer, movie title, music
    lyric, parent, anti-depressant, Internet,
    trench-coat, insult, or whatever else,
Is not the thing at fault.
And no gun policy, censorship, parent in jail,
    drug ban, Web-site check, dress code, sus-
    pension, or whatever else,
Would have removed their every thought.
We must take looks inside ourselves, accept-
    ing looks with love.
For what they didn't like in someone else,
Is what they saw in themselves.

*Jamie Rowen*

# Can That Be?

[AUTHOR'S NOTE: *I would like to submit the enclosed poem by my daughter Kelly, who was a sophomore. Kelly was a beautiful, kind and loving teenager with a heart of gold. She loved to write short stories and poetry, and wanted to become a published author. Kelly's life came to a tragic end, however, on April 20, 1999 when she was shot and killed in the library at Columbine High School. Kelly touched many hearts along her life's journey. A former middle-school teacher described her as "a gentle soul who walked among us that would never be forgotten." Kelly will remain forever in the hearts of those who loved her. This is one of Kelly's poems written in December 1998. Thank you for keeping Littleton in your prayers.*

*God Bless,*
*Dee Fleming]*

> I step outside what did I hear?
> I heard the whispers and
> The cries of people's fear.
> The loneliness of wisdom,
> Can that be?

The sad, sad sorrow that I see,
That is past in the tree.
Is it true? Can it be real?
Can I let them know how I really feel?
The things that I have seen,
The things that I have felt,
The feelings of sorrow that
I hope will soon melt.
I walked through the distances
And thought how it should be,
Of the smiles and the laughter,
That is what I thought it should be.
But can that be?
I walked past the dark houses,
And crossed the open fields.
I walked to the tree to kneel
I took a deep long breath
Then I closed my eyes.
I counted to three,
Then I open my eyes,
I was in my room,
That was a surprise.
But then I had seen that it was just a dream.
I walked to the window and pulled on the string.
What a surprise to see the sunrise.
In the distance were children with laughter and happiness,
That was the thought that I like to see!
But of course can that really be?
Or can this be another dream?

*Kelly Ann Fleming*

# Minutes Like Hours

You walk into the store
and stride down the aisle.
You pick me up and
try to look casual while
you carry me down
to the checkout line.
Pull out your wallet,
you soon will be mine.
Your friends are observing
every move that you make.
The clerk asks for ID—
you show him a fake.
You quickly walk down
to the front of the store.
Your friends are waiting for you
as you step out the door.
You hop in the car
and drive away from the shop.
Then you shut off the ignition,
and pop off my top.
You take a few drinks

and pass me around.
That's when you decide
to take a drive around town.
You turn on your car
and put your foot on the clutch.
*I'm sober,* you think,
*I didn't have very much.*
You pull onto the road
with me by your side,
Taking occasional sips
as you enjoy the ride.
Then the brakes on the car
in front of you squeal.
You try hard to stop,
but lose control of the wheel.
You skid off the road,
and you know you have crashed.
The dashboard is shattered,
the windshield is smashed.
Minutes like hours,
You're in treacherous pain,
that washes your senses,
envelops your brain.
The screams all around you
are faint to your ears,
as life flashes before you,
your hopes and your fears.
Minutes like hours,
you plead and you pray,
*I'll never touch it again,*
*just let me live one more day.*
Your mind starts to go dark,
it falls apart piece by piece.
And then you slip into blackness,
the pain has finally ceased.

Before you entered that store,
you should have thought twice,
for I am the substance
that cost you your life.

*Vidhya Chandrasekaran*

# The Last Song for Christy

Matt never did drugs. He spent his afternoons and nights riding his skateboard through backstreets of the small town that raised him. His friends would experiment with the usual substances, but not Matt.

Christy was his sister; six years older. She and Matt were close. They both liked tattoos and metal guitar riffs. Christy would paint incredible portraits and abstract images, and Matt would jam on his guitar. They shared stories, and they always said "I love you" before bed.

When Matt and I started dating, the first family member I was introduced to was his sister, Christy.

"See this tattoo on my wrist. Christy has it, too. We got them together." He lit up whenever he talked about her.

Matt was at the peak of his skateboarding career, and Christy was still painting. She was beautiful. They looked a lot alike—black hair, blue eyes. Christy was petite—her makeup dark and interesting—her lips, red and passionate. She looked the part she played—the artist, the once-rebel who survived hell and was now back, living life while revisiting the shadows of her past with each stroke of her paintbrush.

When Matt was in junior high, the police took Christy away. His parents wouldn't tell him why, but he found out on his own. Heroin. She had been doing heroin, and they caught her. She was only eighteen. She spent the next several months in rehab while Matt waited, guitar riffs, skate tricks—waited.

When she finally did come home, things were different. Christy seemed distant and Matt didn't know what to say. A few months later, they came again—the police. Matt was sleeping, and they knocked down the door. His sister was screaming as they dragged her away, this time to prison.

I asked Matt what it was like, how that affected him. I tried to imagine hearing her scream. I wondered how it was possible for Matt to sleep when he knew his sister was cold and alone in her cell somewhere.

"I couldn't," he said. "I couldn't sleep."

"Did you visit her?" I asked.

Matt was silent.

"Did you ever talk to her about it, tell her how much it hurt you, tell her that you couldn't sleep, tell her that you were afraid?"

There was a long silence. "She's okay now. She's been clean for eight years. She's great. It's over. The drugs, it's all over." Matt spoke to the wind when he spoke of Christy's past. His voice would fade out into oblivion and then he'd change the subject.

When Christy was finally released from jail and then rehab, Matt's family decided to move. They moved south, away from Christy's reputation and the backstreets where Matt had conquered curbsides and half-pipes in the small town by the sea. Christy was clean and never again did Matt wake up to his sister's arrests, or a cold sweat after the nightmares that plagued him while she was away. She had been clean for six months, and then two years, and then four. Matt went to high school and Christy moved back up north to go to school.

"Were you afraid?" I asked.

"Nope. She was going back to school. I was glad. She was going to pursue her art. She was so talented, you know," Matt whispered.

I knew. I had seen her artwork. It hung in Matt's room, in his kitchen and bathroom. She had even painted straight on the walls. Matt let her paint all over them.

Matt and I dated during my senior year. He was my first serious relationship. Christy came down to visit Matt and the family pretty often, and whenever she came down, Matt would rush to be with her. She was the woman in his life, more than I ever was. Christy and Matt were best friends. They were like nothing I had ever seen. Matt would light up when Christy entered a room. He was so proud of her. She was his angel, his big sister, and everything she said was amusing, brilliant or just cool.

I got the call a few months ago. Even though Matt and I had broken up over a year before, we were still close friends. The call wasn't from him, though. It was from another friend.

"Becca, look . . . I thought I should tell you. Christy died. She overdosed. Heroin. I'm sorry."

The air went numb, and the murmur of the TV in the other room muted. I dropped the phone and stared at the wall for what seemed like hours.

"But she was clean. Ten years now! She was clean . . ." I mumbled softly, my voice tainting the wind that blew on that rainy afternoon. I called Matt. He was with his family up north, where it happened.

I drove up north to be with him at this difficult time. matt told me, "She wasn't supposed to die. She was going to be married in a couple of months. They had the date and everything. We found this picture of her. She was wearing wings. You should see it; she looks like an angel."

He wasn't crying. I searched the blues of his eyes for a tear, but he was hypnotized. The shock. The impossibility of his earth angel lost somewhere in the universe. It was too much.

"The last time I saw her, she was so happy. I had my guitar and I was playing for her, and she was laughing. She was so beautiful and so happy. She was going to be a makeup artist. She would have been the best." Matt was smiling, and I took his hand.

She didn't have to die. She was clean for ten years, and then one day she started up again. Her body couldn't take it. She passed out, and they couldn't revive her. They couldn't make her come back.

Matt spoke during the funeral. His words were soft and eloquent, and he looked out at Christy's friends and family and told them how much he loved her, how much he will always love her. He showed his tattoo, the one that he and his sister got together. Some laughed. Some cried.

The picture that Matt had mentioned to me was perched behind the podium, between lilies and roses. Matt was right. She did look like an angel—red lips and blue eyes, wearing white and angel wings.

That night, after the funeral, Matt and I went down to the cove where he and Christy used to laugh. "How could she do this? Why? Why did she have to do this?" he asked.

He cried. I cried, too.

I talked to Matt the other day. I asked him how he was doing.

"I'm okay," he said. "Most of the time. Sometimes I can't sleep. I'm waiting for Christy to come home or for her to call. Sometimes I have these nightmares. I play the guitar a lot, even more than I used to. I have to practice. I'm in a band now, and we play gigs and stuff. The last song of the set is always the best. That's the song I practice over and over again until it's perfect. It has to be just perfect because I play it for Christy. The last song is always for Christy."

*Rebecca Woolf*

# Defining Myself

*Without a struggle, there can be no progress.*

Frederick Douglass

My dad died when I was four. My brother was two and my sister only one. Soon after, our family grew to five children, as I found myself with a half-sister and then a half-brother. We lived in the poorest part of the city; the projects were only a block away.

My mother, a widow in her twenties with five kids, couldn't handle it. She became an alcoholic and a drug user. Her expensive drug habit caused her to use all the money she could get her hands on for drugs. Although we were on welfare, she didn't use the money for the food we needed. Instead, she used the money to help support her drug habit. Her routine became a normal occurrence: she sent each one of us kids to the store with a food stamp. We'd buy something for a quarter or less, then give the change to her. We soon began to rely on the food given out by homeless shelters in order to eat. We would receive a bag and walk through a line as donated food, such as TV dinners or canned green beans, was dropped in our bags.

Not only were we deprived of a proper diet, but our poverty prevented us from experiencing the normal joys that kids look forward to, such as Christmas. Although we swallowed our pride when we had no choice but to seek food donations, it was hardest during the holidays. Each winter, our thin, hand-me-down clothing and holed shoes forced us to accept free clothes and a voucher for new shoes at the local church, which we then exchanged as Christmas gifts. Knowing that our clothes came from this organization made it impossible to believe in Santa, tainting our holiday spirit.

Soon, my mom began disappearing for days at a time. In a way, it was better when she wasn't around because we didn't have to live in fear of her mental and physical abuse, like the beatings and heartless name-callings. One night, after my mom threw a lamp at me, nailing me on the side of the head, and a plastic vase at my sister, hitting her in the eye, I made the toughest decision that I ever had to make. I called Child Protective Services, while my sisters cried beside me, begging me not to. Although my mom had been reported before for abuse and neglect, we had always been prepared, cleaning the house beforehand and lying about our situation. Since I was a good student and none of us were troublemakers, we were convincing. We made everyone believe that we had a great life. But while we could lie to everyone else, we could no longer lie to ourselves.

We were put into foster care. My sister and I were placed with an elderly couple in the country, my brother stayed in the city with another family, and my half-sister and half-brother went to live with their dads. We were permitted to visit with my mom once a week, that is if she showed up. When she did come to see us, which averaged about once every two months, she promised us that she was getting an apartment so that we could live together once again.

It's been four years now since I made that call. No one

has heard from my mom in over two and a half years. We don't even know if she's dead or alive. Although my brother walked down the wrong path for a while having stolen a car, he was released from detention center early for good behavior and vows to turn his life around. My sister has been adopted by a family who lives in a nice neighborhood. She's on a swim team and finally getting good grades. My half-sister still lives with her father. Her dad remarried a wonderful woman who treats her like her own daughter. Unfortunately, we lost contact with our little half-brother, and we haven't had any luck finding him. He'll be turning six soon.

And me? I'd like to say that I'm doing pretty well. I just turned sixteen, and I have finally found stability in my life, which has helped me excel and succeed in many areas. I've been on the honor roll for five years, and I'm involved in way too many school activities. I'm even in a volunteer group that promotes the fight against drugs and alcohol. I'm a good advocate of the anti-drug campaign because I know from firsthand experience what happens when drugs run your life: they ruin not only your own life, but the lives of those around you. I tell my story and amaze people with my positive attitude, despite all that I've been through. My adoptive mom says, "You've definitely made some sweet lemonade out of all the sour lemons you've been handed."

What I went through, all my hardships and pain, they're part of who I am. I'll always feel like I'm different, and I'll always have to fight the feelings that I wasn't good enough, not even for my own mom. But I'm not going to let those feelings define me. I will only let them make me stronger. And I know that I'm going to be somebody. Actually, I already am.

*Morgan Mullens-Landis*

# 7

# MAKING A
# DIFFERENCE

*It's important to be involved and stand up
for what you believe in.*

*Ione Skye*

# Passing the Dream

She sat on the bench, feeding the birds.
Just throwing crumbs, not saying a word.
I sat down with my beads and braids,
Proclaiming what a mess her generation had made.
I spoke of poverty, and the war in 'Nam.
What is the use of going on?

She replied softly:

"All my life, I have worked for change.
Today, I give you my dream.
You can make a difference, with the small things you do.
The future is entirely left to you.
If things go wrong and you feel down,
Open your eyes and look around.
Don't look for someone to blame.
Search for an inspiration, to rise again.
The changes you make may not always be seen.
But perhaps you can give a child the chance to dream.
So get to work, and maybe find
A small solution to help humankind.

All my life, I have worked for change.
Today I give you my dream."

Today I decided to take a walk.
I passed a teen loudly playing his boom box.
He turned his music down low
And we chatted for a minute or so.
He spoke of the homeless, and the streets filled with crime.
Couldn't my generation have found the time
To ease some of this discord
By feeding the hungry, and housing the poor?

I replied softly:

"All my life, I have worked for change.
Today, I give you my dream.
I hope you make our world a better place.
But you must work diligently; just keep pace
With the changes and dreams of the generation to come.
But with a little luck, a small battle may be won.
Someday, we will merge. And in time you will be
The older generation looking back to see
How you have answered all these questions you ask.
Fixing tomorrow is now your task.
All my life, I have worked for change.
Today, I give you my dream."

*Penny Caldwell*

# The Gravediggers of Parkview Junior High

*People are always blaming their circumstances for what they are. I don't believe in circumstances. The people who get on in this world are the people who get up and look for the circumstances they want, and, if they can't find them, they make them.*

George Bernard Shaw

The most important lessons we are taught in school go beyond answering the questions on a test correctly. It is when the lessons change us by showing us what we are really capable of accomplishing. We can, with the use of band instruments, make beautiful music. We can, with the use of a paint brush and canvas, show people how we see the world. We can, with the hard work of a team, beat the odds and win the game. However, no multiple choice or true/false test will ever teach us the greatest lesson of all: We are the stuff of which winners are made.

Not long after the release of the film *Jeremiah Johnson,*

starring Robert Redford, our seventh-grade class was discussing the story. We talked about the fact that this rough and tough mountain man was also kind and gentle. We discussed his deep love of nature and his wishes to be part of it. Our teacher, Mr. Robinson, then asked us a most unusual question. Where did we think Jeremiah Johnson was buried? We were shocked when he told us the final resting place of the great mountain man was about 100 yards away from the San Diego Freeway in Southern California.

Mr. Robinson asked us, "So, do you believe this was wrong?"

"Yes!" we all chimed in.

"Do you feel something should be done to change it?" he asked with a sly grin.

"Yes!" we replied with an enthusiasm born of youthful innocence.

Mr. Robinson stared at us, and after a few moments of suspenseful silence, he asked a question that would change the way some of us viewed life forever. "Well, do you think you could do it?"

"Huh?"

What was he talking about? We were just a bunch of kids. What could we do?

"There is a way," he said. "It's a way filled with challenge and probably some disappointment . . . but there is a way." Then he said he would help us but only if we promised to work hard and pledge to never give up.

As we agreed, little did we know that we were signing on to the most adventurous voyage of our lives thus far.

We began by writing letters to everyone we could think of who could help us: local, state and federal representatives, the cemetery owners, even Robert Redford. Before long, we started getting answers that thanked our class for the interest, but "there was absolutely nothing that could be done." Many would have given up at that point. Had it not been for our promise to Mr. Robinson not to quit, we would have. Instead, we kept writing.

We decided that we needed more people to hear about our dream so we contacted the newspapers. Finally a reporter from the *Los Angeles Times* came to our class and interviewed us. We shared what we had been trying to do and how discouraging it was that no one seemed to care. We hoped that our story would raise public interest.

"Did Robert Redford ever contact you?" the reporter asked.

"No," we replied.

Two days later our story made the front page of the paper, telling how our class was trying to right an injustice to an American legend, and that no one was helping us, not even Robert Redford. Next to the article was a picture of Robert Redford. That same day, as we were sitting in the classroom, Mr. Robinson was called to the office to take a phone call. He came back with a glow on his face like we had never seen before. "Guess who that was on the phone!"

Robert Redford had called and said he received hundreds of letters every day and that ours somehow had never reached him, but he was very interested in helping us achieve our goal. Suddenly our team was not only getting bigger, it was getting more influential and powerful.

Within a few months, after all the proper documents were filed, our teacher and a few of the students went to the cemetery and observed the removal of the remains. Jeremiah Johnson had been buried in an old wooden casket that had been reduced to a few rotted boards, and nothing but a few bones were left of the mountain man. All were carefully gathered up by the cemetery workers and placed in a new casket.

Then a few days later, at a ranch in Wyoming, a ceremony was held in honor of Jeremiah Johnson, and his final remains were placed to rest in the wilderness he had loved so much. Robert Redford was one of the pallbearers.

From then on, throughout the school, our class was referred to as the "Gravediggers," but we preferred to think of ourselves as the "Dream Lifters." What we learned that year was not just about how to write effective letters, how our government works, or even what you have to go through to accomplish such a simple thing as moving a grave site. The lesson was that nothing can beat persistence. A bunch of kids at the beginning of our teenage years had made a change.

We learned that we were the stuff of which winners are made.

*Kif Anderson*

# The Boy Who Talked with Dolphins

*From what we get we can make a living, what
we give, however, makes a life.*

Arthur Ashe

It began as a deep rumble, shattering the predawn
silence. Within minutes on that January morning in 1994,
the Los Angeles area was in the grip of one of the most
destructive earthquakes in its history.

At Six Flags Magic Mountain theme park, twenty miles
north of the city, three dolphins were alone with their terror. They swam frantically in circles as heavy concrete pil-
lars collapsed around their pool and roof tiles crashed into
the water.

Forty miles to the south, twenty-six-year-old Jeff Siegel
was thrown from his bed with a jarring thump. Crawling to
the window, Jeff looked out at the convulsing city and
thought of the creatures who mattered more to him than
anything else in the world. *I've got to get to the dolphins,* he told
himself. *They rescued me, and now they need me to rescue them.*

To those who had known Jeff from childhood, a more
unlikely hero could not have been imagined.

Jeff Siegel was born hyperactive, partially deaf and lacking normal coordination. Since he couldn't hear words clearly, he developed a severe speech impediment that made it almost impossible for others to understand him. As a preschooler, the small, sandy-haired child was taunted as a "retard" by other kids.

Even home was no refuge. Jeff's mother was unprepared to deal with his problems. Raised in a rigid, authoritarian household, she was overly strict and often angry at his differences. She simply wanted him to fit in. His father, a police officer in their middle-class Los Angeles community of Torrance, worked extra jobs to make ends meet and was often gone sixteen hours a day.

Anxious and frightened on the first day of kindergarten, five-year-old Jeff climbed over the schoolyard fence and ran home. Furious, his mother hauled him back to school and forced him to apologize to the teacher. The entire class overheard. As the mispronounced and barely intelligible words were dragged out of him, he became instant prey for his classmates. To fend off the hostile world, Jeff kept to isolated corners of the playground and hid in his room at home, dreaming of a place where he could be accepted.

Then one day when Jeff was nine, he went with his fourth-grade class to Los Angeles' Marineland. At the dolphin show, he was electrified by the energy and exuberant friendliness of the beautiful animals. They seemed to smile directly at him, something that happened rarely in his life. The boy sat transfixed, overwhelmed with emotion and a longing to stay.

By the end of that school year, Jeff's teachers had labeled him emotionally disturbed and learning-disabled. But testing at the nearby Switzer Center for children with disabilities showed Jeff to be average-to-bright, though so anxiety-ridden that his math test score came out borderline retarded. He transferred from public school to the

Center. Over the next two years he became less anxious, and his academic achievement improved dramatically.

At the start of seventh grade he returned, unwillingly, to public school. Tests now showed his I.Q. in the 130s, the gifted range. And years of therapy had improved his speech. But to his classmates, Jeff was still the same victim.

Seventh grade was unfolding as the worst year of Jeff's life—until the day his father took him to Sea World in San Diego. The minute the boy saw the dolphins, the same rush of joy welled up in him. He stayed rooted to the spot as the sleek mammals glided past.

Jeff worked to earn money for an annual pass to Marineland, closer to his home. On his first solo visit, he sat on the low wall surrounding the dolphin pool. The dolphins, accustomed to being fed by visitors, soon approached the astonished boy. The first to swim over was Grid Eye, the dominant female in the pool. The 650-pound dolphin glided to where Jeff sat and remained motionless below him. *Will she let me touch her?* he wondered, putting his hand in the water. As he stroked the dolphin's smooth skin, Grid Eye inched closer. It was a moment of sheer ecstasy for the young boy.

The outgoing animals quickly became the friends Jeff never had, and since the dolphin area was isolated at the far end of Marineland, Jeff often found himself alone with the playful creatures.

One day Sharky, a young female, glided just below the surface until her tail was in Jeff's hand. She stopped. *Now what?* he wondered. Suddenly Sharky dived a foot or so below the surface, pulling Jeff's hand and arm underwater. He laughed and pulled back without letting go. The dolphin dived again, deeper. Jeff pulled back harder. It was like a game of tug-of-war.

When Sharky surfaced to breathe, boy and dolphin faced each other for a minute, Jeff laughing and the dolphin open-mouthed and grinning. Then Sharky circled and put her tail back in Jeff's hand to start the game again.

The boy and the 300- to 800-pound animals often played tag, with Jeff and the dolphins racing around the pool to slap a predetermined point or give each other hand-to-flipper high-fives. To Jeff, the games were a magical connection that he alone shared with the animals.

Even when there were summer crowds of 500 around the pool, the gregarious creatures recognized their friend and swam to him whenever he wiggled his hand in the water. Jeff's acceptance by the dolphins boosted his confidence, and he gradually emerged from his dark shell. He enrolled in a course at a nearby aquarium and devoured books on marine biology. He became a walking encyclopedia on dolphins and, to his family's amazement, braved his speech impediment to become a volunteer tour guide.

In 1983 Jeff wrote an article for the American Cetacean Society's newsletter, describing his experiences with Marineland dolphins. He was unprepared for what followed. Embarrassed by the extent to which he'd been playing with the dolphins without the park's knowledge, Marineland management revoked his pass. Jeff returned home numb with disbelief.

For their part, Jeff's parents were relieved. They could see no benefit to the time their strange, misfit son was spending with dolphins until a day in June 1984 when Bonnie Siegel took an unexpected long-distance phone call. That evening she asked her son, "Did you enter some kind of contest?"

Sheepishly, Jeff confessed that he'd written an essay for a highly coveted Earthwatch scholarship worth more than $2,000. The winner would spend a month in Hawaii with dolphin experts. Now, telling his mother about it, he expected a tirade. Instead, she said quietly, "Well, you won."

Jeff was ecstatic. Best of all, it was the first time that his parents realized he might achieve his dream of someday sharing his love of dolphins.

Jeff spent the month in Hawaii, teaching dolphins strings of commands to test their memories. In the fall, he fulfilled another condition of the scholarship by giving a talk on marine mammals to fellow students at Torrance High School. Jeff's report was so enthusiastic that it earned him, at last, grudging respect from his peers.

After graduation, Jeff struggled to find work in marine research, supplementing the low pay with minimum-wage moonlighting. He also earned an associate's degree in biology.

In February 1992 he showed up in the office of Suzanne Fortier, director of marine-animal training at Six Flags Magic Mountain. Though holding down two jobs, he wanted to do volunteer work with Magic Mountain's dolphins on his days off. Fortier gave him the chance—and was immediately amazed. Of the 200 volunteers she'd trained in ten years, she'd never seen anyone with Jeff's intuitive ability with dolphins.

In one instance, her crew needed to move a sick 600-pound dolphin named Thunder to another park. The animal had to be transported in a nine-by-three-foot tank. During the journey, Jeff insisted on riding in the truck bed with Thunder's tank to try to calm the anxious animal. When Fortier later called from the cab of the truck to ask how Thunder was doing, Jeff replied, "He's fine now. I'm cradling him." *Jeff's actually in the tank with Thunder!* Fortier realized. For four hours, Jeff floated inside the cool tank, holding Thunder in his arms.

Jeff continued to amaze co-workers with his rapport with the animals. His favorite at Magic Mountain was Katie, a 350-pound, eight-year-old dolphin who greeted him exuberantly and swam with him for hours.

Once again, as at Marineland, Jeff could interact with the dolphins and find affection in return. Little did he dream how severely his love would be tested.

As Jeff struggled to reach Magic Mountain on the morning of the earthquake, freeways were collapsing, and caved-in roads often forced him to backtrack. *Nothing is going to stop me,* he vowed.

When Jeff finally reached Magic Mountain, the water in the twelve-foot-deep dolphin pool was halfway down, and more was draining from the crack in the side. The three dolphins there when the quake hit—Wally, Teri and Katie—were in a frenzy. Jeff lowered himself to a ledge five feet down and tried to calm them.

To ease the dolphins through the continuing tremors, Jeff attempted to distract them by playing games, but it didn't work. Worse, he had to reduce their food: The pool's filtration system had shut down, creating the additional risk that an accumulation of their body waste would further contaminate the water.

Jeff remained with the dolphins that night as temperatures fell into the thirties. He was still there through the next day, and the next, and the next.

On the fourth day a road opened, and staffers secured a truck to transfer Wally, Teri and Katie to the dolphin pool at Knott's Berry Farm. But first, someone had to get them into their transport tanks. Transporting a dolphin is normally a routine procedure, after it has been safely guided through a tunnel and hoisted on a canvas sling. But the water level in the connecting tunnel was too low for the animals to swim through. The three dolphins would have to be caught in open water and then maneuvered into canvas slings.

Staffer Etienne Francois and Jeff volunteered for the jobs. As much as he trusted the dolphins, Jeff knew the likelihood of getting hurt or bitten by them in an open-water capture was almost 100 percent.

Wally was easily removed from the pool, but Teri and Katie became erratic. Each time Jeff and Etienne closed in on Katie, the powerful dolphin fended them off with her hard, pointed beak.

For almost forty minutes the men struggled as Katie butted and whacked them with her thrashing tail. Finally, just before they maneuvered her into a sling, she sank her needle-sharp teeth into Jeff's hand. Ignoring the bleeding, Jeff helped capture Teri and hoist her into the transport tank.

When the dolphins reached Knott's Berry Farm, Katie was exhausted but calm. Later, Fortier told friends that Jeff's courage and leadership had been essential in safely transporting the dolphins.

Today, Jeff is a full-time dolphin trainer at Marine Animal Productions in Gulfport, Mississippi, where he organizes programs for schools.

One day, before he left for Mississippi, Jeff gave a demonstration to sixty children from the Switzer Center at one of the aquariums where he had taught. He saw that a boy named Larry slipped off to play alone. Realizing Larry was an outcast, as he himself had been, Jeff called him forward and asked the boy to stand next to him. Then Jeff plunged his arms into a nearby tank and hauled up a harmless but impressive three-foot horn shark. As the children gasped, he allowed Larry to carry the dripping creature proudly around the room.

After the session, Jeff received a letter reading: "Thank you for the magnificent job you did with our children. They came back glowing from the experience. Several told me about Larry getting to carry the shark. This was probably the happiest and proudest moment of his life! The fact that you were once a student here added to it. You are a model of hope that they, too, can 'make it' in life." The letter was from Janet Switzer, the Center's founder.

For Jeff, that afternoon held an even more gratifying moment. As he spoke, he saw his mother and father in the audience, watching intently. From the look on their faces, Jeff could tell they were proud of their son at last.

Jeff has never earned more than $14,800 a year in his life, yet he considers himself a rich man and an exceptionally lucky one. "I'm completely fulfilled," he says. "The dolphins did so much for me when I was a child. They gave me unconditional love. When I think about what I owe the dolphins . . ." His voice trails off momentarily, and he smiles. "They gave me life. I owe them everything."

*Paula McDonald*

# For You, Dad

"Here we go!" Dad would say, and I'd climb on his back. "There! Look! See London Bridge?"

Lying on the floor with his arms outstretched, he was my Superman and together we were weaving our way around make-believe clouds. But like those clouds, my moments with Dad always vanished too quickly—because there was something stronger than love in Daddy's life, something that was stealing him away. It was an enemy I would end up fighting when he no longer could. . . .

"He's sick," my mother would say when Dad passed out. "It doesn't mean that he doesn't love you."

I knew he did. He could make us laugh with his funny faces and cartoon drawings. I loved him, and I wanted to believe Mom still did, too. As my little brothers and I grew, she explained that Dad hadn't always been "this way." He was just a little wild when they'd met in high school. And with his wavy hair and wide smile, I could understand how he'd captured Mom's heart.

But soon he must have been breaking it. Sometimes we didn't see him for weeks. One day, he called to say he wasn't coming home again. "I'm not far. We'll see each other on weekends," he said after he'd moved out. "I'll swing by and get you Saturday."

"Mom," I called out. "Can we go with Daddy?"

Grabbing the phone, Mom said, "No, John, you have to visit them at the house. You know I won't let them get into a car with you."

I thought of the commercials I saw on TV—the ones with the twisted metal and chalk outlines. And the words *Drunk driving kills.* Could that happen to Daddy? *Please God,* I'd pray at night, *help Daddy get well.* But too often, when he pulled into the driveway, we could smell the booze.

"Daddy, don't drive like that," I'd plead. Usually, he tried to shrug off my worries, but once he pulled me close, his eyes heavy with sadness. "I wish I wasn't like this," he said. "I wish I was a good dad."

I wished that, too. I hated alcohol for what it had done to all of us.

At first, I was too embarrassed to tell my friends the truth about my dad. But as I started to see kids drinking, I couldn't hold back. "That's why my dad isn't around," I'd say, pointing to the bottles.

All Dad's visits were brief. In between hugs and kisses, he drew pictures for us, and we crammed in stories about school and friends. "I'm getting help," he'd say. Maybe my brothers, Justin and Jordan, believed it—but I didn't. And yet with all my heart, I wanted to believe. I can still feel the rocking of the porch swing and my father's arm around my shoulder.

"The day you turn sixteen," he once said, "I'm going to buy you a car." I nuzzled closer to him. I knew he'd give me the world if he could. But I understood that no matter how much he wanted to, he couldn't.

Then one night during my senior year of high school, I got a call at the store where I worked part-time.

"Heather?" Mom's voice was strained. I knew what was coming. "There's been an accident."

I raced to the hospital; Dad's motorcycle had hit a mini-van. Blood tests showed he'd been drinking and doing drugs that night. The other driver was fine, thank God.

"I love you, Daddy," I sobbed, sitting by his bed. Though he was unconscious, his heart monitor quickened at the sound of my voice. He had found a way to let me know he'd heard me, and that he loved me. But there was something I had to make sure that he knew.

"I forgive you," I choked. "I know you did your best."

Moments later, he was gone. An accident killed my father, but his death was not sudden.

Everyone told me I needed to grieve, and for a while, I did. But in a sense, I'd been grieving for Dad all my life. Now I needed to do something that would help me feel less powerless against the enemy that had stolen him.

I went to the library to find what I could on substance abuse. *Almost every family is affected. . . . Children may repeat the patterns,* I read. My heart broke even more. My father's life hadn't amounted to very much. Maybe his death could.

That afternoon, I picked up the phone and called the area schools. "I'd like to talk about substance abuse," I began. "I've lived with it in my own family, so I think I can help."

Before I knew it, I was standing before a sea of young faces ready to speak, in a presentation called "Drug-Free Me."

"People who do drugs and alcohol aren't bad," I began. "They've just made the wrong choice." Then I asked the kids to draw pictures of what they wanted to be. They drew firemen and doctors and astronauts.

"See all those pretty dreams? They can never come true if you turn to drugs and alcohol." Their eyes grew wide. *I'm reaching them,* I thought. But I knew it wasn't that simple—I'd have to keep trying every day if I really wanted to make a difference.

Since then, I've used cartoon characters to get the message to younger kids. I've organized a tuxedo-stuffing program, sticking statistics on drunk driving into pockets of prom-goers. And I've joined Mothers Against Drunk Driving and the National Commission on Drunk Driving.

Today, as a college junior, I do presentations at middle and high schools. I also speak at victim-impact panels, sharing stories of loss with people convicted of driving under the influence. Most people on the panel have lost loved ones to people like my father. But I was a victim, too, and maybe my story hits harder.

"It's hard to think of a faceless stranger out there you may kill," I tell the offenders. "So think about the people you are hurting now—like a child at home who will miss you forever if you die."

I'd been missing my father long before he was taken for good. I remember once he said that we, his children, were the only things he'd ever done right in his life. Daddy, because of you, I'm doing something very right in mine.

*Heather Metzger*
*As told to Bill Holton*
Woman's World Magazine

# Somebody Loves You

*Don't forget to be kind to strangers. For some who have done this have entertained angels without realizing it.*

Hebrews 13:2

One miserable rainy night, a man named Mark decided to end his life. In his mid-fifties, Mark had never been married, had never experienced the joy of having children or spending holidays with his family. Both his parents had been dead for seven years. He had a sister but had lost contact with her. He held a menial job that left him unfulfilled. Wet and unhappy, he walked the streets, feeling as if there was nobody in the entire world that cared if he lived or died.

On that same soggy night, I was sitting in my room watching the rain hit my window. I was six years old, and my life revolved around my Star Wars action figure collection. I was dreaming of the day when I'd have earned enough money to add Darth Vader to my new collector's case. To help me make money, my father paid me to jog with him. Every day, at seven o'clock, we jogged together.

And every day, I was fifty cents closer to getting Darth Vader.

When I heard the doorbell ring, I jumped from my chair and raced out of my room to the top of the steps. My mother was already at the door.

Opening it, she found herself face-to-face with a very disheveled-looking man with tears streaming down his face. My mother, overcome by pity, invited the man inside, and he sat with my parents in our living room.

Curious, I snuck downstairs so that I could get a better look. I couldn't understand what they were saying, but the sight of the rumpled man, holding his head in his hands and crying, made my chest ache. I raced back upstairs to my room and stuck my hand into my money jar. Pulling out the Kennedy half-dollar I had earned that day, I ran back downstairs.

When I reached the door of the living room, I walked right in. The three adults looked at me in surprise as I quickly made my way over to the stranger. I put the half-dollar in his hand and told him that I wanted him to have it. Then I gave him a hug and turned and ran as fast as I could out of the room and back up the stairs. I felt embarrassed but happy.

Downstairs, Mark sat quietly with his head bowed. Tears streamed down his face as he tightly clutched that coin. Finally looking up at my parents, he said, "It's just that I thought nobody cared. For the last twenty years, I have been so alone. That was the first hug I have gotten in—I don't know how long. It's hard to believe that somebody cares."

Mark's life changed that night. When he left our house, he was ready to live instead of die. Although my family never saw Mark again, we received letters from him every once in a while, letting us know that he was doing fine.

Being a six-year-old kid, I hadn't thought about what I

was doing that night. I had just reacted to the sight of someone else's pain. On our morning jogs, my dad and I had talked about the importance of giving, but I hadn't had any idea of what it really meant. My life changed that night, too, as I witnessed the true healing power of giving. Even if it's only a gift of fifty cents.

Before Mark left, my parents asked him why he had knocked on our door. Mark said that as he'd walked the streets that rainy night, hopeless and ready to die, he had noticed a bumper sticker on a car. He'd stood in the driveway and wondered about the people who lived in the house where the car was parked. Then, in a fog of unhappiness, he had made his way to the front door. It's hard to imagine that a bumper sticker and fifty cents could change two people's lives, but somehow they did.

The bumper sticker on our car read: SOMEBODY LOVES YOU.

*Wil Horneff*

# A Street Kid's Guide

When I was asked to address a high school graduation in a nearby community, my mind boggled.

"Me!" I gasped. "You want me?"

After they assured me they did, I felt honored. Just think of it! Me! A guy who never went to high school was being asked to speak to a group of kids on such an important occasion.

*What will I say to them? What profound words can I impart that would stay with them, and perhaps help them with life's choices?* The more I thought about it, the more I realized that if I was not careful, I stood a good chance of adding my name to a long list of boring, over-the-hill, has-been speakers that came before me. These kids didn't need that. They didn't need any more long-winded speeches of how it was done in the past, nor did they need to be deluged by a barrage of useless platitudes.

I thought and rethought all sorts of ideas, but came up with nothing. It wasn't until the night before the address that it suddenly dawned on me. *Don't tell these kids what you did. Tell them what you learned while you were doing it.*

As I gathered these new thoughts, I drifted back to my

past. I grew up—or rather, was dragged up—in dozens of foster homes and institutions. It was hard to tell where one home left off and another began. Through those same years, I fumbled my way through seven different grade schools. Somehow I missed the fourth grade entirely. But that really didn't matter. Nobody paid very much attention to me. I had no books, no pencils and no paper. And as far as anyone was concerned, I was passing through.

By the time I was eleven, I was in the fifth grade and unable to read. A nun took pity on me. She kept me after school every day to teach me what she could. For the brief time I was with her, I learned a lot. I wish I could have stayed with her, but I knew I couldn't. I was in "the system." I was sent where they wanted to send me, and stayed until they sent me someplace else. I learned early to obey any and all rules, and to never question authority. The system was designed to teach unquestioned discipline, but it was really containment and control. It worked very well.

By the time I was fourteen, I was finished with school—or, rather, it was finished with me. In either case, I was tossed out, told I couldn't be educated, and given a job.

At first this was very frightening. I was alone and on my own. There was no one to turn to if I got into trouble, no one to guide me or show me the way. It was hard. I had to become street smart in a hurry. I got tough quickly; I learned to show no fear and to keep my mouth shut. I chose my roads by trial and error. Whenever I stumbled, I got up and tried again. I was determined not to quit and not to be beaten. I did alright. I got through.

About a dozen or so years ago, a friend who knew about my past and the way I grew up encouraged me to write it down. He told me it was important for people to know what it's like to grow up the way I did. And so, with much stress and difficulty, I somehow found the strength to reach back forty years to relive all the pain and all the tears. I revisited the fear and the loneliness. I wrote my autobiography, *They Cage the Animals at Night*. It was reading this book, and responding to it, that prompted those in charge of the graduation ceremony to invite me to address their kids.

It was a warm June morning when I stood at the podium. All eyes were fixed upon me. The kids were dressed in their caps and gowns and sticky from nervous perspiration. From time to time, they'd glance over to the sections reserved for parents, family and friends. They were trying to locate the proud and smiling faces of those whom they belonged to. When they did, they would smile as a faint blush filled their cheeks. They were just as proud as their parents.

I began to speak. I told them I was honored to be addressing them, but not having been in high school, or graduating from anything, I didn't feel qualified. I then made an unusual request. I asked them if there was any way in which I could take part in their moment, if they might let me be one of them: a graduate. Their applause took me into their ranks, and their eyes took me into their hearts.

I choked back my tears as I said, "This is a street kid's guide on how to get from here to there." Maybe a word here or a line there that might help you get through a rough time: I hope so. . . .

### A Street Kid's Guide
### (How to get from here to there)

*It's hard to get from here to there*
*If you never get out of bed.*
*You lie a lot to fool your friends*
*But you fooled yourself instead.*

*It's harder to get from here to there*
*If you set your goals too high;*
*Then nothing ever works out right;*
*Too soon, you no longer try.*

*But the hardest way to get from here to there*
*Is when all you ever do*
*Is count up the years, and miles to go.*
*Then you're through before you're through.*

*So how do you get from here to there?*
*Well, you first must believe you can*
*Let no one tell you differently—*
*It's your life and it's in your hands.*

*Then turn your dreams into your goals*
*And see what you need now*
*To satisfy the requirements:*
*The why, the where and how.*

*At first you're overwhelmed, of course;*
*There is so much you don't know.*
*But keep your faith, be strong and sure,*
*For you do have a way to go.*

*Take careful steps and do them right,*
*Take pride in each thing done.*
*Don't look too far ahead of yourself,*
*Just that next step yet to come.*

*Before you know it you'll be there, friend,*
*Your dream will then be real.*
*And you'll be standing where I am now,*
*Telling others how good it feels.*

*You'll tell them not to quit themselves,*
*To have faith, though it's hard to bear.*
*So they will know it can be done—*
*They, too, can get from here to there.*

*Jennings Michael Burch*

# An Open Heart

We had to take a malaria pill every week for eight weeks and get a shot of gamma globulin. We were told to bring old clothes, flashlights, bug repellent and an open heart.

I think the last item was the most important: an open heart. That is what those kids really needed.

Honduras is a small country in Central America. The majority of the population is dirt poor, hungry, homeless, parentless and in need. This is where I, along with eighteen of my peers, had committed to spending two weeks of our summer vacation.

I am sixteen years old. This trip was not the vacation trip most teens dream of. It was sponsored by Mrs. Patricia King, whose two sons were adopted into her family from this third-world country. Through her love we were able to help those in need.

We spent our time at an orphanage with children who won our hearts the very moment we met them. How could you not adore a child who wants only a multi-colored pen for his fourteenth birthday? For two weeks we shared our souls with these children. We lived in their world, relying only on bare necessities. The heat was often unbearable and the smell of raw sewage was constant. Dirt clung to everything and we had to close our eyes and hold our breath to shower in the contaminated water. It was our job to repaint the boys' room and the hard iron bunk beds. We washed and braided the girls' hair and painted their nails. We exchanged hugs, high fives, kisses and eventually good-byes. We came home different—better.

We learned that the best of all blessings is to be able to give to others. I feel lucky that I'm sixteen and I know that we can make a difference. That's not just something that celebrities say on TV. Every day I am grateful that I learned an open heart is a happy heart.

*Sandy Pathe*

# 8

# GROWING UP AND SELF-DISCOVERY

*Who in the world am I?*
*Ah, that's the great puzzle.*

*Lewis Carroll*

# The Girl Next Door

Do you remember
Many years ago
When we were young,
How we used to play together
Every day?

It seems like yesterday—
The childhood world
Of clowns and cotton candy
And summer days
That never seemed to end
When we played hide 'n' seek
From four o'clock till dusk
Then sat outside on someone's stoop
And listened to the crickets
And slapped away mosquitoes
And talked about our dreams
And what we'd do when we grew up
Until our mothers called us in.

And do you remember
That one winter when it snowed
For days and days on end
And we tried to build an igloo
Like the Eskimos?
Or when we made a game
Of raking leaves
All up and down the street
Until we'd made the biggest pile
The world had ever seen
And then we jumped in it?
Or how about the time
We gathered honeysuckle
From your yard
And sold it to the neighbors?
And the grand day when finally
The training wheels came off our bikes
And we were free
To explore the whole world
In an afternoon
So long as we stayed
On our own street.

But those days passed by furtively
And we grew up, as children do
Until we reached a day when we
Assumed that we were too grown-up
To play amid the trees on summer nights . . .
and when I see you now
You've changed in ways I can't explain
You're like a rose that blooms before its time
And falls a victim to
The February frost.

Because the waist on your jeans is getting tight
Symbolic of a youth that's not your own
And your face is pale and green—
You don't look well.
I see you scowling at the street
From the window in your room,
It's so rare to see you smiling anymore.
And when a car pulls up outside
You run downstairs and out the door
With a suitcase in each hand
And the car speeds away
And the girl next door is gone.

And I long once more
For the summer days
When I stood on your porch
And banged on your door
And bade you come outside to greet
the afternoon's adventures.

Won't you come out to play, once more?
For we are still so young . . .

*Amanda Dykstra*

# Wonder, to Me

One morning, I woke up later than usual. The night before had been difficult. My eldest daughter, Carla, and I had exchanged harsh words. At sixteen years old, she was challenging my parenting skills. I'm sure that I must have scolded her about the type of friends she was hanging around with, her choice of social activities, even the clothes she wore.

When I walked into the kitchen, I saw an unfamiliar piece of paper on the kitchen table. Carla had already left for school. I thought maybe this was some homework that she forgot. Instead, it was a poem she had written:

> *Wonder, to me,*
> *Is the worst place to be.*
> *Situations get complex,*
> *You're afraid of what's next.*
> *Starting out fresh and brand-new,*
> *Stepping in another shoe.*
> *Wondering how you'll turn out,*
> *Having all sorts of doubt.*
> *Turning over a new leaf,*
> *Sometimes wanting to leave . . . sometimes do!*

As I read her words, my heart ached for the pain she was feeling. I recalled my own youth and teenage struggles. Now I felt that I had let her down somehow. A single mom, raising five children on my own and working two jobs, I was dealing with my own set of problems. But she needed me! How could I reach her?

Suddenly, all my own selfish worries left me. I grabbed a piece of paper and penned a reply that I hoped would bring her some comfort.

That afternoon while I was at work, she came home and found the poem that I had left. That evening there were hugs and maybe a few tears. It seemed that perhaps I had made some progress in narrowing the generation gap.

Days and months passed. We still had the typical mother–daughter disagreements, but with a special bond of respect and understanding for each other. It wasn't until a year later that I realized the full impact of our special relationship.

It was Carla's graduation. I was sitting in the bleachers, so very proud to see my own daughter's name on the program for the class speaker. As she approached the podium, I felt a sense of accomplishment in knowing that, through it all, I must have done something right to have such a vivacious, beautiful daughter who was providing her classmates with advice for their future.

She talked about leaving the security of school and venturing out on your own. Then I heard her share the story of her own struggles, doubts and fears. She was telling the entire audience about that difficult day when she left the poem on the kitchen table. And then, the words of advice to her classmates ended with the reply that I had given her so many months ago.

*Dearest Carla,*

*Wonder, to me, is a good place to be.*
*It helps you to think, it helps you to see.*
*Life's full of twists and turns will abound,*
*But wonder and insight can guide you around.*
*Explore what you may and fill up your mind,*
*And hold in your heart the mysteries you find.*
*Wonder is only saying you yearn*
*To know and select the things that you learn,*
*And making a choice in which way you turn.*
*The best path you take will always be right,*
*'Cause if you were wrong, you CAN make it right.*
*Each new step you take when you listen and hear*
*Will give you more courage and freedom from fear.*
*So wonder my child, rid of your doubt,*
*And you will rejoice with how you turn out.*
*And though you may fall and struggle, too,*
*Know that I've been there, and will always love you.*

I sat there, stunned. The entire auditorium was silent, listening to her message. My eyes welled with tears; everything was a blur. When I finally blinked, I saw the entire roomful of people on their feet, cheering and applauding. Then she ended her speech with her own inspired summary of "You can turn YOUR wonder into wonderful!"

*Jill Thieme*

# New Beginnings

## June, 1996

Dear Graduate,

Well, this is it! Graduation is over and you're ready to begin life's journey! I know you have lots of mixed feelings. That's the weird thing about most of life's big moments—very rarely do they consist of one emotion. But that's okay. It helps to make the good times more precious and the not-so-good times bearable.

I've spent a lot of time trying to figure out what sage advice I could pass along. That's one of the hard parts about being a parent—determining what should be said and what should be left for you to discover. I finally decided just to offer a little insight to life's basic questions. Some people go through their whole lives without ever giving them any thought. Too bad—as you search for the answers, you can make some wonderful discoveries. They can also be frustrating; just when you think you've found the answer, you'll find the need to ask another question. (Which explains why even at my incredibly advanced age, I still don't have any answers!) At any rate, I hope that sharing this little piece of myself and my soul will somehow help to carry you through when the questions come along.

*Who?* It took me a while to realize that this is probably the most important question of all. Take time to discover who you are and be your own person. Strive to be honest, respectful and happy. When you are at peace with yourself, everything else will fall into place. Just be careful not to wrap your identity in possessions. Allow yourself to grow and change. And remember always that you are not alone—you have your family, your friends, your guardian angel and God (not necessarily in that order!).

*What?* This is a tricky one, and at first this question had me fooled. I thought the question was, "What will I do today?" However, I found that things really got interesting when I instead asked, *"What is my passion?"* Discover what it is that burns inside and keeps you going, then nurture it. Take it apart and build it back together. Do whatever you want with it, but never let it from your sight. Do it because that's what you love to do. The joy it brings you will keep you going through some of the doldrums of life.

*When?* This is the sneaky one. Do not ignore it. It will keep you balanced. Some things are best done now. Procrastination usually just creates more work. But keep in mind that there is a season for everything, and some things are better left for another day. As hard as it may be, remember to take time to rest and enjoy the miracle of each new day. With practice, you will learn the pleasure of doing some things now and the unique delight of waiting and planning for others.

*Where?* Surprisingly, this is the easiest one. You will always have the answer with you if you keep your home in your heart and put your heart into wherever you call home. Be an active part of your community and you will discover the special charm that will endear it to you.

Remember always that the simplest act of kindness can make an enormous difference, and that you *can* change the world.

*Why?* Never stop asking this one. It's the one that will keep you growing. Let it. Let it challenge you when you've become too complacent. Let it shout at you when you are making decisions. Let it whisper to you when you lose sight of who you are or where you want to be. But you also need to be careful with this one. Sometimes the answer does not come for years, and sometimes it doesn't come at all. Recognizing that basic fact can keep you sane and allow you to move on.

*How?* Ah, this is the one on which I can't advise you! This is the one you will answer in your own special way. But you've come so far in the past few years, I know that you'll do fine. Just remember to believe in yourself and in miracles. Remember that the greatest discoveries come after stumbling over questions. And please remember—always—that I love you.

Congratulations on your new beginning.

Love,
Mom

*Paula (Bachleda) Koskey*

# How Much Does It Cost?

The six teenagers sank onto their beanbags in the group counseling room. Today there was none of the usual raucous punching and good-natured exchange of insults. I knew they didn't want to be at school this week any more than I, their counselor, did.

For three days they had received counseling, comfort, sympathy and lectures. Ministers and psychologists had come to the school at a time when the kids' world seemed to have ended. It had indeed ended for four of their schoolmates, who had died in a car accident on the way home from a keg party in celebration of graduation.

What was there left for me to say? Only that these six would go on living, barring a tragedy like this one—a tragedy that didn't have to happen.

My mind searched for words to fill the silence. Finally I said, "I remember a day when I was about your age, seeing a fancy Levi's jacket and jodhpurs in a store window. Since I was to be riding in the girls' rodeo competition the following month, I figured I simply couldn't live without that outfit. I went into the store, found the garments in my size and bought them without asking how much they cost. I practically had a heart attack when the clerk told me the price. There went all the spending money I had saved practically forever. In fact, I had to go home and rob my piggy bank and then go back to the store for my purchase."

At that point in my story, I paused long enough to note that the group members were staring at me with questioning eyes. After all, what did a stupid rodeo costume have to do with their grief?

So I babbled on. "Was the outfit worth that much? No way, I concluded during the following months, when I had to do without several things I needed or wanted, including a class ring."

My counselees continued to look at me with a so-what? expression.

"I did learn from that experience," I said finally. "I learned to ask, 'What does it cost?' before buying. During the years following, I've learned that looking at price tags is a good idea when it comes to actions, also."

I told them about a time when I went on a hike with friends without telling our parents where we would be. The price was heavy. My fellow hikers and I got lost, and it was many terrifying hours before we straggled back to town to face our frantic parents and the drastic punishments they decided we deserved.

Now it was the kids' turn to talk, and they did, relating some of the times when their bad judgment had not been worth the cost of the consequences.

I gently reminded the students at this point that their friends' graduation celebration had cost too much. I mentioned the frequency of teen tragedies, many involving alcohol and other drugs. Then I read them parts of an editorial about an accident that had occurred a few months earlier. The article had been written by the town's chief of police:

*Close to a thousand people were there that day, all sitting in front of a smooth casket topped with flowers and a high school letter jacket. Jason was president of the senior class, a star athlete, a popular friend to hundreds, the only son of successful parents, but he drove into the side of a fast-moving freight train at the city square on a beautiful Sunday afternoon and was killed instantly. He was eighteen years old. And he was drunk.*

*You never get accustomed to or forget the horror on the faces of parents when you break the news to them that their child is forever gone from this earth.*

*We know there will be both youth and parents who don't like our enforcement posture. There will be verbal and maybe physical abuse against the officers. Some parents will complain about our enforcement of underage drinking laws. But we can live with that a lot easier than telling parents that their son or daughter has been killed.*

Four of the six students were crying by the time I finished reading the editorial. Crying for Jason, crying for their dead schoolmates and their families, crying because of their own loss.

Then we talked about the four friends they had just lost.

"Can any good come out of our tragedy?" I asked. "Or do we just let it end like a sad movie?"

It was Mindy, the shyest member of the group, who suggested in a wispy voice, "Maybe we could make a pledge or something."

Ordinarily, the three boys in the group would probably have ridiculed the idea, but this day was different.

"Hey!" Jonathan said. "Not a bad idea."

"Something like pretending there's a price tag on things grown-ups think we shouldn't do, then maybe deciding if we're ready to take the chance anyway," Laurel added.

Paul said, "The problem with that is, we can't know for sure what that price would be. Maybe nothing bad will happen even if we take the risk."

"That's a point," I admitted. "Suppose instead of 'How much *will* it cost?' we asked ourselves, 'How much *might* it cost?' Then we'd at least look at the possible outcomes."

"I'll buy that," Kent said.

A week ago, these kids would have shrugged off such suggestions, but today—well, today they weren't quite the same people they had been last week.

*Margaret Hill*

# No Longer a Child

Jordana was a twelve-year-old girl like every other; she worried about her clothes, hair and boys. She always had a smile on her face and a warm hug to share. What most people did not know about her was that this little girl had some very grown-up problems. Her father caused these problems. He had sexually abused her when she was five and physically abused her for years after. The emotional scars left her in hidden shambles. Her mother and father divorced when Jordana was eight, leaving her mother with sole custody.

When we met in seventh grade, years after the abuse had stopped, she seemed like every other twelve-year-old girl. We became instant best friends, gossiping about movie stars, rock bands and boys. Jordana seemed happy living with her mother and stepfather, and when I asked about her father she only told me that she did not see him anymore.

One June day, I found out one of her biggest secrets. It was hot that day after school, and we went in Jordana's backyard to tan in tank tops and shorts. It was then that I noticed cuts on her arms, mirrored by scars of cuts that had already healed. When I asked her where she received the cuts, she turned to me and began to cry stories of the past, horrors flowing from her lips as fast as the tears fell from her eyes. Jordana told me that she had cut herself because she felt so much anger towards her father. She told me about the nights of terror, about beatings and the bruises. I didn't know what to do so I just listened, consoled and counseled to the best of my ability.

Not until I had gone home did I realize what had just happened. Jordana had trusted me with information that she had hidden deep inside for a dozen years. She had chosen my hand to reach out to and pleaded silently for me to reach back.

As the weeks went on the cuts became more frequent, as if she was using her body as a personal canvas. I became increasingly scared. I was too young to handle this myself. I realized soon that I did not have the means to help her, and my decision lay before me like a shallow grave. That day after school when Jordana was at basketball practice I went to her house and knocked on the door and reached out the only way I knew how, "Mrs. Brown, I have something I have to tell you." It was then that I realized I was no longer a child.

*Hilary E. Kisch*

# I Won't Be Left Behind

I run my fastest
But still get beat.
I land on my head
When I should be on my feet.
I try to move forward,
But I am stuck in rewind.
Why do I keep at it?
I won't be left behind.

The harder I am thrown,
The higher I bounce.
I give it my all,
And that's all that counts.
In first place,
Myself, I seldom find.
So I push to the limit—
I won't be left behind.

Some people tell me you can't,
Some say don't.
Some simply give up.
I reply, I won't.

The power is here,
locked away in my mind.
My perseverance is my excellence,
I won't be left behind.

Make the best of each moment,
The future is soon the past.
The more I tell myself this,
The less I come in last.
Throughout my competitions,
I've learned what winning is about.
A plain and clear lesson—
Giving up is the easy way out.

So every night before I go to bed,
I hope in a small way I have shined.
Tomorrow is a brand-new day,
And I won't be left behind.

*Sara Nachtman*

# I Am Loni

*To be nobody but yourself in a world that's doing its best to make you somebody else is to fight the hardest battle you are ever going to fight. Never stop fighting.*

e. e. cummings

Why do I even try? If there's one thing I should have learned, it's, try or not, I'll probably screw up. Mom says, "Loni, a lady shouldn't say things like 'screw up.'" That just proves my point. I even screw up how to tell you that I screwed up.

I know, I have so much going for me. Don't even go there. Dad brags about my grades, and Mom's proud of the person I am and all my activities. Grandma goes on and on about my pretty face. *Yeah, too bad about the rest of me,* I think to myself.

I'm not, like, big enough to be featured as The Amazing Amazon Teen in *The Guinness Book of World Records,* but I am big enough not to like shopping with my friends. "How cu-u-u-u-ute!" they squeal over every rack of clothes. They know they'll fit into anything. I can't commit until I scan the plastic circle dividers to see how high the sizes go.

I pretend that clothes don't matter to me. That explains my semi-grunge look everyone takes for my chosen style. No outfit is complete without a sweater, flannel shirt or sweatshirt tied around my waist to cover up . . . oh . . . everything.

So, when we go to the mall, I'm the designated shopper. You know, like the designated driver who goes to a party but doesn't partake. I stand outside the changing rooms to *ooh* and *aah* when they emerge for the three-way mirror check. Only after a careful inspection do I reassure them that their thighs, legs, waist or bottom do not look too big in that outfit; otherwise, it would be taken as insincere.

It takes all I have not to roll my eyes when they hand me a piece of clothing and plead, "Can you see if this comes in a smaller size?" Give me a break. Where should I look? The children's department?

I really did screw up, though. Being a self-appointed good sport, I tried out for the volleyball team with my friends. Here's the bad part: I made it.

It seems I have a killer serve. I use it for self-defense. The harder I ram the ball, the less likely it will be returned and force me to clod around the court keeping it in play.

To make matters worse, we keep winning. This is the first winning season of any girl's sport in our school's history. Volleyball fever took over, and attendance soared. Just my luck. And those pep rallies. There's a thrill. Jumping around high-fiving while my name echoes over the PA system.

In our small town, making it to State Finals is newsworthy. Our team was pictured sitting in the bleachers in a "V for Victory" formation. I was the connecting bottom of the "V," front and center in all my glory.

"Loni Leads the Charge to State!" read the headline. Not

bad. I didn't even pretend to protest when Mom bought copies for the relatives. I was pleased when the team framed the picture and hung it in the tunnel between our locker room and the arena. It soon became our team gesture to blow kisses at our picture every time we passed it.

It was the night of the final game, and we had home-court advantage. The series was tied two games to two. I led the team's run for our triumphant entrance. Cheers stormed down the tunnel to meet us. We glanced at the banners posted along the walls, taking energy from the words.

YOU GO, GIRLS! YES YOU CAN! WE'RE #1!

We were ready to blow kisses at our picture when shock froze me. Two words were written in red on the glass. Two words that totally changed the headline.

"Loni THE BULL leads the charge to State!"

The horns drawn on my head completed the insult.

I felt myself emptying until I wasn't me anymore. I was nobody. The team bunched behind me.

"Who did this?"

"Who would be so mean?"

Their questions had no answers. They thought they were as upset as I was, but they were wrong. I wasn't upset at all. I was in shock.

*So this is the truth,* I thought. *This is who I am.*

And all the words around me didn't heal the hurt because nobody said the three words I needed to hear most: "That's not true."

The team moved me down the tunnel. There was no time to sort myself. What was real seemed like a dream, and I couldn't shake myself awake. The chants of "Loni! Loni!" sounded hollow. I let the cheers of the many be muted by the jeers of the few.

We won the coin toss and took to the court for my first serve. Around me the team was pumped and ready to go.

I rolled the volleyball in my palms to get its feel and mechanically went into my serving stance. All I could see were the words . . . THE BULL. THE BULL. THE BULL.

I tossed the ball up, but before my fist made contact the shout "OLE!" hit me. I stutter-stepped and missed the ball. I told myself not to look, but my eyes were drawn anyway. I couldn't pick out who it was. The team tried to buck me up with back slaps and "that's okays." But it didn't help.

I went through the rotations until I was at the net. My concentration scurried between the game and the bleachers. When the ball skimmed the air above my head, a loud snorting sound came from the front row.

"That's taking the bull by the horns!" someone yelled. The player behind me made the save and set up the ball for me to spike. But I wasn't looking at the ball. I was staring into the faces of the five high-school guys who were mocking me. My humiliation only fueled their taunts.

"Give me a B, give me a U, give me a double L, too. What's that smell? LONI! LONI! LONI!"

Why didn't someone shut them up?

The coach called a time-out. "Loni, can you get your head in the game?"

I shrugged.

"Why are you letting a few people who don't even know you decide for you who you are?"

I shrugged again.

"Loni, you're valuable as a person and to your team. Unkind words don't change who you are unless you decide they change you," she said.

*Sounds good in theory,* I thought, *but this is the real world.*

"I'm keeping you in, but if you can't work through this I'll pull you."

I nodded.

I walked past the boys to take my place in the game. With each step I took, they stomped their feet to shake the floor. I got the point. Very funny.

I also had to walk past my teammates, and in spite of my weak showing, they were still rooting for me. "You can do it." "You're the best."

Something in me gave way. The quote on a magnet on my grandma's refrigerator popped into my thoughts: "God don't make no junk."

I knew what I knew, and I knew myself—I wasn't junk. I felt my value to the very depths of my soul. Who was I anyway? What did some immature boys know about me? There were so many people who loved and supported me, and it was time to do my best for them and for myself.

And just like that, I was free of them. Oh, they continued to stomp their feet with each of my steps. I didn't like it, but it didn't matter. They were powerless over my life.

The game was close, and we played hard. The winning serve fell to me. It was my moment, and I took it. The ball went up, my fist came forward and hit it right on. It was a perfect power serve unreturnable by the other team. The crowd went wild. The pep band started beating out our school song. The team huddled around me.

Shouts of "Loni! Loni!" vibrated the arena. The funny thing is, the cheers didn't feed me like they used to. They were great, but the joy I felt, the freedom I felt, the sense of myself I had filled me more than any cheers.

There was more than one victory that day, and the game was not the most important one.

*Loni Taylor*
*As told to Cynthia Hamond*

# An Athlete's Prayer

It was right before the big one and the football player said,
"Excuse me guys for just a sec while I go bow my head."
And in the quiet of that room
The football player prayed,
"Oh God if nothing hear me now
I know that fate is made."

"So help us Lord to win this game,
It's the big one, man, you see,
If we lose this game that's it for us ,
Please do this, Lord, for me."

And as his body knelt in prayer,
He looked up to the sky,
"And while I'm here, and have some time,
I need to ask you why?"

"They say you never help teams win,
Just do it once I pray,
We will pay you back in kinder deeds
Or in another way."

"The reason I can't help you win,"
The Lord just then replied,
"Is as you're asking me to win,
So is the other side."

"I'm everybody's father and
I must not take one side,
So games are played all on your own
Or they would all be tied."

"But that doesn't mean you shouldn't pray,"
He answered him with care,
"You can pray that players don't get hurt
And that all the calls are fair."

"And then I won't just watch the game,
I'll bless it with my care,
Because dear son you need to learn
That life's not always fair."

And while the player heard this voice,
He bowed his head in prayer,
"I pray for fairness," said the boy
"And for your tender care."

"You shall be blessed," the Lord replied,
"Your team and you the same,
And now will you excuse me boy,
I cannot miss this game."

*Sandy Dow Mapula*

# Applying Myself

*Those who dream by day are cognizant of many things, which those who dream only by night may miss.*

Edgar Allen Poe

At thirteen years old, I was like any other kid my age. I liked computer and Nintendo games. I complained about too much homework, and I hated when my little brother ate the last Fruit Roll-Up in the box. I guess I looked like any other kid my age, too. I wore baggy pants and over-size T-shirts—you know, the typical middle-school prison garb. However, inside I harbored a secret that made me feel different and weird.

You see, I was diagnosed with ADD. This is the hip term for attention deficit disorder. I couldn't even get the cool-kid type where you're hyper. I had to get the dreamier, "space-cadet" type. I can look straight into your eyes and not hear a word you're saying. It's sort of like in the Charlie Brown TV specials. All the adults' voices in the cartoon sound like endless droning. "Mwop, mwop, mwop, mwop." I appear to be listening while all the while my mind is somewhere miles away.

After extensive and boring tests, the doctor explained to my mom that I was what they called "dual exceptional." It sounds pretty cool, doesn't it? No, it doesn't mean that I have any special dueling abilities like the swordsmen in *The Three Musketeers*. It also doesn't mean that I have a major psychiatric disorder like multiple personalities. That might be kind of cool in a weird sort of way. What "dual exceptional" means is that I am what they call "gifted." This means I'm pretty bright, and yet I'm also learning disabled. This makes school challenging for me.

Yes, you can be gifted and learning disabled at the same time. The two words are not a contradiction in terms. I once heard a comedian refer to the words "jumbo shrimp" as one of these conflicted phrases.

I've learned to accept the fact that I'm an enigma to some. Still, it is a bummer to be misunderstood. The whole syndrome can sometimes make me feel like I am on the outside looking in. Everyone else seems to be getting it, and I'm not.

What really burns me up, though, is when teachers don't get it. In middle school, I took Language Arts with Mrs. Smith. She had piercing brown eyes that made you feel like you had done something wrong. Her no-nonsense, rigid posture made her look as though she'd forgotten to take the wire coat hanger out of her dress. Her face was angular, stiff and white, like a freshly starched and laundered hanky. A smile rarely creased her well-powdered complexion. I could imagine only an intermittent smirk grazing those thin red lips as she X'd her way through someone's failing test paper with her glorious red marker.

I was enrolled in Mrs. Smith's gifted section. That first day, she not only set down the rules of her cellblock, but she handed out copies of them for us to memorize and be tested on the following day. I knew right away that I had better "advocate" for myself. This is just some big, fancy-shmancy term that means to stand up for yourself. In my case, trying to explain, for the umpteenth time, about my learning disabilities. Basically, I have lousy reading comprehension and my handwriting is the pits. So I told her that I have ADD and that I might need to take home some reading assignments because my concentration is better when I am in a quiet setting. I went on to explain to her about my "fine motor skill" problems, which make my handwriting look like chicken scratch. I asked her if I might be able to use my word processor at home to do written assignments.

As I explained all this to Mrs. Smith, she gave me a squinty-eyed look down her bespectacled nose and said, "You are no different from anyone else, young man. If I do for you, I have to do for all the others." She snorted once and then added, "I will not give you an unfair advantage over your peers!" And with that, the bell rang and a herd of students swept me away to my next period.

The comprehension packets were rough. You had to read them, digest them and write an essay on them, all within the forty-five-minute allotted time. Not only couldn't I finish the reading, I couldn't write my essay fast enough or neatly enough to be legible. The result was that each paper came back decorated by Mrs. Smith's flaming red pen. She was like the mad Zorro of red X's.

One day, after she had handed me back my fifth X'd-out paper of the term, I approached her desk for the second time.

"Would you mind very much if I completed the next packet at home, Mrs. Smith? I think I might do better where there is less distraction." Then I backed away from her desk as though I were within firing range of her loaded mouth.

Mrs. Smith bit her thin red lips as her trademark smirk spread across them. "It's against school policy, young man. No unfair advantages. I have treated all students the same in the thirty years I have taught here." Then she flared her nose, clicked her heels and turned away from me, in more ways than one.

So I did what any other kid would do in my situation: I smuggled the packet out of the classroom. I felt like I was doing something illegal, and yet my motives were pure. I had to prove to her, or rather prove to myself, that I could do the work under the right conditions.

I secretly unfolded the contraband on my bed that night. The story, which had seemed so confusing in class, became quite clear to me in the still of my room. I not only got it, I could even relate to it. It was the true story of Louis Braille. He lived in the 1800s and was blinded by a childhood accident. During this time, society shut off the blind from having much of an education. Many were left with the bleak future of becoming homeless beggars. Despite much misunderstanding of his disability, Louis Braille "advocated" for himself. He developed a reading system of raised dots for the blind, which enabled him to read on a par with his peers. A world of books and knowledge opened up to him that he and others like him were literally blind to before. I was like Louis in my classroom setting. I was being made to learn like the other students who were sighted in a way I wasn't.

That night I sat down at my word processor. My thoughts spilled out so fast that my fingers danced across the keyboard, straining to keep up. I explained myself in terms of Louis, in hopes that Mrs. Smith would finally understand me. Funny thing is, somewhere along the line I began to understand myself in a way I never had before.

I cited many other famous people who were in some way different in their learning styles and abilities throughout history. Hans Christian Andersen was said to have been learning disabled, and yet he wrote some of the best fairy tales of our time. I summed it all up by asking, "If I were a student with a vision impairment, would I be seated in the back of the room?" I questioned, "Would I have my glasses taken away from me so that I would not have an unfair advantage over other, glassless students?"

Mrs. Smith never looked at me as she handed my paper back facedown on my desk that day. She never even commented that my work was done on the word processor. As my eyes focused in on the white page, I found an A decorating the margin instead of her customary X. Underneath were her neatly red-penned words: "See what you can do when you apply yourself?"

I took the paper, tucked it away in my folder and shook my head. I guess some people will never get it!

*C. S. Dweck*

# The Blank Page

The pencil moved ever so slightly in my hand as I stared at the blank page that would become my completed homework assignment: a five-paragraph essay on the meaning of life for Mr. Neal's English class.

I had no idea that a person's palms could sweat as much as mine were gripping that pencil. I almost needed sunglasses to shade the glare of the blank notebook paper. I had been sitting at my desk pondering the various aspects and meanings of life for nearly an hour. Thus far, I was clueless as to what to write. *What does Mr. Neal expect?* I wondered. *I am only fourteen.*

I thought about everything that had happened previously in my life. I began high school this year, ran cross-country and played girls' soccer. However, I was sure that the meaning of life had nothing to do with any of these things.

I stretched my arms above my head and looked around the room. My room was so *me*. The mark of Jenni was everywhere to be seen, from my posters and paintings of Europe to the many vibrantly colored CDs that littered my floor. My gaze then fell upon a photograph of me standing beside a girl. Our arms are raised above our heads in an imitation of cheerleaders and we both flash blindingly bright smiles. I froze. Immediately, tears began to well in my eyes. The girl in the photograph and I had been best friends for nearly two years when a sudden disagreement planted a rift in our friendship that still had not been mended. It saddened me beyond measure that an argument could put so much distance between such close friends.

The pencil now moved fluidly across the paper.

When I again looked up, I happened to glance at the varsity *A* I had received for completing cross-country season. Memories now rolled through my mind and flooded my brain: remembrances of long, loud bus rides; water fights with our archrival; memorable trips to various fast-food eateries after the races; the stinging words of many arguments; the tinkling giggles of many laughs gone by.

Again, the lead scraped the clean white paper.

As I went to bed that night, my homework assignment still incomplete, I ran over in my mind what I had written so far. Fitful dreams revealed new stories and thoughts to be explored.

In my dreams, I remembered when my family moved to the beach—tearful good-byes rang in my ears. I reexperienced the velvety voice of my former crush during our first phone conversation, which was a major breakthrough, even though it only lasted five minutes. I remembered how excited I felt after that conversation—I drifted on cloud nine. I relived how happy and proud I felt walking across the Albemarle High School stage to receive my varsity *A*. Even in my sleep, a lone tear's salty track burned my cheek: Albemarle, my life in the past and also now, beginning anew.

I awoke early the next morning to finish my essay. When it was complete it read as follows:

*When you asked us to write about the meaning of life*
*in a five-paragraph essay, Mr. Neal, I wondered how I*

*would ever fill so much empty space. I sat thinking it over for nearly an hour before I even knew how to begin. When I began to write, however, the problem became not how to fill the space, but how to make use of what little I had.*

*There is so much more to life than cross-country meets, soccer games, and the transformation from middle-schooler to high-schooler. What matters most is what you make of your life. If how you feel from day-to-day is based upon what others think and how they judge you, then your life has no basis. If you are a person who wakes up in the morning and dreads the day ahead, then your life has no meaning.*

*However, if you wake up every morning eager to start the new day, then your life has meaning, for it has a purpose. My life certainly has a purpose. Every day is a struggle to survive: building new friendships, fixing old ones, learning how to deal with complicated emotions and accepting new surroundings. I find that every day is a journey of finding out who and what you are.*

*I believe that the question "what is the meaning of life" is too broad. I don't think that anyone will ever truly discover the exact reason why we were put here and what we must do now that we are here. Personally, I do not care to discover the reason. I prefer to leave each day to its own devices.*

*Every day is an adventure in discovering the meaning of life. It is each little thing that you do that day— whether it be spending time with your friends, running in a cross-country race or just simply staring at the crashing ocean—that holds the key to discovering the meaning of life. I would rather be out enjoying these simple things than pondering them. We may never really discover the meaning of life, but the knowledge we gain in our quest to discover it is truly more valuable.*

My hand ached and my pencil was but a stub, by my essay was finished. I had discovered many things while writing this essay, although maybe not the exact meaning of life. *I don't need to find that out yet,* I thought, smiling. *I have things to do along the way.*

My notebook page, as well as my mind, was no longer blank.

*Jenni Norman*

# An Ode to Shoes

Shiny look-a-likes are they,
empty night time, full all day,
travel miles along the street,
though they only move two feet.

When I was thirteen
I stepped
Off my horse
Out of my tall, black leather boots
And into
Running shoes
Into high school
And high-school track
Into high heels and high-school parties
Strutting
Running
Away from the chaos
And back
Strutting
Swinging my legs, my hips
Just enough
Just so, to get the looks

Not the bad ones,
The good
Expensive boots
All the girls have them
Like all the boys have egos
Fake ones
Like fake plastic heels I would never wear
Call me ritzy
I'll call you cheap
In orange, green, and clear
Four-inch heels
little skirts
and I remember
When no one really cared
When our calves hadn't developed into
The sexy, sloping
Line we exploit
When I tied my LA Gears with
One pink shoe lace
And one chartreuse
Like my socks
Like the style
Before the decade turned
Spun into
Steve Maddens and Doc Martins
And Mary Janes
Each with two names
And we all had two faces
Sometimes more for more occasions
Meaning more shoes
Overflowing our closets like muddy water
Like the muddy circle
The track I run in the spring rains
In the new Nikes
Glossy white leather flushing to red-brown

That cracks and dries in the summer sun
The heat
That beats down in a country where
These shoes are manufactured
By small, brown fingers
Crescents of dirt under unkept nails
Working fine threads into my shoes
Working from dawn until dusk
In a place where nobody knows
Steve Madden or Doc Martin
Or any other doctor that the baby's mother cries for
And the children cry here
For a new pair of shoes
Here in
Distorted Reality
In crowded
Walk-in closets
Full of shoes.

*Jessica Pinto*

# Happiness from Within

*Finish each day and be done with it. You have done what you could; some blunders and absurdities have crept in; forget them as soon as you can. Tomorrow is a new day; you shall begin it serenely, and with too high a spirit to be encumbered with your own nonsense.*

Ralph Waldo Emerson

Having been raised Catholic by parents who worked hard for every penny they earned, I was taught at an early age that money cannot buy happiness. As much as my parents and the church tried to teach me these values, I had to learn through my own experiences that happiness comes from within and cannot be measured by material possessions.

As a child, I would sit in church, trying to concentrate on the words of the priest, but my attention was soon diverted by the sparkle of the gold and diamonds worn by the Sunday churchgoers. As my eyes began to wander, I noticed men dressed in their tailored suits and monogrammed shirts, accompanied by women in their designer dresses with matching handbags and shoes.

My family, on the other hand, was the opposite of glamorous. Our hand-me-down clothes had been washed so many times that the colors had become dull and lifeless and the material frayed around the seams. Although our clothes revealed the money struggles of our large family, our faces were always washed, our hair neatly combed, and we each tossed our twenty-five cents in the basket even when there was a second collection. As my family piled into our big green and white VW bus after the service, I fantasized about the glamorous lives led by those driving their brand new BMWs, wishing I were more like them.

I continued these fantasies when I was an adolescent attending Catholic school. Since it was a private school, most of the children came from wealthy families. As a result, I constantly felt inferior to the rest of my classmates. Although I could hide my lack of wealth at school by wearing our mandated school uniforms, my poverty was embarrassingly apparent on weekends when my classmates wore designer jeans, and I had no choice but to wear my sister's outgrown jeans. Once, because I could not afford a birthday gift, I gave one of my own used CDs to a friend in school. When she opened the gift, her face twisted into a strange look as if she did not know whether to laugh or say thank you. It was times like these, when the other kids laughed at me and talked behind my back, that convinced me that if I only had the new clothes, the nice house and other such material possessions, then maybe I would have a chance to fit in. Then I would be happy.

I began to believe so much in the material world that I started my first job when I was fourteen so that I could afford those "things" that were going to make me happy. Soon I was working two jobs in order to fulfill my needs.

I began to purchase the clothes, the jewelry and the perfume. Each purchase was a sign of hope. Each time I thought, *This is it, this is really going to make me happy.* Within a few days, sometimes as little as a few hours, that feeling of emptiness came over me again. I would dream bigger and set my goals higher to purchase something even better. Each time I thought it was going to be different, but it never was.

Unfortunately, it took many of these disappointing and painful experiences, not to mention the amount of money spent, for me to realize that what I admired in other people was not about their clothes, their hairstyles or the car they drove. It was their self-confidence. I admired the way they carried themselves, their ability to take on new challenges and the way they looked people in the eye during conversations instead of staring down at their toes as I often found myself doing. I began to notice that it was the qualities that they possessed inside themselves that I was lacking. I knew then that I would never be a complete person until I started to do some work on the inside.

There was no lightning bolt or voice from God that brought me to this realization. I had to go all the way down the wrong road in life to realize that I was headed in the wrong direction. As a result, I now possess those qualities that I had always admired in other people. Long gone are the days of remedying my problems with new clothes and makeup. I confess I still get caught up in the excitement of shopping sprees, but there is a difference today: I know each time I put on a new outfit and look in the mirror, the same person will be underneath it all. I now carry myself with an air of confidence, and I can look people in the eye, for I have no reason to look down.

*Dianna McGill*

# The Plaster Shell

Intense feelings of embarrassment and absurdity filled my entire body. These feelings were not helped by the fact that I was slathered in baby oil, clad in a T-shirt and lying in my basement, in fifty pounds of plaster. I stared down at the warm plaster that embraced my midsection and slowly crept up toward my chest, and I tried to remember why I had chosen to make a plaster cast of my entire body. For a moment, I simply concluded that I was an utter fool, but I soon remembered my motives. And while the plaster dried, I certainly had the time to think about it.

The insecurities of my freshman year in college, combined with my poor body image, made me feel like an oaf. Here I was surrounded by all these lithe, long girls who wore the latest fashions really well. Was there some mold that churned out these girls? And where in the world did I come from?

That was the beginning of the question that led me to my plaster ensconcement. It all began 506 years ago, when my forebears were thrown out of Spain. They migrated to Eastern Europe and developed the stocky, bosomy shape consigned to overstuffed chairs. Though my tall, slender parents seemed to have defeated this pernicious (certainly in my eyes) shape, it continued lurking in the depths of the family gene pool and flung itself into existence again with the arrival of their firstborn child—me. It gifted me with wide hips, a nonexistent waistline, powerful shoulders and ample breasts. Very reminiscent of a long line of intimidating German matriarchs.

Built to survive harsh winters and to breed children, I certainly wasn't near anything I saw in fashion magazines —or like any of my new college peers. I loathed my shape and cursed my past. Though I was always an independent person who disregarded the edicts of popularity and fashion, I could not ignore our culture's concepts of beauty. The rancor I had for my body made my freshman year of college really hard. Clothing seemed made for those generic stick figures I sat next to in class. That was when Dorothy, my slightly eccentric art teacher and mentor, originated the idea of body casting.

Consequently, on a lovely May morning, I found myself sitting in a dark basement, encased in plaster. I lost all sensation in my legs at approximately the same time that the plaster hardened. After an additional uncomfortable twenty minutes, I slipped out of my plaster shell. At first, I was rather depressed by the sight of the powder-white and headless torso lying on an old towel. It looked more like a sea creature stranded by the tide than a human shape. My eyes squinted, trying not to take in the entire picture of my shape, which was even more exaggerated by the plaster. I thought about how I would never be graceful or delicate, how two-piece swimsuits were absolutely out of the question and how I would never be conventionally beautiful or fashionably thin.

As I stared at the empty outer shell of myself, a great realization hit me—I realized that I had been completely wrong about my body image. For the past nineteen years, I had believed that my linebacker-like shape would discourage others from noticing my additional attributes. How would they ever see my love of science and books, my creativity or my offbeat sense of humor?

All this time I had wanted to be fashionably svelte, but that would not make me a better person. I recognized that confidence was much more important to others than a dainty appearance and that if I had confidence, they would notice my talents. More important, I realized that I did not actually want to be thin and bikini-clad. I was quite content using my powerful build to lug around sixty-pound scenery pieces, and I liked my one-piece, practical bathing suits. My physical appearance had shaped my personality in a largely positive way. It contributed to my dislike of conformity. It gave me my somewhat self-deprecating sense of humor. And it gave me that strong will that I cherish so much. The misconception I was holding all these years, along with the exaggerated body cast that lay there on my basement floor, was suddenly so hilarious to me. I laughed for five minutes straight.

The body cast currently resides in Dorothy's attic, under a large blanket. I never actually used it in any art piece; I felt it had served its purpose. The process of body casting had been far more important than the product.

Since that day three years ago, I have not resented my ancestral build. I have also discovered that being comfortable in my body has given me increased confidence and assertiveness, something many girls, and women, lack. Perhaps they should all be given the opportunity to make their own body casts. When the shell of the body is separate from the person, it is obvious that it is severely lacking. Without the wisdom, sense of humor and heart, it really has no shape at all.

*Miriam Goldstein*

"I think it's so cool that you don't care if you're cool."

*Reprinted with permission of Dave Carpenter.*

# Out of Step

*The roots of true achievement lie in the will to
become the best that you can become.*

Harold Taylor

I wanted to find my niche. I wanted to fit in so badly
with some group, any group in high school. Sports didn't
really work for me. I sucked at just about all of them. In
fact, I dreaded those times in PE when the captains picked
teams. Fights sometimes ensued between captains about
who would have the misfortune of ending up with me on
their team. I was the guy who had a full-scale neurotic
episode if you threw the ball to him.

I did run track for awhile. This was a pretty good sport
for me because it required very little coordination, and I
already had some practice running: away from bullies, their
girlfriends and any ball thrown in my general direction. But
I wanted to run sprints and only the football players got to
run sprints. I was relegated to middle distance—the half-
mile, which really didn't work for me. It took about two
minutes to run, and the extent of my ability to exert myself
athletically was about thirty seconds.

But one day, a girl I liked and sometimes stalked (although we didn't call it stalking back then—just a playful crush) happened into the band office to sign up. Because I had a "playful crush" on Jaclyn, I was hiding behind a tree and noticed her sign up for the band. Okay, sure, the uniforms were pretty dorky and being in the band didn't exactly give you the best reputation in school (which in my case couldn't really get much worse), but I could learn to play the drums and there *was* Jaclyn. I would later learn that many of the greatest musicians of our time were motivated to music by some girl whose name they most likely don't remember anymore.

It was not just the band, but the marching band. I picked the drums for two reasons: (1) It seemed pretty easy, and (2) I thought it would make me look cool. I later found out that the drums are actually quite difficult and that little or nothing could make me look cool. I wanted to play snare drum, but because of my lack of experience I was relegated to the tenor drum.

The first thing to learn was how to hold the drum and play it. We all had to learn the cadence which, to this day, I can still perform with two pencils and a paper cup, which really wows them on job interviews. Holding the drum and playing it is not as easy as it might look. I did, after several private lessons, learn the cadence. Next, as if that weren't difficult enough, I had to learn how to play it while not only walking, but marching.

We were required to march the equivalent of five miles per practice day, while carrying our eighty-pound drums (it was then I wished I had picked the flute) and wearing our big, shiny, black military shoes, in the 104-degree summer heat. And then one day, they delivered the Shakos. For those of you who may not be familiar with high school marching band terminology, the Shako is that really tall, furry-looking hat that you wear with a strap around your chin. Now I was marching five miles a day in my shiny shoes, carrying my eighty-pound drum, playing the cadence about six thousand times, in 104-degree heat, and wearing a big tall, white, furry hat.

Finally, at the end of the summer, our uniforms arrived. The band uniform is a sacred attire. It is carefully sized to fit the individual, hand sewn, and acquired through twenty-seven or so fundraising activities such as car washes, bake sales and door-to-door sales of things like half-melted candy bars at inflated prices. It is cleaned after each use and worn with pride. It is also 100 percent wool. Add now to the excruciatingly painful military shoes, the eighty-pound drum, the silly hat and the 104-degree heat, what I estimate to have been about forty pounds of long-sleeved, neck-to-toe, pure wool.

I forgot to mention something. In addition to an inability to play sports, I was also not so good at marching. If you were not in step, the band director would yell in a loud and embarrassingly annoyed voice, "OUT OF STEP!" It was at this point that I began to question my decision to join the band. How do playing music and marching around in silly formations, all "in step," go together?

The day of our first competition finally arrived. It was the Mother Goose Parade, an annual Thanksgiving Day event in my town. High school bands from all over the county marched while all the people in town lined the streets in lawn chairs and watched them march by. Although the parade didn't start until 9:00 A.M., we had to meet at 6:00 A.M. to get our uniforms from the "band boosters"—those selfless, dedicated parents who provided comfort and assistance to the members of the band.

At 6:00 A.M., to this day, I am not really in existence. Oh sure, you can get me out of bed and dress me, and I will walk and talk, but inside my brain is fast asleep, waiting for a more reasonable hour. I was standing around waiting for my Shako to be cleaned when I noticed a big urn of coffee. *Coffee? That wakes you up, doesn't it?* I poured myself a cup—my first-ever cup of coffee. It tasted pretty bitter, but I had to wake up. I dumped in three sugars and three packets of that white, milky powder that is supposed to scientifically simulate cream. It still tasted bitter but drinkable. I just had to wake up so I could be "IN STEP." After about ten minutes, I was awake. I WAS REALLY AWAKE. I went over to the corner and put on my drum. I wanted to see how fast I could play the cadence. Pretty fast. I started marching around in circles until one of the band boosters came over with a look of concern on her face. She suggested I sit down and rest until it was time to line up. That's when I learned to play the cadence with pencils and a paper cup.

Finally, the moment of truth. They lined us all up and we waited for about forty-five minutes. I had my coffee, and I was raring to go. The drum major blew his whistle and off we went. I beat the cadence out with all my heart. I marched with the precision of a brigadier general. For about the first hour. Then, something happened. Suddenly all my energy drained away. I began to feel sleepy and I fell "OUT OF STEP." No one noticed at first and I tried to skip back into step. But nothing worked. Then I saw one of the band boosters talking to another one and pointing at me. They looked very concerned. They enlisted a third booster and suddenly, to my horror, they all three pointed at me and motioned for me to leave formation. I complied; after all, they had rank. I walked over to them as the band marched on. They told me what I already knew, I was "OUT OF STEP," and would have to stay out of the formation until the band passed the judging stand. I could rejoin the band after the judging stand, but only if I followed along on the side of the road.

I couldn't believe it. Now, I not only couldn't march

with the band, but I had to climb over the lawn chairs, popcorn and arms and legs of my fellow townspeople for the next mile to keep up with the band, in my shiny shoes, carrying my drum and wearing my Shako. I would like to say this was the single most humiliating moment of my life, but unfortunately there were more to follow. But this one did rank pretty high up there on the list.

I never did learn to march "IN STEP." But it hasn't really come up that much in my adult life. I also never did find a niche in high school, but I got through it. As an adult, I have found several niches that I fit into quite nicely, and I look for new ones every day. And I always ask if there is any marching competition before signing up.

*Tal Vigderson*

# The Essence of Adolescence

I yelled at Mom yesterday
'Cause she told me I'm going through
A difficult age
And I'm not.
So I slammed the door extra hard
When I got up to my room.
And then I yelled at God for a while
Just for good measure
'Cause he made it snow but
Wouldn't close school.
Besides
He parked that damn streetlight
Just where
He knew it would shine in my eyes
Every night when I'm trying to sleep.
And I yelled at the light, too
'Cause it's too bright
And besides
It lights up the snowman
That the kids next door made.
I was too old to make a snowman this year

But that's okay
I've always hated snowmen anyway.
I yelled at the snowman, too
Before I sat down at my desk
Where this old box was sitting . . .
It had a bunch of
Stupid treasures from when I was little.
Inside was a cotton ball
And some acorns, a dead bee
My eraser collection, and a pen
That had my name on it.
I picked up the box and
Threw it away
'Cause it's dumb to keep that sort of stuff
I put my phone and a romance novel
On the desk instead.
I have to keep my priorities straight.

Then I got home from school today
And I sat down at my desk
I looked for my box.
It wasn't on my desk or in the trash
'Cause today was garbage day
And I sat back down and I guess,
I started to cry.
It's too complicated being mad at the world.

*Anne Gepford*
*Submitted by Katie Shaw*

# Teenagers' Bill of Rights

## Our Rights with Friends:

We all have the right and the privilege to have friends. We can choose our friends based on our own likes and dislikes. We don't have to like the same people everyone else likes or not like someone because they aren't in our "group." Friendship is a personal thing.

We can ask from our friends that they be trustworthy. If we share something with them and ask them not to tell everyone, we can expect that they will keep it just between us. We will give them the same right. If they don't, they have betrayed our trust and our friendship.

It is okay to be honest with our friends. If they do something that hurts us or concerns us, we can talk to them about it. We will be open to their being honest also. This does not mean it is okay to be mean to each other, just that we can talk honestly about our feelings.

We have the right to be respected for the decisions we make. Some of our friends may not understand the choices we make, but they are our choices. In return, we take responsibility for them.

## With Parents and Other Adults:

We have the right to have our feelings respected and not compared to the feelings of puppies . . . or any other such put downs. Our feelings are strong and sometimes confusing. It helps if you take our feelings seriously and listen to us before disregarding them.

We feel we have the right to make decisions (some, not all) for ourselves. If we make mistakes we will learn from them, but it is time for us to be more responsible.

Whenever possible, exclude us from your fights. We understand that fighting is part of every relationship, but it is painful for us to be involved. Don't put us in the middle of *any* problem you have with each other.

We agree to treat you with respect and ask that you respect us in return. This includes respecting our privacy.

## With Everyone:

We have the right to be loved unconditionally, and our goal is to love you the same.

We have the right to speak our minds, love ourselves, feel our feelings, and strive for our dreams. Please support us by believing in us rather than fearing for us.

*Lia Gay; Jamie Yellin;*
*Lisa Gumenick; Hana Ivanhoe;*
*Bree Able; Lisa Rothbard*

# Center Stage

Once upon a time, my life was as orderly as the inside of my locker. I took detailed notes, never talked out of turn, helped put away library books during my free periods, and went to track practice after school. But all that changed the day Mr. Soames made Sara McGee my partner in biology.

"If he thinks I'm touching this, he's dreaming," Sara whispered after Mr. Soames told us to make the first incision into the earthworms we were dissecting. She pushed her bangs—they were orange today as opposed to last week's green—out of her face and frowned.

I took the knife from her hand and split the earthworm neatly down its center.

"Thanks," she said. She rolled up her sleeves and her silver bangles clattered. "I know I'm a baby, but cutting open animals makes me sick."

I finished dissecting the worm, and when the period was over, Sara slipped her backpack over her shoulder and asked me to eat lunch with her.

"Okay," I said, surprised. I followed her to her locker,

where she opened a tube of tomato-red lipstick and thickly applied it.

"Want some?" she asked, but I shook my head "no."

"Just a tiny bit?" she asked again, and before I could stop her, she dabbed it on. Then she removed the tortoise-shell barrette I always wore and lifted my hair into a high ponytail, pulling two tendrils down on either side of my ears.

"Stunning!" she said, standing behind me so that I could see both of us in the little mirror that hung from a hook. Stunning? I wasn't so sure.

Soon, whenever Sara chewed Juicy Fruit gum in class, I did, too, even though I was careful not to get caught. I wore long skirts like Sara's, and dangle earrings. She hid in the stacks during study hall and read old magazines and, consequently, so did I. She took me to Papa Jimmy's and introduced me to double caffé lattes and biscotti dipped in chocolate. She liked to start arguments in world history class about personal freedom and even though I never could do that, I did find myself, miraculously, volunteering to read out loud in Mr. Bernard's English class.

It was Mr. Bernard, in fact, who pulled me aside and told me I had a flair for drama (we were reading *Romeo and Juliet*). He also said I should try out for the part of Laura in the junior class production of *The Glass Menagerie*.

"No way. I could never do that," I told Sara as soon as we left the room. Secretly, though, I was pleased he had asked.

"Of course you can. You'll be great," Sara said. "You have to try out!" She bugged me until I finally agreed.

At the audition, I read a scene with Joe Greenlaw, who I'd never said a word to before. I doubt he knew who I was, but I could recite his activities as if they were listed in alphabetical order under his picture in the yearbook: junior class vice-president; photo editor for the Park

Ridge *Banner;* captain, debate team; soccer goalie.

After we finished, Mrs. Layton, the director, just smiled and said, "Thank you *very* much," and the next day the casting list was posted on the bulletin board and there was my name, second from the top, with Joe Greenlaw's just above it.

I had play rehearsal almost every night, and so I had to use all my free time to catch up on my schoolwork and hardly ever had time to go to Papa Jimmy's with Sara. Slowly, though, a strange thing began to happen. Homework and chores, babysitting, and even Sara started to fade in importance, but the time I spent at rehearsals was as vivid as the glow-in-the-dark stars on my bedroom ceiling.

Joe talked to me, calling "Laura" from way down the hall. This made me so happy that I didn't even mind when I saw Rachel Thompson, who had waist-long hair that was shiny as glass, put her arm across his shoulder. One night, during dress rehearsal week, we were standing together on the fire escape outside the auditorium watching the snow flakes gather on the iron railing. Joe told me that deep down inside he was really shy and that he was glad he could be himself with me. "Maybe we should do things together," he said. "Go running, go to a dance, I don't know." And then we heard Mrs. Layton calling for us, so we ran back inside.

The next day, Sara stood by my locker just before homeroom. "Hi," she said.

"Hi."

"I never see you anymore. Except in classes, and that doesn't count." She tugged on one of the four stud earrings that lined her ear.

"I know," I said. "It's the play. I'm really busy. It'll be over soon." I looked closely at Sara, past her makeup, and her jewelry, and the long black cape that covered her shirt and her thick, black hiking boots. She always seemed so bold, the way she stated her opinions as if they were facts, and looked anybody in the eye. But now she was quiet, more like the old me than Sara. I gave her a hug.

"Let's do something," she suggested. She looked at the poster on the bulletin board just behind us. It was a drawing of a flapper girl twirling a strand of pearls. "Let's get a bunch of people together and crash the Winter Carnival dance. We'll go to the thrift shop and get some beaded dresses."

A dance. I thought of Joe and of our conversation the night before. And even though I knew, deep down, that it would be a white lie to say he'd invited me to that particular dance, I told her I was busy. "I can't," I said. She looked at me and waited. "Joe Greenlaw asked me."

"Yeah, right," she said.

"I'm sorry," I told her. "He did." Sara picked up her backpack from between her feet and started to walk away.

"Sara!" I called after her.

"Let me know when you can fit me into your busy schedule," she hissed.

* * * *

This is the part of my story that is really embarrassing—the part that I wish I could tell in third person, as if it really belonged to somebody else. A week after the play was over Joe found me during sixth-period study hall. "I'm sorry," he said.

I looked at him, not understanding.

"Sara McGee asked me if it was true we were going to the dance together. I'm sorry. I'm going with Rachel."

I looked down at my feet. The new me was going away, like a picture on a computer screen that fades out. I was sure my ears were bright red.

"I'm sorry," Joe continued. "It's nothing personal." He turned and looked like he was leaving, but then he came back. He put his hand on my arm. "Don't be embarrassed," he said. "You know, I should have asked you. I wish I had." And then he left.

Now Sara passed me in the hall without speaking. I spent most of my free time studying or practicing my sprints. I went back to wearing my plain, comfortable clothes and threw away my makeup. And I only talked when teachers called on me. As if nothing had changed.

But that wouldn't be true. To Sara, I might have looked the same. Still, deep inside, where she couldn't see, there was another me. I was brave, I was fun. I got a standing ovation in the middle of a stage, and a boy regretted not asking me to a dance. And it was Sara I had to thank for introducing that girl to me.

*Jane Denitz Smith*

# Automobile Ambivalence

*Life consists not in holding good cards but in playing those you hold well.*

Josh Billings

I know it sounds a little strange since I live in Detroit, the Motor City, but from the time I bought my first car as a new teenage driver I've been afflicted with an apparently unique condition. Automobile ambivalence.

When I got my driver's license I was excited beyond belief. I'd saved some money to buy a little unsightly, plodder of a vehicle, so appearance didn't matter to me. Of course, not having much money, appearance really couldn't matter. This was a classic clunker car.

It didn't matter what it looked like; I was no longer chaperoned. I could drive to school, and I could pick up my friends. (Okay, I admit some of my friends wouldn't be caught in my car for fear of picking up some strange germs or being convinced the whole thing was just going to fall apart, without warning, at any instant.)

On the other side of the carburetor, my not-that-much-older brother had a passion for cars. He subscribed to all the auto magazines, washed and waxed his car every Saturday morning and kept the inside of the vehicle pristine clean. Our two cars, sharing the driveway, were pretty much the Odd Couple of autos.

Fearing that some strange occurrence would happen to his car being parked too closely to mine, my brother put a blanket over his every night, kind of like one of those jackets the X-ray technician wears to avoid exposure to radiation. My brother was convinced my car was sending out some type of harmful emissions well beyond what came out of my broken muffler.

I admit that his car was clearly the Homecoming Queen, while mine was, well . . . mine was pretty much the end-of-the-bench junior varsity football player who got his uniform dirty because he fell in the mud on the way to the locker room after the game. Not much talent, not much speed, dirty as can be, but still able to move in the right direction. Most of the time.

When I first heard the term "all-purpose vehicle" I believed they were actually referring to my car. My vehicle was multifunctional: It served as a mobile closet, storage area for sports equipment, stockpile for non-perishable food items and a portable periodical section of newspapers and magazines. Every "purpose" was utilized when an impromptu basketball game was organized for the park after school and I needed my gym clothes, a pre-game snack, a basketball and shoes.

My automobile ambivalence did create a few problems on the homefront. This was clear when my brother was required to borrow my car because his princess of a vehicle was in the shop for probably some type of face lift or tummy tuck.

I gave him the latest briefing as he sprayed a few layers of disinfectant throughout and laid a clean towel over the driver's seat. The info I provided included don't lock the door because the key won't open it, the driver's side window doesn't roll down, the trunk light remains permanently on and don't park in a position where you'll need to back up to leave. Getting the car to go in reverse is usually a fifty-fifty proposition. It's not worth playing the odds given the potential difficulties of having to enlist the services of a passerby to push your car into a position where you can actually drive away.

When my brother returned from his jaunt in my jalopy I knew that something was amiss when he threw down the keys and simply stared at me.

"Problem?" I meekly proposed.

"You didn't tell me it stalls at most stops!"

"I guess I forgot to mention that little peculiarity. However, if you pump the accelerator twice, pull the passenger-side seatbelt once, turn the radio to country music and roll down the rear passenger-side window, it should start right up."

He was as amused as the time I had to confess to him that I'd backed out of the garage into his car parked in the driveway. I had seen his pride-and-joy vehicle as I'd entered mine but, apparently, my short-term memory wasn't in full operation that morning. As I heard the sound of metal on metal, I knew it wasn't a good sign. I told him that maybe having Dad put up some traffic signals in our driveway would be a good idea. He wasn't amused.

One of the benefits of automobile ambivalence is there isn't an overwhelming disappointment when a little body damage occurs. Heck, with my car, I'd have been hard-pressed to notice anything. The dents and dings throughout made it resemble one of those antique-looking candelabras you hammered away at in seventh-grade shop class.

Before going to advise my brother of the two-car pile-up in the driveway I surveyed the injuries. I remember actually being somewhat pleased that I'd accidentally achieved some symmetry given that the previous huge dent on the rear driver's side now matched the new dent on the opposite side. I thought, for whatever reason, that maybe I'd now get better gas mileage. Kind of some new aerodynamic action. More wind resistant.

After having had this first car for a couple years, I recall feeling a little sentimental as we approached an important milestone—one hundred thousand miles. Despite my general ambivalence, I did love my car, warts and all. I recall thinking for this big event I'd do something really special. I first thought a drive-thru car wash would be nice, but I was a little hesitant since I felt some of the dirt and rust may actually be holding the whole darn thing together.

I finally decided on a drive-in movie. Just a teenager and his car. In years since, I've had more cars and my auto ambivalence remains. But you only have one first car and although it's no longer intact, my memories are.

*Bob Schwartz*

# Minimaxims for My Godson

*The purpose of life is a life of purpose.*

Robert Byrne

Dear Sandy,

Your nice thank-you note for the graduation present I sent you a few weeks ago just came in, and I've been chuckling over your postscript in which you say that such presents are great but you wish someone could give you "half a dozen foolproof ideas for bending the world into a pretzel."

Well, Sandy, I must admit, I don't have any very original thoughts of my own. But through the years I've encountered a few ideas of that kind—not platitudes but ideas sharp-pointed enough to stick in my mind permanently. Concepts that release energy, make problem-solving easier, provide shortcuts to worthwhile goals. No one handed them over in a neat package. They just came along from time to time, usually from people not in the wisdom-dispensing business at all. Compared to the great time-tested codes of conduct, they may seem like pretty small change. But each of them has helped to make my life a good deal easier and happier and more productive.

So here they are. I hope you find them useful, too.

1. *If you can't change facts, try bending your attitudes.* Without a doubt, the bleakest period of my life so far was the winter of 1942 to 1943. I was with the Eighth Air Force in England. Our bomber bases, hacked out of the sodden English countryside, were seas of mud. On the ground, people were cold, miserable and homesick. In the air, people were getting shot. Replacements were few; morale was low.

   But there was one sergeant—a crew chief—who was always cheerful, always good-humored, always smiling. I watched him one day, in a freezing rain, struggle to salvage a fortress that had skidded into an apparently bottomless mire. He was whistling like a lark. "Sergeant," I said to him sourly, "how can you whistle in a mess like this?"

   He gave me a mud-caked grin. "Lieutenant," he said, "when the facts won't budge you have to bend your attitudes to fit them, that's all."

   Check it for yourself, Sandy. You'll see that, faced with a given set of problems one man may tackle them with intelligence, grace and courage; another may react with resentment and bitterness; a third may run away altogether. In any life, facts tend to remain unyielding. But attitudes are a matter of choice—and that choice is largely up to you.

2. *Don't come up to the net behind nothing.* One night in a PTA meeting, a lawyer—a friend and frequent tennis partner of mine—made a proposal that I disagreed with, and I challenged it. But when I had concluded what I thought was quite a good spur-of-the-moment argument, my friend stood up and proceeded to

demolish it. Where I had opinions, he had facts; where I had theories, he had statistics. He obviously knew so much more about the subject than I did that his viewpoint easily prevailed. When we met in the hall afterward, he winked and said, "You should know better than to come up to the net behind nothing!"

It is true; the tennis player who follows his own weak or badly placed shot up to the net is hopelessly vulnerable. And this is true when you rush into *anything* without adequate preparation or planning. In any important endeavor, you've got to do your homework, get your facts straight and sharpen your skills. In other words, don't bluff—because if you do, nine times out of ten, life will drill a backhand right past you.

3. *When the ball is over, take off your dancing shoes.* As a child, I used to hear my aunt say this, and it puzzled me a good deal, until the day I heard her spell out the lesson more explicitly. My sister had come back from a glamorous weekend full of glitter, exciting parties and stimulating people. She was bemoaning the contrast with her routine job, her modest apartment and her day-to-day friends. "Young lady," our aunt said gently, "no one lives on the top of the mountain. It's fine to go there occasionally—for inspiration, for new perspectives. But you have to come down. Life is lived in the valley. That's where the farms and gardens and orchards are, and where the plowing and the work are done. That's where you apply the visions you may have glimpsed from the peaks."

It's a steadying thought when the time comes, as it always does, to exchange your dancing shoes for your working shoes.

4. *Shine up your neighbor's halo.* One Sunday morning, drowsing in a back pew of a little country church, I

dimly heard the old preacher urge his flock to "stop worrying about your own halo and shine up your neighbor's!" And it left me sitting up, wide-awake, because it struck me as just about the best eleven-word formula for getting along with people that I've ever heard.

I like it for its implication that everyone, in some area of life, has a halo that's worth watching for and acknowledging. I like it for the firm way it shifts the emphasis from self to interest and concern for others. Finally, I like it because it reflects a deep psychological truth: People have a tendency to become what you expect them to be.

5. *Keep one eye on the law of the echo.* I remember very well the occasion when I heard this sharp-edged bit of advice. Coming home from boarding school, some of us youngsters were in the dining car of a train. Somehow the talk got around to the subject of cheating on exams, and one boy readily admitted that he cheated all the time. He said that he found it both easy and profitable.

Suddenly, a mild-looking man sitting all alone at a table across the aisle—he might have been a banker, a bookkeeper, anything—leaned forward and spoke up. "Yes," he said directly to the apostle of cheating. "All the same—I'd keep one eye on the law of the echo, if I were you."

The law of the echo—is there really such a thing? Is the universe actually arranged so that whatever you send out—honesty or dishonesty, kindness or cruelty—ultimately comes back to you? It's hard to be sure. And yet, since the beginning of recorded history, mankind has had the conviction, based partly on intuition, partly on observation, that in the long run a man does indeed reap what he sows.

You know as well as I do, Sandy, that in this misty area there are no final answers. Still, as the man said, "I think I'd keep one eye on the law of the echo, if I were you!"

6. *Don't wear your raincoat in the shower.* In the distant days when I was a Boy Scout, I had a troop leader who was an ardent woodsman and naturalist. He would take us on hikes, not saying a word, and then challenge us to describe what we had observed: trees, plants, birds, wildlife, everything. Invariably, we hadn't seen a quarter as much as he had, nor half enough to satisfy him. "Creation is all around you," he would cry, waving his arms in vast inclusive circles, "but you're keeping it out. Don't be a buttoned-up person! Stop wearing your raincoat in the shower!"

I've never forgotten the ludicrous image of a person standing in the shower with a raincoat buttoned up to his chin. The best way to discard that raincoat, I've found, is to expose yourself to new experiences in your life *all your life.*

All these phrases that I have been recalling really urge one to the same goal: a stronger participation, a deep involvement in life. This doesn't come naturally, by any means. And yet, with marvelous impartiality, each of us is given exactly the same number of minutes and hours in every day. Time is the raw material. What we do with it is up to us.

A wise man once said that tragedy is not what we suffer, but what we miss. Keep that in mind, Sandy.

Your affectionate godfather,

*Arthur Gordon*

# All the More Beautiful

At seventeen, I wanted desperately to be an adult, and believed I was making progress. I shaved almost every other day, and had my own wheels. The only thing I needed was the girl.

I saw her from a block away. She was tall, with long brown hair. We went to the same public school, but she often wore this plaid skirt, like a private-school girl. I drove up from behind, in my car, the only place I didn't feel short, and something amazing happened. She looked back at me. It felt just like one of those cheesy movies, slow motion, hair flowing, a halo of light surrounding her. She followed me with her eyes as I passed. That day, I felt tall wherever I went.

My luck didn't stop there. It turned out that she and my cousin were friends. He gave me her name and number. That afternoon, my sweaty, shaking hand picked up the phone, and I spoke to Kristen for the first time. That weekend, I drove down the same street where our eyes first met, to pick her up for our first date, my first real date ever.

I pictured myself sitting next to this perfect girl, in her perfect living room, being interrogated by her perfect parents. I arrived, and all my expectations began to be challenged. There was no playful dog in the front yard, and no white picket fence to keep him from running away. Before I could knock on the door, Kristen opened it just enough to slip out. Then she smiled and all was perfect again. We went miniature golfing and laughed together for the first time.

After that night, we were inseparable, sickening all our friends. She made me feel like a big man, even though she called me her little guy. I had never felt so close to anyone before. But some mornings, when I'd pick her up for school and she'd slip out her door, something was different. She wouldn't have that perfect smile. She'd stare out the window and she seemed lost. I'd ask her what was wrong, and she'd say, "Nothing."

No answer could have been worse. It drove me crazy. I wanted to help. I wanted her to smile. Most of all, I wanted to be let inside. If I was an adult, it was time to start acting like one.

I confronted her; told her I knew there was something wrong. I knew she had problems at home, and I knew I could help if she'd just let me. Then she started to cry. I felt utterly helpless.

She put her arms around me and pressed her face into my chest. I felt her hot tears seeping through my shirt.

I soon learned that Kristen suffered from anxiety and depression. At home, she couldn't escape her past. Outside, with me, she could pretend all was perfect. When she started crying, she stopped pretending, and let me inside. I also stopped pretending. There were times when I didn't feel strong, when I didn't feel wise. There were times when I didn't feel like an adult.

During these past six years, Kristen and I have shared many laughs and tears together. I have had time to study her smile. I realize it is not perfect and, therefore, all the more beautiful. She continues to challenge and surpass all my expectations, teaching me more about life than I ever imagined there was to know. We talk about marriage and a family of our own, but we're in no hurry to grow up.

*Marc Gaudioso*

# Rolling Down Summer's Hills

*Every human being on this Earth is born with*
*a tragedy, and it isn't original sin. He's born*
*with the tragedy that he has to grow up. A lot of*
*people don't have the courage to do it.*

Helen Hayes

We run through the August night with only fireflies
lighting our way, feeling the freedom of time that only
children of summer ever know. The echo of our laughter
sails through darkness, while we chase each other in tag.
Soon we become silent, hunting through the tall, damp
grass punctuated only by the beating of our hearts.

A hand pierces through the night, grabbing me. Our
two bodies fall entwined into a huddled mass of legs and
arms with her gaining the upper hand because I let her.
She pins me down upon my back, her hands holding
mine outstretched upon the moist grass. Straddling my
chest with her knees, I sense her head slowly growing
ever nearer. We're so close that I can feel the ins and outs
of her breath upon my lips. She covers my mouth with
her own and I am lost in the newness of my first kiss.

Before I can speak or think, she pulls away. Running off, she leaves me there dazed. That was how the night ended; this is how it began.

It's the summer of my thirteenth birthday, and I'm enjoying these majestic Pocono days. Our cabin overlooks the endless rolling hills carpeted by sweet-smelling grasses and black-eyed Susans. My younger brother Mikey and I climb to the highest point and then, lying down on our sides like two bowling pins, we close our eyes rolling wildly down to the bottom. It's a dizzying sensation to feel the world spin around and around this way. Sometimes I lose control and go careening off into some unplanned foreign destination.

And so it is when I first see Carly, hanging out among the other girls at Lake Wallenpaupack. I didn't know then that I'd go careening off sideways and smack straight into her world.

She hangs with this group of thirteen-year-old girls who've teamed up more out of convenience than common interest. Her long black hair falls in waves against her pale white skin, and she has this unique ability to smile at me with her eyes.

My posse looks like an odd assortment left over in some thrift-shop clearance box. First off, there's me. I had a major growth spurt this summer, and my limbs feel way too long. It's weird to suddenly tower over your own mother, the person you've looked up to your whole life. Now a good three inches taller than she, I can easily pat her on the head. Yet no matter how much I eat, my pants hang low on my gangly, 105-pound frame. Everything is changing around me and inside me. I can't even count on feeling comfortable in my own skin, which is now riddled with acne.

Then there's my ten-year-old brother, Mikey. He hasn't found any other kids his age around, and appears to be going through severe Nintendo withdrawal. It's my responsibility to watch out for all four fast-moving feet of him. We make an unlikely pair. Although only three years come between our ages, almost two feet separate our heights.

Finally there's Ron, who's fourteen, a full year older than I and so much more wise in the ways of the world. He shoves his Mets cap low on his head to shield his eyes from the sun and any parent's watchful gaze. In his left ear he sports a fake diamond stud, which denotes the coolness he envelops.

Ron and I sit on the dock, dangling our feet in the water's edge, while Mikey floats carelessly in his black inner tube. Once in a while we have the nerve to dart our eyes over to the girls who are taking turns diving into the water in their bright bikinis, giggling and trying to peek over at us as well.

Ron shares his experiences with women and I wonder how much of it is really true, but I listen closely just in case it is. Some of his stories are funny, and others are just really gross, but I tuck all of what he tells me safely away in the annals of my mind for future reference.

My only other experience hearing about sex was back in health class, and there it seemed like such a crude joke. There was this one jerk in the back of the room who'd laugh whenever the teacher mentioned anything sexual. He was the same guy who'd repeat over and over that there was going to be a "teste" on Monday and then die laughing at his own wit.

At home, my parents speak in strictly medical terms. The way they tell it, the whole thing sounds more like a painful procedure for wisdom teeth removal than a pleasurable experience. Here, sitting on the dock with Ron, it seems a lot more real. I watch Carly in her red two-piece. Her shining black hair reflects the noonday sun, and I wonder what it would be like to kiss those peach-colored lips. So far it's taken all the courage I can muster just to say hi as we pass each other every day at the lake.

Soon, night falls and Dad calls us around the dinner table to have an informal family meeting. He says he wants to talk about our "future." The cabin is hot and noticeably un-air-conditioned. The sweat on the back of my legs causes my skin to stick to the vinyl-covered dining chairs.

My dad sits at the head of the table with his elbows resting on the yellow Formica. He hasn't shaved since we arrived here, and the gray stubble on his cheeks and chin make him look old. My mother sits at the other end of the table still wearing the same swimsuit she wore earlier today down by the lake. She pulls the seat of her suit down over each thigh, fidgeting more than her usual calm demeanor allows. Mikey sits lazily dipping his Oreo cookies into a large glass of milk and then sucking them down over his wet lips.

My dad tells us he's been laid off from work—straight out with no beating around the bush. I can't say I'm shocked; we all saw the writing on the wall. Dad's a textile man, and the industry is dying. I know this because I've heard the hushed conversations between my mom and dad. With most labor now going overseas, there's just not enough work to keep the U.S. sewing factories alive. It's not as if Dad has a profession where he can just slip comfortably into a new opportunity. Finding another job at forty-six years old is rough.

Mikey just keeps sucking down his cookies. He's too young to understand that there is no magic that will make everything better, and that Dad doesn't have all the answers.

In between frantic thoughts, I hear Dad saying something about our home; using words like "scaling down" and "tightening belts." All I keep wondering is, *How is this going to affect me? Will I still be able to afford to go to the movies with my friends, or will I be left at home? And where will my home be?* I hear Dad saying something about our horrendous taxes and the possibility of moving to a smaller apartment.

I want to grab him and yell, "Stop! Don't you know you're ruining my life? I can't move . . . this is where all my friends are . . . this is where I go to school. We had a deal, remember? You would take care of me, and I would never have to worry about these kinds of things, because I'm just a kid."

And then this feeling gives way to a sickening rush of guilt for being so selfish. I look over at my parents who seem small and vulnerable. Who are these pathetic imposters whose words change everything for all of us, and how should I react to these strangers that I love so much? Should I lie and tell them everything will be okay? And is that what they need to hear, or is that really what *I* need to hear? I suddenly feel like the parent.

That night I run out to play tag with all those kids whose lives are still unchanged. I run through the night hoping to knock the wind out of myself—running to forget about my dad or maybe to stumble onto an answer that will save us. That's when Carly's arm reaches out to grab me. She kisses me, and I forget for one moment about all the uncertainty.

Then she's gone, and I lay there in the pitch-black darkness with my head spinning the same way it did when I rolled down those long summer hills. I feel that same dizzying disorientation lying there alone in the darkness, and I realize that sometimes there are no real answers, and life goes on.

*C. S. Dweck*

# $\overline{9}$

# LETTERS FROM READERS

*T*o send a letter is a good way to go
somewhere without moving anything
but your heart.

*Phyllis Theroux*

# My Sister's First Love

*Dear* Chicken Soup for the Teenage Soul,

*I am sending you a story my sister wrote for your consideration for a* Chicken Soup *book. My sister, Jodi, underwent a very emotional, psychological and spiritual struggle as she dealt with the fact that her long-term boyfriend, Tim, was dying from an inoperable brain tumor. She helped Tim fight his cancer in every way imaginable, but unfortunately on Valentine's Day in 1997, Jodi sat by Tim's side as he took his last breath.*

*Although her story is tragic, she was able to gain a whole new outlook on the meaning of life and death. She wrote this story about her experience, and it touched me deeply. The power of her words is simply breathtaking, and I wanted to share them with you, and, hopefully, others, as well.*

*Sincerely,*
*Kristi Vesterby*

# Immortal

*When someone dies, you don't get over it by forgetting; you get over it by remembering, and you are aware that no person is ever truly lost or gone once they have been in our life and loved us, as we have loved them.*

Leslie Marmon Silko

His dizziness and headaches began during the summer; they worried me a little, but I never thought they would amount to anything serious. I look back now and wonder if he knew they were signs of what was to come. Tim and I had been dating for over a year; we'd become best friends. We were in that phase of our lives when we thought nothing could go wrong. We were going to be together forever and live our perfect high-school-sweetheart love story with a white picket fence and all. When his symptoms persisted, I think we both knew that something was wrong, but I never could have imagined just how wrong.

By basketball season, things were considerably worse. It was his junior year, and Tim had hoped he would finally be starting on the varsity team. I would sit in the stands and cheer with the rest of my friends, but inside I was constantly wondering who this impostor was that was taking over Tim's body. He bobbled the ball as he'd dribble up the court, or tip over on the backs of his heels while attempting to play defense. His frustration increased with each day of practice, so when his mother, Ann, suggested he see a doctor, Tim agreed. The local clinic scheduled an appointment for him to have a scan of his brain the next time the "MRI-Mobile" came to Olivia, our small, unequipped town. The scan later showed a tumor growing on the base of Tim's brain, and from then on our lives were never the same.

We all sat crammed in an incredibly small room they called a doctor's office, waiting for the arrival of some overly busy neuro-oncologist. He was going to interpret the complicated X rays that were beyond the capability of the doctors at Prairie Family Practice. This room was as close to hell as I've ever been, and without even knowing what was ahead of me, it was difficult to find a way to pass the time. None of us wanted to think about why we were there, so we mostly occupied the passing minutes with the idle talk of basketball and history class. The oncologist finally graced us with his presence as he walked into our crowded room. He introduced himself and started discussing what we already knew from the scans. Tim had a tumor invading his brain stem. He went on to say that it was inoperable, which meant very little to me at the time. As he went into medical jargon, his words became mere background noise as I turned my attention toward Tim.

He sat in the chair directly across from me, listening to every word the doctor was saying. He was motionless; even his eyes seemed to be staring into a place that had somehow captured his whole being. Tim hated his eyes. He often joked about their "ugly" tint, which he called green-brown-yellow-orangish. I always had to remind him that despite their lack of definite color, his eyes were one of his best features. They disclosed his every emotion. All I had to do was look at them and I could actually see his love for me. His eyes revealed his kindness, his cocky and somewhat rebellious nature, and, of course, his spark of determination. Now they were vacant.

Ann, Tim's mother, asked a question, and I was thrown back into the conversation at hand. Dr. So-and-So answered by discussing the options that could be attempted to shrink the tumor. I wondered why none of his so-called options sounded promising. As this thought meandered through my mind, his mother, with a voice that attempted to hide the quivering, asked how long Tim was expected to live. Her words snuck up from behind me and grabbed my throat. I looked at her as though she was a murderer with no conscience. How could she ask such a question? Tim was not going to die, and she had no right to even suggest that he might. In a detached voice void of all emotion the doctor said, "One year to eighteen months with treatment."

As he spoke these words, the grip around my neck tightened to the point of choking me. I struggled for a breath, and the already tiny room closed even more. I needed space, and the first thought that crossed my mind was to run, not only from the room, but from the whole situation. I could escape now before I got hurt. I was confused and angry, but most of all I was consumed by the incredible fear of losing someone I loved so much.

I looked at Tim who sat motionless; he didn't say anything and neither did anyone else. The room was filled with an uncomfortable silence, and I could feel the pulse of my heart pounding in my ears. I was sure that everyone could hear me sucking in each breath. I don't remember what the doctor said before he left the room—I couldn't even look at this man who had just sentenced Tim to death. When we were alone, Ann crossed the room and gave Tim a hug. The rest of us sat and cried. Tim looked up and with a smile said, "I'm not going anywhere." It was his declaration of war.

I was nervous, and I didn't know what I should do. I was just the girlfriend; I didn't know if I had any business being a part of this ordeal. As I was thinking that this was a time their family should be alone, Ann left Tim's side and he motioned for me to come over. I sat down on his knee and, wrapping my arms around his neck, rested my forehead against his. When I opened my eyes they met his, and I saw the emotion in them that had been missing up to that point. Water welled up on the brim of his lids, and finally a single tear fell, gliding down his cheek in slow motion.

Tim had always had the fighter attitude, and I believed him completely when he said he was going to beat the odds that were stacked against him. The battle was on. He was going to do everything he could in order to conquer the cancer threatening to overtake the life that he wasn't done living. His life became a quest to find a physical cure. He viewed it as a challenge he needed to overcome, and there was no doubt in his mind that he would do it.

His battle was viewed as courageous; he became a local hero. Why is it that people with terminal illness are so respected for fighting for a cure until the end? Do they even have a choice? The focus always lies in finding a physical remedy. Do everything and anything you can to battle the disease. What have you got to lose? Don't give up. Rarely do you find people looking for a type of healing that restores the soul. I guess that's just not good enough. Death meant failure, and that was unacceptable. So along with everything else, I encouraged Tim to stay strong and fight. I wanted him to do whatever he could to beat the cancer. I didn't realize that it didn't have to be a war. Nobody had to be the loser. I wish I would have known that then.

He was bombarded by alternative healing options, some more "far out" than others, but all promising a miraculous cure. There was no way he could try all of them. Tim choked down over seventy pills a day: shark cartilage, herbal remedies, beta this and turbo that, each one offering a way to fight his growing tumor. He forced himself to drink glass after glass of carrot juice despite the thick texture, pungent odor and lingering aftertaste. He tried some positive-imagery techniques and then there was that magnetic contraption. The list goes on.

The traditional medical world was also involved in the battle, despite their lack of confidence in a cure. Surgery was out of the question because of the tumor's location, so the doctors suggested other treatment options. The Duke University brain-tumor team provided a protocol that involved heavy doses of radiation therapy, shooting directly at the base of his brain stem two times a day for several months. The tumor shrunk by half, but it wasn't annihilated; in fact, it was fighting back. Eventually chemotherapy, a word that had quickly became as taboo as profanity in church, was attempted as a last resort. It didn't work.

I was included in Tim's battle against cancer in almost every way possible, and the Orth family always made me feel welcome. I went where Tim went. I don't know if his parents always approved (or mine for that matter), but as long as it kept Tim happy, they didn't complain. I went along on all the hospital visits. I went on family trips. I spent more time at their house than I should admit, but it was worth it. I rapidly evolved from my "just a girlfriend" status to member of their clan. I loved them, and still do.

Tim's health declined rapidly during the last months of his life. His former physique was reduced to a loose layer of skin covering his skeleton. It was difficult to keep him comfortable, and he spent most of his days hunched on the reclining sofa in his living room. I spent most of my days in the seat beside him watching him sleep. Sometimes the selfishness in me would overpower my good sense, and I would wake him from a peaceful sleep so that I could talk to him.

In a matter of months I watched my boyfriend turn into an eighty-year-old man. He went blind, he couldn't walk, he couldn't remember, but he could still laugh. I

experienced a crash course in Nursing 101, quickly learning all of the details involved in caring for someone who
is terminally ill. However, I soon realized that my most
important "job responsibility" was to keep a smile on
Tim's face. It's difficult to maintain dignity when you can't
do anything for yourself. He had to cope with issues of
aging as a teenager. He was nineteen years old and had to
deal with the fact that his girlfriend had to help him go to
the bathroom. I cracked jokes and teased him about silly
things to lighten his mood. I basically treated him like I
always had; I was the person who didn't minister to him
like he was dying. I made him laugh. It was the only thing
I could do to help in a seemingly helpless situation, but it
wasn't enough. I wanted to help him be at peace, even
though I wasn't. One day after waking up from a regular
afternoon nap, I noticed that Tim's eyes were focused in a
dreamlike manner on something in the upper-right corner of the living room. He was mesmerized by what he
was seeing, and the slight grin across his face suggested it
was something awesome. It took me a few seconds to
remember that Tim was blind because the tumor was
slowly overtaking the optic nerve's space in his brain. I
wondered what he could be looking at.

"Tim, what are you staring at?" I asked, though I wasn't
sure I was ready to hear his answer.

"Just the light up there," he replied, continuing to stare
ahead. The tears raced to my eyes, but I blinked to keep
them from falling. I knew in my heart what he was seeing,
but I wasn't satisfied with his vague answer. I wanted
more.

"I can't see it. What is it like?" I asked.

"It's beautiful. You're not supposed to see it, though."

"Tell me about it," I probed with a combination of curiosity and fear. Tim didn't take his eyes off the spot in the
corner of the room. He had several false starts before he

was finally able to form the words he was searching for.

"I'm going up there . . . soon." The tears that had been welling in my eyes up to that point were released like floodgates. For the first time, I was grateful for Tim's blindness; I didn't want him to see me cry. I cleared my throat, in an attempt to get rid of the lump that had formed there, and took a deep breath, letting it out slowly to help me relax. This might be my last opportunity to talk to Tim about facing death, and I wasn't going to allow my emotions to let it slip away. I had so much I needed to tell him, for my own sake and for his. I wanted Tim to experience a peaceful death, and I did not want to be the one who was holding him back. I told him he could leave whenever he was ready. I explained that I would be okay after he left.

"I love you so much," I said, "and I am going to miss you more than you could possibly imagine. It will be so hard to live the rest of my life without you here, but I know that one day I'll see you again." Tim's attention was finally diverted from the heavenly focus. He reached over and held his hand out for me to hold. A smirk took over the peaceful expression that had been occupying his face and he let out a weak chuckle.

"That part is up to you," he said, completely amused with his insinuation that I had better be good while he was gone if I wanted to join him in eternity. He could never pass up a good smart remark. I laughed and cried. I felt a sense of relief. There was no way I could have said everything that needed to be said, and of course, everything didn't come out the way I intended it to. However, Tim and I were able to share an experience that offered us both a sense of closure. It was the closest to heaven that I have been in my lifetime, and I'll never forget it.

I left Tim's house on February 13 feeling disheartened. I always got a kiss from Tim before leaving; it was a custom I'd grown used to. He would sit with his eyes closed and his lips puckered, waiting for me to bend down and say good night. Tonight things were different. Tim had slipped into a comalike state and was still incoherent as I prepared to leave. I bent down to kiss him good-bye, and his labored breathing was magnified. My lips touched his, and all hope for a response was lost. As I put on my coat and boots, I remembered that the next day was Valentine's Day. I had told him earlier that the best gift he could give me was for him to be at peace. As I closed the front door behind me, I wondered if he heard.

With a bunch of red and white balloons in hand, I entered the Orths' house the next morning. I knew he wouldn't be able to see the gift I'd brought, but I needed to bring something. Tim was lying lifeless in his high-tech hospice bed, but I could see his chest moving as he took each breath, and was relieved that he hadn't gone without me by his side. I spent the morning curled up next to him in his bed, holding his hand. Around 12:30, Tim took his last breaths. I don't recall the exact moment he died; I only remember opening my eyes and he was gone. His mother proclaimed, "Oh, Tim, no more seizures, no more headaches. Now you can see. Now you can laugh. Now you can run. Now you can fly! We love you!"

I didn't have any profound words; I'm not good with good-byes. I whispered, "See ya later."

Although Tim's life on earth ended on February 14, 1997, he continues to live on in so many other ways. Tim helped me to be the person that I am today. He taught me that the most important part of living is to find happiness in everything. I look back on all the memorable moments we shared together, and I recall his immortality. I remember all the fishless fishing trips. I remember eating popcorn and playing endless games of cribbage at my kitchen table. I remember cringing every time a song by Prince came on the radio because I knew he would sing along. I remember keeping my parents up all night with our outbursts of laughter, and I remember falling asleep on the couch listening to his heartbeat.

I know I will experience love again, but I will never find a replacement for what I had. Instead, I will take Tim with me as I continue to live my life. He will be with me when I graduate from college. He will be with me when my father walks me down the aisle at my wedding. He will be with me when I teach my first child to throw a softball. Eventually we will be together again when it's my time to leave this Earth.

*Jodi Vesterby*

# Getting the Most Out of Life

*I have gone through many difficult experiences in my life, barely squeezing around the obstacles in my way. But with those challenges came a great deal of learning. If I had to go back and do it all over again, I would not change a single thing. What I have come to learn is too valuable.*

Marissa Angel

Dear Authors of *Chicken Soup for the Teenage Soul,*

I love your books! They are so wonderful!

When I started the first *Teenage Soul,* I was going through a really hard, depressing time, and suicide had popped into my head more than once. I read the stories about teenagers who had committed suicide, or attempted suicide, and they really made me think. I realized how incredibly stupid it would be for me to end my life for my own selfish reasons, just so I didn't have to face my problems and reality. I would have hurt so many people who love me. I thank you from the bottom of my heart for making me wake up and face my reality.

I'm fifteen years old, and I have cystic fibrosis. It's not contagious—I was born with it. This disease affects the lungs, the respiratory system and the digestive tract. I have been in the hospital several times, and it can be a lonely feeling. A part of me has felt alone all my life because of this disease. Sometimes my friends say, "Oh, I understand," but they don't really. No matter how hard they try, or how hard they want to, they can't understand what it's like to live with a life-threatening disease. I'm lucky, though: On the outside you can't tell anything is wrong with me. Some people with this disease aren't as lucky because they can look anorexic. Some die young, in their twenties. I am a very healthy cystic-fibrosis kid. Sometimes I even forget I have it, but other times I can't help but be reminded.

During one of my first stays in the hospital, I made friends with a girl my age who had cancer. I remember her shiny bald white head in contrast to her bright blue hospital gown. We played together all the time, racing down the hospital corridors on our IV poles, kinda like scooters. The nurses would just laugh and let us have fun. I can't remember exactly why, but she went away and we didn't see each other anymore.

Later, I was moved to a different room. I shared it with another CF girl, Kate, who was sicker than I was. Even though I was in the hospital, the time we spent together was one of the best times of my life. It was cool just to have someone like me with the same illness. We would take our medicine together and have therapy together. She taught me how to blow smoke rings out of my nebulizer. We spent an endless amount of hours just talking and hanging out with one another. Our friendship was special. My health eventually improved, and I was able to go home. Kate was not so fortunate. She had to remain in the hospital. I lost contact with her after I left the hospital.

The following summer I found out she had died. I was so sad not knowing how she died—or if she died alone. The whole time I was in the hospital I never really saw anyone come visit her, maybe a telephone call once in a while but that was it. She was only fourteen when she died. When I think about it sometimes it scares me to know that she died at fourteen and I am now fifteen. I get this lonely feeling that sometimes smothers me. None of my friends have to think about or wonder if they will live to see their sixteenth birthday. I do, almost every day. I think about Kate and the fact that she will never get to drive or freak out over SATs. She will never marry or have kids. I live in two worlds—one of which is very lonely and scary. But no matter how lonely or scary it may seem, I will survive. I've promised myself many times that I will live to see another day.

Today I enjoy playing soccer for my high-school team. I long jump and throw the javelin. I act, sing and dance. I love to read and write, and I live my life to the fullest. From reading your books, I have learned that it's possible to do anything you want to, and that everyone is made of "Tough Stuff."

Sincerely,
*Emily R. Monfort*

# Sharing an Intimate Moment

*Dear* Chicken Soup,

*I have lived in Southern California my whole life. I was never part of the popular crowd in high school. I never had the best grades or kept up on my who-is-dating-who gossip. The only things that interested me were hanging out with my friends and being on time for my horseback riding lessons. I didn't set foot in an airport until I was sixteen and had my first boyfriend when I was seventeen.*

*I have never had much luck with guys. I don't like the idea of breaking up over something dumb and crying for a week about how much he hurt me, so I usually end things early. Just before my eighteenth birthday, I met the most beautiful guy. He was really sweet to me so I thought maybe he would be different from other guys. I really let myself like him; I trusted him.*

*On my eighteenth birthday, I went to school because I had two tests to take, one of which I failed. My friends had brought me balloons, but the wind took the biggest and prettiest one. Then the rain began to pour down on me. My birthday was not going very well, and worst of all, when I went to my boyfriend's house he broke up with me!*

*For the next day, I stayed in my room until my mom offered to take me to lunch. She presented me with* Chicken Soup for the Teenage Soul. *Reading the stories made me feel so much better. Even though I didn't know the people who wrote the stories, I felt connected to them. They made me feel good inside.*

*I have written about something that happened to me at summer camp that I would like to share with others in hopes that they too can get something positive from it. I hope it makes at least someone feel better, like others have done for me.*

*Sincerely,*
*Emily Ferry*

## Camp Confidence

"Mike! Camp question," Reese declared. "Now, the camp question, for those of you who don't know, is: Out of all the counselors at Meadow Oaks summer camp, who would you get together with?"

Mike sat for a second contemplating his decision. "Well, I could take the easy way out and say Monica," he grinned, "but I am not going to do that." He paused again before saying, "I would have to say the horse girl, Emily."

Okay, this is where I have to back up a bit. See, my name happens to be Emily. The conversation taking place above happened at a Meadow Oaks summer camp campout. It was two weeks before the end of camp, and my friend Reese and I had decided to attend the campout. When the kids were all asleep, the counselors made their way to the arts and crafts building where we all sat in a big circle and played Truth or Dare . . . without the dare.

The people in the circle ranged in age from sixteen to their early twenties. This game made me feel as if I was back in high school, but it was fun to find out what people thought about everyone else at camp.

Since Reese and I worked in the area of horses we didn't see or hear much of what went on with the other counselors. Mike certainly never came down to see us. We attended camp parties and staff events and had gotten to know a lot of the counselors, but we were still pretty much out of the loop. I had had a crush on Mike all summer, but he was a part of the really popular clique and I deemed him untouchable since he could pretty much have anyone he wanted. But during the last week of camp he paid more attention to me than before. Reese insisted he liked me, but I paid it no mind. Well, the campout certainly changed my view. This is where I return to the previous conversation.

". . . the horse girl, Emily," Mike said.

I sat in the darkness not sure what to think. Mike had just picked me out of all the other girls at camp. I sat for a minute while Reese chimed in my ear with, "I told you so." A few minutes later, Mike stood up and told me to follow him. I asked where we were going, and he said to follow. I heard the quiet oohs from the people in the circle as I stood and followed him to the back of the arts and crafts building.

He stood in front of me for a minute and turned his toe in, smiling like a little boy. "I can't believe I told all those people I like you," he said. I smiled at the sight of his twenty-three-year-old shyness, but when I began to say something back he pulled me close and kissed me sweetly. Now, at nineteen I had received my share of kisses, but something about Mike's kiss was different. It seemed more sincere than any I had gotten in the past. I felt as if I would float away.

Mike left for a teaching job in San Diego two days later. I have seen him a few times, but nothing ever came of our night at the campout. Circumstance wouldn't allow for it. But ever since that night I have walked with my head a little higher and looked in the mirror at a face I finally see as pretty . . . all because I was picked by one seemingly unattainable boy.

*Emily Ferry*

# A Plea for All of Us

*Dear Kimberly,*

My parents have been foster parents for over ten years, but for about the past five years we've taken in mostly teenagers. Many are pregnant teens or unwed moms. It hasn't always been easy, but it's always been worth it, and I've learned a lot about people over the last several years. One of the things that has benefited me the most is learning to see where people are coming from. It's much easier to love someone, and much harder to get hurt, if you can understand the reasons that people act the way they do—whether it's fear, pain, or just plain not knowing any better. I wrote this poem from the perspective of my foster sisters, but I believe that, to some degree, all of us can relate. Very few people show all of their true selves, and everyone is crying out for someone to care enough to see past the outer shell to what's really there behind it. This is a plea to all of us from everyone around us who is hurting. Thanks, Kimberly.

*Sincerely,*
*Rachel Bentley*

## Stone by Stone

I have a wall you cannot see
Because it's deep inside of me.
It blocks my heart on every side
And helps emotions there to hide.
You can't reach in,
I can't reach out.
You wonder what it's all about.

The wall I built that you can't see
Results from insecurity.
Each time my tender heart was hurt
The scars within grew worse and worse.
So stone by stone
I built a wall
That's now so thick it will not fall.

Please understand that it's not you,
Continue trying to break through.
I want so much to show myself,
And love from you will really help.
So bit by bit
Chip at my wall,
Till stone by stone it starts to fall.

I know the process will be slow,
It's never easy to let go
Of hurts and failures long ingrained
Upon one's heart from years of pain.
I'm so afraid
To let you in.
I know I might get hurt again.

I try so hard to break the wall,
But seem to get nowhere at all.
For stone upon each stone I've stacked,
And left between them not a crack.
The only way
To make it fall
Is imperfections in the wall.

I did the best I could to build
A perfect wall, but there are still
A few small flaws, which are the key
To breaking through the wall, to me.
Please use each flaw
To cause a crack,
To knock a stone off of the stack.

For just as stone by stone was laid
With every hurt, with every pain;
So stone by stone the wall will break,
As love replaces every ache.
Please be the one
Who cares enough
To find the flaws, no matter what.

*Rachel Bentley*

# Life Is a Bumpy Road

Dear Kimberly,

*Chicken Soup for the Teenage Soul* was such a blessing for me. The quotes and stories really opened my eyes to all new perspectives in life. I am only twenty-three, and I have been incarcerated for seven years. This book has given me the courage to share my story with you.

When I was sixteen, I had my mind set on two things: having fun and being cool. One Saturday night, a friend and I knocked off from work at a local grocery store and could think of nothing better to do than ride around and get drunk. I never expected how drastically my life would change before that night ended.

After I was intoxicated, I came up with the "coolest" idea to show off in front of my older friend. "Hey man, let's go get my gun and find someone to scare by shooting at them." My friend didn't see anything wrong with the idea, so we went and got the gun. The alcohol, and now the gun, gave me all the "courage" I needed to show off. We finally passed a boy walking by himself along the road, and I just pointed the gun out of the window and started firing. He was fatally wounded and died right there on the side of the road.

I have now been paying for those actions for the past seven years as I sit in the Louisiana State Penitentiary serving a mandatory life sentence without parole. Like a lot of teens, I never worried about the consequences of my actions. I didn't care what happened tomorrow. I just wanted to have all the "fun" I could have today, but there was a price to pay. I'm afraid too many of us are making foolish decisions that come at such a high price, and we will never be able to clear ourselves of the consequences.

I am often asked what's the most important lesson I've learned, or what would I tell teens if I could only say one thing to them. It would be this: Life is a bumpy road with many regrets and very few second chances, so think before you act.

I have missed a lot of things in life. But reading all the stories in *Chicken Soup for the Teenage Soul* has taught me many things. I am thankful for the wonderful work y'all have done. Please keep up the awesome job. I can hardly wait for the new one to come out.

Thankfully yours,
*Gary LeRoux*

# The Violence Needs to Stop

Dear *Chicken Soup for the Teenage Soul,*

I am not going to start out this letter like most. I am writing for one reason and one reason only: to get my point across. I have held in so much for the past two years—so much frustration, so much pain and so much confusion. Nobody seems to care that teens today are dealing with so many tough issues in our communities and schools. I am a teen with strong opinions about the world we live in. I have ideas about the changes that need to be made, but I don't even know where to begin. I feel like I have no one to talk to about it all. No one seems to want to listen. So I'm not used to expressing myself. I've learned to stay quiet, and that hurts.

Two years ago, during the summer before ninth grade, I was attacked and beaten up by two girls I didn't even know. I was hanging out in my hometown with my boyfriend and some of my friends when these girls started verbally harassing us. Supposedly I "looked" at them wrong. Suddenly things escalated and they were yelling—and I was punched in the face over and over. It all happened so fast and I don't remember much, but I do remember looking at my friends and my boyfriend while I was being punched. They just stood there and didn't do a thing. These girls were tough and powerful in our high school, so my friends must have been scared. I hit the ground and blacked out. When I woke up I was in so much pain it was overwhelming. I had bruises all over me, and I couldn't move my jaw. I couldn't understand how this could have happened to me.

I had always led a relatively easy life. Until that day, violence or hatred did not even exist in my world. But I now know that they exist everywhere—and their long-term effects are powerful.

After the attack, I became depressed and cried all the time. All I wanted to do was stay in my room where I was safe. Ninth grade was painful. I felt like I had been stabbed in the back by most of my friends. Whenever I saw them at school, they just looked away. Fortunately, my best friend, Michelle, was there for me and helped me to get back on my feet in more ways than one.

I started to notice the problems all around me. I became sensitive to the remarks of others and started to notice that certain kids at my school were continually picked on and harassed by older, more powerful kids. Fights broke out all the time, and it seemed like there were certain kids who would wait for any excuse to beat somebody up. The verbal harassment was brutal. Nobody was safe from the taunting and teasing. We even had police officers at our school, but their presence did little good. They seemed to be more interested in chatting with the teachers than patrolling the hallways, where all the trouble was going on.

I started to dread going to school. My grades dropped dramatically. I couldn't talk to anyone about what I was experiencing so I became more and more quiet. My parents and I finally talked about what I should do, and we all decided that changing schools would be the best thing for me. We decided that I would attend an alternative, independent-study program.

That decision seemed to jumpstart something inside of me. By this point, I was sick and tired of feeling depressed all the time. So I made a decision. I decided to get well. I wanted to be whole again, to experience my life to the fullest. And to be joyful. I tried to make the most of what was left of my freshman year by meeting people and reaching out. My success in making new friends gave me more energy and helped me to stop crying and start laughing and smiling once again.

Now that I am a junior in high school, I have spent a lot of time thinking about my experience and what changes need to be made to make the world a safer place for children. Ending violence in our schools is something that is extremely close to my heart, for obvious reasons, and something that I am very committed to in my lifetime. It's not fair that people have to walk home from school and be afraid for their lives. It's not fair that young teens go to school feeling scared inside and feeling like they need to "watch their back" because their peers make them feel like they're two inches tall and don't amount to anything. It's not fair that teens are afraid to speak their mind for fear that others might get mad and try to "throw down" and pick a fight. The truth is, teen violence is everywhere, and kids don't feel safe even in my small town.

I have a lot more time on my hands than the average teen since I am in an independent-study program, so I have spent the last year writing letters to people who might be able to help—congresspeople, community leaders, teachers and now you. I am trying to get the word out to as many people as possible that things need to change—and they *can* change. It is possible. We all need to stand up and do something about it. Teens need role models, more counselors, conflict resolution skills and anger management classes. How hard would it be to take just an hour every other day to work on these issues in the schools? Kids need to come together and learn how to get along and try to make amends. We need a place where we can talk freely about our life, how our day is going, about our families and our friends, and about our feelings and emotions. We need help in coping with all our feelings and our fears. We need peer communication skills classes in our schools. We need community centers where teens can get together and help each other out. We need adults who can teach us how to help each other and teach us how to take a stand against violence and hatred.

Coincidentally, I happened to be watching UPN today and a show called *Teen Files* came on. It was about teen violence and was hosted by Leeza Gibbons. The show made an incredibly positive impression on me. I would do anything to be able to meet those courageous teens, to thank them for opening my eyes even further to the problem and for helping me to see ways to begin solving the problem. The solution is kindness. These teens are committed to leading a life of kindness and service to each other after all they have been through and seen. And that is what matters most—that we learn to treat each other with kindness and respect.

Two years ago I was brutally beaten by girls who didn't stop to think about the emotional and physical pain they were causing. I was left to feel hurt and alone. I am now committed to preventing my experience from happening to other teens. I am going to work to make all of our lives better, and I am starting with this letter. I want to make a difference, and I need help. Please help me to get my message out to other teens so that we may all begin to work together for safe streets and safe schools. Help me to be heard.

Sincerely,
*Ashley Sims*

[EDITORS' NOTE: *If you also want to make a difference in your community and work toward safer streets and schools, here are some resources that we have found to be both useful and inspiring:*

Be a Global Force of One! 202 Common Sense, Portable and Human Ways to Restore Our Communities, Our Schools and Ourselves. *John T. Boal, PacRim Publishing, March 1998.*

Can Students End School Violence? Solutions from America's Youth. *Jason Ryan Dorsey, Archstone Press, LLC, November 1999.*]

# Cotton Candy

*When you're young you're told to be more responsible and act mature. If I knew being mature meant realizing all the hardships both in the world and in my life, I would have stayed three years old.*

Claudia Cicciarella

Dear *Chicken Soup for the Teenage Soul,*

I was only eight years old when I was forced to grow up. My childhood dreams quickly became adolescent responsibilities. In September of 1991 I realized that the world is full of suffering, and it took me seven years to realize that it is also full of overcoming it.

My parents had separated that year. My sisters and I spent the first few months after the separation with my mom at her friend's house. Eventually we settled into a condominium of our own. We lived with my mom during the week and my dad on the weekends. Fridays were so hard. It was always so difficult to say good-bye to my mom. I could see the pain and anger in her eyes each time we would leave. My heart would ache tremendously. It always seemed like she looked at me as if it was the last time she would ever lay eyes on me. That made me even sadder.

One weekend, I decided not to say good-bye; I guess I was just trying to spare myself the pain. I got in the car with my father and we left, but as we were pulling away, I caught her sorrowful eyes as she watched us drive out of her life.

That weekend, my dad took us to a carnival at our synagogue. He seemed to be acting kind of strange, but we just tried to enjoy ourselves anyway. My dad was strict when it came to eating sugar, but on this day he let us eat cotton candy. I remember being flawlessly happy at that moment and my sisters' faces smiling at me with big bites of pink cotton in their mouths and joy in their eyes. Unfortunately, the happiness ended when we got home. My father sat us all down in the family room. As he spoke, his voice quivered in an obvious attempt to contain some unimaginable pain. He told us to always remember how happy we were that day and to never lose that. He then told us that our mother had committed suicide that morning.

The unbearable and intense pain I felt that day stayed with me for several years, and as the sorrow turned to anger, I learned to hate. I was furious with the idea that my mother had abandoned us. We were left to go through the turmoil of adolescence alone and unguided, to raise ourselves. From this loss, I learned not to trust anyone, for no one stays around forever. I constantly tested my friends' loyalty by pushing them away to see if they would come back. In the end, I always ended up alone. I hated everyone for leaving me—my friends, my mother, and even God. I was too bitter and too empty to realize that life can go on, but somewhere in the hollowness of my heart I finally found the strength to move forward. Heart Warrior Chosa once said, "In the darkest hour the soul is replenished and given strength to continue and endure."

I was touched by Jack Cavanaugh's story, "I'll Be Back,"* in *Chicken Soup for the Teenage Soul* about a boy who had lost his leg in a car accident. The boy, who was once the starting center on his high-school varsity basketball team, was hospitalized, had three operations, and ended up getting a prosthetic leg. He kept his spirits up and shunned anyone who told him that he would never play again. With determination, he did play basketball again. He wasn't bitter or angry, and he never pitied himself. He thanked God for saving his life, rather than hating God for taking his leg.

That's when I realized that I have everything it takes to overcome my anger and loneliness. God gives every soul the strength to endure; what was blinding me was my negative frame of mind. I now believe that anyone who experiences the kind of pain I did is also given the potential to overcome it. Seven years ago my mother died, and it is only recently that I have been able to overcome my anger, and trust my family, my friends and God once again. One day I hope to again feel as happy as I was with my first taste of cotton candy.

Thanks so much,
*Michelle Sander*

---

*"I'll Be Back," by Jack Cavanaugh, Chicken Soup for the Teenage Soul, pp. 279–286.*

# Bonding with Notebooks

*Today could be the day that my mom realizes I'm growing up and gives me some more responsibility.*

Jenny Gleason

Dear *Chicken Soup for the Teenage Soul,*

I have always been a real fan of your books and the important lessons of love and understanding that are shared in each of the stories. They have helped me to see things that were not so clear to me. I have received a great deal of comfort from reading many of the stories.

I had been going through some difficult times not so long ago dealing with the pressures of growing up and trying to communicate with my parents, particularly my mother. Our relationship had suffered because of this. When I would get frustrated or angry it seemed like we would end up in some sort of confrontation with each other and not talk about what we were really feeling. I feel like I have overcome those obstacles now, but not without a certain turn of events.

A while back I ran away from home so that I could be far enough away to vent my anger and release some of the pain bottled up inside of me. I stayed away for many hours, well into the night, before I finally decided to return home. When I walked through the front door of my house, I immediately saw all the pain, anger and disappointment on my parents' faces, especially my mother's. For days after the incident, my mom and I were on unfirm ground, to say the least. Everything we did or said was filled with tension until we both eventually snapped. We knew we desperately had to have a talk. We agreed to have breakfast together the next morning. That morning will remain etched in my memory forever. It was a turning point in both of our lives and our relationship.

We decided to go to a local café. On our way to the table I noticed that my mother had two notebooks and some pens. I asked her what they were for. She explained to me that sometimes it is easier to write down our feelings rather than try to talk about them. She then proceeded to hand me a notebook of my own and she kept one for herself. The "rules" for that talk were that she would pick a topic, and we would write down our feelings about the topic in the form of a letter. It could be as long or as short as we wanted. Our first topic was: "Why I am so angry." I had written a half page worth of stuff, and my mom filled up nearly three pages. I watched tears stream down her face as she wrote. I never realized anyone could hide so much anger and frustration. It could have been that I never paid much attention, either. Sometimes we think we are the only ones with problems, but I was reminded that morning that other people can be hurting just as much.

After she was finished writing we exchanged our notebooks and read what the other had written. As soon as I started reading my mother's words, I began to cry and so did she. When we were finished reading we discussed our feelings. Amazingly enough, it felt like all the anger I had welled up inside of me drained from my body. Our talk helped me realize so many things I had never thought of before, not only about my mother but about other people as well.

My mother and I continue to use our notebooks as a means of communicating our anger and frustrations, and our happiness also. We know that no matter how we feel about each other, our notebooks are a safe place to express it. We have made a pact that at the end of each letter we write, "I love you." Here are two of our more recent entries:

*Dear Mom,*

*I just wanted you to know that some things I do are not meant to hurt or spite you. When I yell at you it's not because I hate you. And when I tell you I hate you, you should know that I really don't, although at times I feel like you hate me. Sometimes you just make me really mad and frustrated, and I don't know what to do with it. Like when you tell me you don't believe me even though I'm not lying, or when you do things that invade my privacy without my permission that you know I won't like. For instance, the other day you searched my room without me knowing or being there. I just wanted to hate you so much then. Then today you yelled at me, and it made me so mad. I really don't think there is much more to say right now. I love you.*

*Katie*

And my mother's response to my letter:

*Dear Katie,*

*I realize that you get mad and frustrated, but I do, too. I don't want you to think that since I am an adult I don't have feelings. As much as you think that I might like it, I don't like yelling at you. I just wish you would help out a little more with the family and around the house. It would make things easier on me. Some things I do, like searching your room or not believing you, are not done to be mean. I only do those things if I have good cause. Sometimes you worry me, but it's just because I care. Although you might not think so, you yell at me as much as I yell at you. It hurts my feelings as well. Sometimes I just want to cry. I'm glad you told me how you felt about all those things. I'll try to work on my temper with you, and I'll try to be more patient if you will return the same courtesy to me and help me out a little around the house. If this is not okay, tell me and we can try to work something out. I love you.*

*Mom*

We gained a special gift that day at the restaurant and we continue to be blessed with each other's everlasting love and patience. I am now a firm believer that we all need to express our feelings in order to live healthy lives. Thank you so much for letting me share this with you.

Sincerely,
*Katie Benson*

# Never Count Me Out

*I understand I am not perfect and life won't always wait for me. I say "life is what I make it!" I dream of tomorrow, not of yesterday. I try to be successful and bold and brave. I hope tomorrow creates a new foundation because I am young and making my own roads.*

Deanna Seay

Dear *Chicken Soup for the Teenage Soul,*

I am writing to thank you for your books. They have given me the confidence to overcome any obstacle—and I have faced a lot of them. My mom tells me I am the kind of person who has always had plenty of challenges, and when I didn't encounter enough I could be counted on to create some of my own.

My first challenge was not self-chosen, however. I was born with my umbilical cord wrapped around my neck. I wasn't breathing. After the doctors were able to resuscitate me, they discovered that something else was wrong. My right leg was twice the size of my left one, with barely any muscle tissue. They assured my mother that it was not too serious and that it would eventually work itself out and grow to the size of a "normal" leg. Unfortunately, it never did.

When I was in sixth grade, my family moved to Washington State. Adjusting to the move was difficult enough, yet suddenly I was experiencing back pain that wouldn't go away. I saw a doctor who took X rays and noticed something very uncommon. My spinal cord had attached to a piece of tissue that was pulling my back out of alignment. It would require surgery.

The surgery was agonizing. It was a complicated procedure, and I went through a lot of pain. The doctors found nerve endings that were damaged, and for some reason I lost the ability to urinate and had to be hooked up to a catheter. It was one of the most unpleasant experiences I have ever faced and one I never could have gotten through without the support of my family. They were always by my side.

After the surgery, I had to slowly regain mobility in my legs. The nurses and my mom would help me to slowly walk the halls until I could walk further and further every day. I was determined to grow strong once again. Finally, they sent me home.

I was told that I was going to need help walking for a while, but I wasn't about to just accept that as the final word. The first morning I woke up in my own bed, I decided I wasn't going to need anybody's help. I wanted to go downstairs and say good morning to my mom—on my own. I swung my legs to the side of my bed, and I fell to the floor. I pulled myself up and walked to the stairs, holding onto the walls for support. When I reached the stairs I told myself there was no going back. I held onto the railing and slowly walked down the steps, one at a time. Finally, I reached the bottom. When my mom saw me, she was so shocked and so proud that she started crying. It was in that moment that I decided I would never let my physical challenges get in the way of my accomplishments.

Much to my parents' chagrin, as my physical therapy sessions were coming to a close my football career was just getting started. I had always wanted to play football, but when I found myself all padded up for my first practice I was terrified. I almost quit. I made it through practice that day, though, and when I got home my dad had me watch the movie Rudy with him. It is about a guy who beats all the odds against him to become a star football player at the University of Notre Dame. That movie changed my life.

I'm now sixteen and have been playing for our high school team, despite my physical challenges and my size. I am only 5'3" and 125 pounds, so I'm not much of an offensive threat. My coach lets me play in the games, though, and I've had so much fun with my teammates. My hard work and determination has earned me their respect, and they've even taken to calling me "Rudy." My goal is to attend Notre Dame and play on their football team. I hope they call me "Rudy."

Your books with stories of triumph and busting through barriers have reinforced my determination to get the most out of my life. Thank you for showing me that we all have within us the power to achieve beyond our wildest imaginations.

Sincerely,
*Dan Mulhausen*

# More Chicken Soup?

Many of the letters, stories and poems that you have read in this book were submitted by readers like you who have read *Chicken Soup for the Teenage Soul* and the other *Chicken Soup for the Soul* books. In the future, we are planning to publish *Chicken Soup for the Teenage Soul IV, Chicken Soup for the Teenage Soul on Love and Relationships, Chicken Soup for the Teenage Boy's Soul* and *Chicken Soup for the Teenage Christian Soul*. We would love to have you contribute a story, poem or letter to one of these future books.

This may be a story you write yourself, or one you clip out of your school newspaper, local newspaper, church bulletin or a magazine. It might be something you read in a book or find on the Internet. It could also be a favorite poem, quotation or cartoon you have saved. Please also send along as much information as you know about where it came from.

Just send a copy of your stories or other pieces to us at this address:

**Chicken Soup for the Teenage Soul**
P.O. Box 936
Pacific Palisades, CA 90272
e-mail: *stories@iam4teens.com*
Web site: *www.iam4teens.com*

# Who Is Jack Canfield?

Jack Canfield is a bestselling author and one of America's leading experts in the development of human potential. He is both a dynamic and entertaining speaker and a highly sought-after trainer with a wonderful ability to inform and inspire audiences to open their hearts, love more openly and boldly pursue their dreams.

Jack spent his teenage years growing up in Martins Ferry, Ohio, and Wheeling, West Virginia, with his sister Kimberly (Kirberger) and his two brothers, Rick and Taylor. The whole family has spent most of their professional careers dedicated to educating, counseling and empowering teens. Jack admits to being shy and lacking self-confidence in high school, but through a lot of hard work he earned letters in three sports and graduated third in his class.

After graduating college, Jack taught high school in the inner city of Chicago and in Iowa. In recent years, Jack has expanded this to include adults in both educational and corporate settings.

He is the author and narrator of several bestselling audio- and videocassette programs. He is a regularly consulted expert for radio and television broadcasts and has published numerous books—all bestsellers within their categories—including more than twenty *Chicken Soup for the Soul* books, *The Aladdin Factor, Heart at Work, 100 Ways to Build Self-Concept in the Classroom* and *Dare to Win.*

Jack addresses over one hundred groups each year. His clients include professional associations, school districts, government agencies, churches and corporations in all fifty states.

Jack conducts an annual eight-day Training of Trainers program in the areas of building self-esteem and achieving peak performance. It attracts educators, counselors, parenting trainers, corporate trainers, professional speakers, ministers and others interested in developing their speaking and seminar-leading skills in these areas.

For further information about Jack's books, tapes and trainings, or to schedule him for a presentation, please contact:

**The Canfield Training Group**
P.O. Box 30880 • Santa Barbara, CA 93130
phone: 800-237-8336 • fax: 805-563-2945
e-mail: *speaking@canfieldgroup.com*
Web site: *www.chickensoup.com*

# Who Is Mark Victor Hansen?

Mark Victor Hansen is a professional speaker who, in the last twenty years, has made over four thousand presentations to more than two million people in thirty-three countries. His presentations cover sales excellence and strategies; personal empowerment and development; and how to triple your income and double your time off.

Mark has spent a lifetime dedicated to his mission of making a profound and positive difference in people's lives. Throughout his career, he has inspired hundreds of thousands of people to create a more powerful and purposeful future for themselves while stimulating the sale of billions of dollars worth of goods and services.

Mark is a prolific writer and has authored *Future Diary*, *How to Achieve Total Prosperity* and *The Miracle of Tithing*. He is the coauthor of the *Chicken Soup for the Soul* series, *Dare to Win* and *The Aladdin Factor* (all with Jack Canfield) and *The Master Motivator* (with Joe Batten).

Mark has also produced a complete library of personal empowerment audio- and videocassette programs that have enabled his listeners to recognize and better use their innate abilities in their business and personal lives. His message has made him a popular television and radio personality with appearances on ABC, NBC, CBS, HBO, PBS, QVC and CNN.

He has also appeared on the cover of numerous magazines, including *Success, Entrepreneur* and *Changes*.

Mark is a big man with a heart and a spirit to match— an inspiration to all who seek to better themselves.

For further information about Mark, please contact:

**Mark Victor Hansen & Associates**
P.O. Box 7665
Newport Beach, CA 92658
phone: 949-759-9304 or 800-433-2314
fax: 949-722-6912
Web site: *www.chickensoup.com*

# Who Is Kimberly Kirberger?

Kimberly is an advocate for teens, a writer for teens, a mother of a teen, and a friend and confidante to the many teens in her life. She is committed to bettering the lives of teens around the globe through her books and the outreach she does for teens on behalf of her organization, Inspiration and Motivation for Teens, Inc.

Kim's love for teens was first expressed globally with the publication of the bestselling *Chicken Soup for the Teenage Soul*. This book was a true labor of love for Kim, and the result of years of friendship and research with teens from whom she learned what really matters. After the success of the first *Teenage Soul* book, and the outpouring of hundreds and thousands of letters and submissions from teens around the world, Kim went on to coauthor the *New York Times* #1 bestsellers *Chicken Soup for the Teenage Soul II* and *Chicken Soup for the Teenage Soul III*, *Chicken Soup for the Teenage Soul Journal*, *Chicken Soup for the Teenage Soul Letters* and *Chicken Soup for the College Soul*. Kim's empathic understanding of the issues affecting parents led her to coauthor the recent release *Chicken Soup for the Parent's Soul*.

In October 1999, the first book in Kim's *Teen Love* series was released. *Teen Love: On Relationships* has since become a *New York Times* bestseller. Her friendship and collaboration with Colin Mortensen of MTV's *Real World Hawaii* produced the much-loved *Teen Love: A Journal on Relationships* and *Teen Love: On Friendship*. She recently released *Teen Love: A Journal on Friendship*.

Her nonprofit organization, Soup and Support for Teachers, is committed to teens and teachers having available to them inspiring and supportive reading materials.

When she is not reading letters she gets from teens, Kim is offering them support and encouragement in the forums on her Web site, *www.iam4teens.com*. She also enjoys nurturing her family, listening to her son's band and hanging out with her friends.

For information or to schedule Kim for a presentation, contact:

**I.A.M. 4 Teens, Inc.**
P.O. Box 936
Pacific Palisades, CA 90272
e-mail for stories: *stories@iam4teens.com*
e-mail for letters and feedback: *kim@iam4teens.com*
Web site: *www.iam4teens.com*

# Contributors

Some of the stories in this book were taken from previously published sources, such as books and magazines. These sources are acknowledged in the permissions section.

Most of the stories were contributed by readers of our previous *Chicken Soup for the Soul* books who responded to our requests for stories. If you would like to contact the, you can reach them at their e-mail addresses provided below.

**Liz Alarie** passed away since submitting her story at the age of fourteen. Her family, which includes her mom and dad, one sister and two brothers, reside in Petersburg, Ontario, Canada. They can be reached at RR#2, Petersburg, ON., Canada, N0B 2H0 or via e-mail at *ralarie@continuum.org*.

**Kif Anderson** is establishing a reputation as a unique speaker who blends magic, motivation and merriment to lift his audiences to new heights of inspiration. He writes a monthly column for the on-line magazine *Lighten Up! America* and is an author of many works on magic. Kif is presently working on his first major book, titled *Reaching Beyond Perceived Realities*. In 1991 he was honored with the distinguished Comedy Magician of the Year Award. Kif can be reached at P.O. Box 577, Cypress, CA 90630, by e-mail at magicalmotivator @the mall.net, or by calling 562-272-7363.

**Sarah Barnett** is a student and freelance writer in Ft. Worth, Texas. She has written many poems and other works for various publications including The National Library of Poetry and the Iliad Press. Her story was told to continually remind herself and others that such a simple thing, brought on by a simple person, can conquer so much. There are no limits. She can be reached via e-mail at *Duchess305@aol.com*.

**Katie Benson** is a student at Central High School in Little Rock, Arkansas. She likes to play soccer, snow ski and spend time with her friends. Katie can be reached by e-mail at *Katrisha@hotmail.com*.

**Rachel Bentley** is one of eight adopted/permanent foster/birth sisters. She has spent over fifteen years helping her family minister to over forty foster kids, primarily troubled teen girls. Now in her twenties and married, Rachel still ministers to teenagers and is very outspoken on pro-family issues. She is also very involved in music and enjoys her eleven (so far!) nieces and nephews. She can be reached at *a2jc4life@yahoo.com*.

**Sarah Bercot** is currently a freshman in high school in Indiana. She has had poems published in three different compilation volumes and a cartoon published in *All About You*. Her recent letter to the magazine's editor sparked a local television appearance. Her passions include drawing, painting, writing and reading.

**Shashi Bhat** is fourteen years old and a student from Ontario, Canada. She enjoys writing, reading and both playing and listening to music. Shashi has had her stories and essays published in various newsletters.

**Laura Bloor** is a student in high school in Ohio. Her hobbies include playing tennis, piano, writing, listening to music and being an active participant in many school clubs. Her future aspirations include writing for *Rolling Stone* or aiding in communications for MTV Network. Her story is dedicated to Colleen, whom she hopes never gives up on such an emotionally and mentally challenging disease. She can be reached via e-mail at *LoBlo311@aol.com*.

**Jason Bocarro** is currently pursuing his doctorate at Texas A&M University. Originally from London, England, Jason has spent the last five years working with troubled youths in Nova Scotia, New Hampshire and Texas. He is the coauthor of the monograph *Alternatives to Incarceration: Prevention or Treatment* and is currently working on a new book, *Humorous Stories Within Education*. He can be reached at 306 First St., College Station, TX 77840 or by calling 409-846-8207.

**Alicia M. Boxler** is an honor roll student. She is involved with her school marching band, church, youth group and Youth Alive. Alicia enjoys spending time with her boyfriend, friends, shopping, talking on the phone and going to concerts.

**Jennings Michael Burch** is an internationally recognized author and speaker. His autobiography, *They Cage the Animals at Night*, chronicles his childhood experiences living in orphanages and foster homes. He speaks to children and adults about family, values, kindness and honor. He strives to eliminate the ridicule of children by other children and succeeds. He can be reached at 2 Elm St., Chappaqua, NY 10514 or call by calling 914-238-3031.

**Martha Campbell** is a graduate of Washington University School of Fine Arts, and a former writer-designer for Hallmark Cards. Since she became a freelancer in 1973, she has had over two thousand cartoons published and has illustrated nineteen books. You can write her at P.O. Box 2538, Harrison, AR 72602 or call 870-741-5323.

**Dave Carpenter** has been a full-time cartoonist since 1981. His cartoons have appeared in a variety of publications, including *Reader's Digest, Barron's, Harvard Business Review*, the *Wall Street Journal*, the *Saturday Evening Post, Better Homes and Gardens, Good Housekeeping, Forbes, Woman's World*, as well as numerous other publications. Dave can be reached at P.O. Box 520, Emmetsburg, IA 50536.

**Vidhya Chandrasekaran** is a freshman in high school in Rockford, Illinois. She hopes to pursue a career in medicine. She has been writing short stories and poetry most of her life, and her various works have been published in books and local newspapers. Vidhya has also enjoyed playing the violin and dancing for a number of years and plans to continue. She can be reached via e-mail at *Vidhya85@aol.com.*

**Diana L. Chapman** has been a journalist for fourteen years, having worked at the *San Diego Union,* The Los Angeles Copley Newspapers and the *Los Angeles Times.* She specializes in human interest stories and is currently working on a book involving health issues, since she was diagnosed with multiple sclerosis in 1992. She has been married for nine years and has one son, Herbert "Ryan" Hart. She can be reached at P.O. Box 414, San Pedro, CA 90733 or call 310-548-1192.

**Dan Clark** is the international ambassador of the "Art of Being Alive." He has spoken to over 2 million people worldwide. Dan is an actor, songwriter, recording artist, video producer and award-winning athlete. He is the well-known author of seven books, including *Getting High—How to Really Do It, One Minute Messages, The Art of Being Alive* and *Puppies for Sale and Other Inspirational Tales.* He can be reached at P.O. Box 8689, Salt Lake City, UT 84108 or by calling 801-485-5755.

**David Coleman** is known nationwide as "The Dating Doctor." He received the 1997 National Lecture Entertainer of the Year from the National Association for Campus Activities and the 1996 and 1997 Reader's Choice Lecture Program of the Year from *Campus Activities* magazine. He was nominated for six straight years and is currently the number-one ranked entertainer in America by *Campus Activities* magazine. David received his bachelor's degree from Bowling Green State University, Ohio. He is the author of a self-syndicated column on relationships and a book entitled *101 Great Dates.* He is currently working on two more books: *Prescriptions from the Dating Doctor: Answers to the Most Common Relationship Questions* and *When the Heart Is Unavailable: Putting a Stop to Revolving Door Relationships* (with Richard Doyle). David can be reached at *www.dating-doctor.com* or by calling 513-583-8000. He is represented in the college market by Umbrella Productions, Inc. at 407-649-6448.

**Danielle Collier** is a freelance writer and published fiction writer. She has a B.A. from Columbia University and an M.F.A. from the Iowa Writers' Workshop. Her story is dedicated to her parents and brother. She can be reached at *booxbabe@yahoo.com.*

**David Cooney**'s cartoons and illustrations are published in a variety of magazines including *USA Weekend, American Legion, Mutual Funds* and the *Chronicle of Higher Education.* Through the scientific journals that feature his work, his cartoons are seen in over fifty countries. David's cartoons are also published in *The New Breed,* a cartoon feature distributed by King Features Syndicate. His cartoons run in numerous newspapers under the title *Twisted View.* David lives with his wife Marcia and two children in the small Pennsylvania town of Mifflinburg. His Web site is *www.davidcooney.com* and he can be reached via e-mail at *david@davidcooney.com.*

**Liz Correale** is a New Jersey native who currently attends college in New England. She is a psychology major with high hopes of a career in governmental intelligence. Liz attributes much of her inspiration to her deep faith and her mother's lively sense of humor. She remains happy by writing, running and guessing what color her sister's hair will be this week—fuchsia or royal blue?

**Cheryl Costello-Forshey** is a freelance writer, poet and songwriter who resides in Ohio. Her poem, "Making Sarah Cry," appears in *Chicken Soup for the Teenage Soul II* and *Stories for a Teen's Heart*. Cheryl's poetry can also be found in other *Chicken Soup* books: *A 4th Course, A 5th Portion* and *College Soul*, as well as the upcoming book, *Stories for a Faithful Heart*.

**Brad Dixon** was born when his mother was twenty-two years old. She later divorced his father who then left him and his sister. Their mother remarried and they were raised by a man named "My Dad." He was his best friend growing up and laid down a foundation for him and his sister surrounded by love. Brad has had a nice life and is still learning.

**Stacey Doerner** is seventeen years old and will be a member of the high-school graduating class of 2000. She enjoys playing soccer, running, spending time with her friends and family as well as reading and writing. She has been elected class treasurer the past three years and is a member of the NHS. Currently, she is looking forward to graduating and attending college.

**Elisa Donovan** first garnered the attention of filmgoers when she co-starred as the tippity, completely misguided slave-to-fashion, Amber, opposite Alicia Silverstone in the feature film *Clueless*. She also stars in the television series "Clueless" that airs on UPN. Next, Elisa will emerge in the Paramount feature *A Night at the Roxbury*, slated for release in October. Elisa was born in Poughkeepsie, New York, and raised on Northport, Long Island. Elisa began acting at the age of seven and became engrossed with New York theater. Some of her theater credits include *The Baby, Mad Love, Mad Forest, Dark Hours, Chamber Music* and *Treading the Boards*. Other credits in television and film include *Blossom, Encino Woman, Beverly Hills, 90210* and *Powder Burns*. Elisa currently resides in Los Angeles.

**Kristina Dulcey** goes to a Catholic high school and enjoys playing softball. She dreams of becoming a plastic surgeon so that she can help people whose external appearances do not conform with what society deems as acceptable. She would like to specialize in reconstructive surgery rather than cosmetic as she feels cosmetic is "superficial." "After all," she says, "it's what is on the inside that counts."

**C. S. Dweck** is the author of I.A.M. 4 Teen's "Little Voice" column. His writing has appeared in such publications as *MH-18 Magazine, Real Kids, Real Adventures #12* and *The Market Guide for Young Writers, 6th Edition*. He aspires and perspires to have his own book published. Reach him by e-mail at *dweck@ptdprolog.net*.

**Amanda Dykstra** has always wanted to be a writer. This is her first published poem. She can be reached at *Minerva382@aol.com.*

**Danielle Eberschlag** is an OAC graduate and will be entering the University of Toronto. She enjoys writing poetry, short nonfiction stories and formal essays during her spare time. She can be reached via e-mail at *tayskiss_scottslove@themoffatts.com* or *hansonlives@hotmail.com.*

**Dale** and **Dar Emme** started the Yellow Ribbon Suicide Prevention Program after losing their youngest son, Mike, seventeen, to suicide in 1994 and are dedicated to saving lives. They are in high demand giving presentations, workshops and in-services to youth, parents, teachers, staff, churches and communities across America and internationally.

**Emily Ferry** is a nineteen-year-old college student at Moorpark Junior College. She plans to transfer to CSUN to get her B.A. in Child Psychology. In her spare time she wants to write, sing for her brother's band, run her own restaurant and start a horseback-riding school. Although all of these might seem like a far-off, impossible fantasy she plans to try to do them all and hopes that a few of them will happen.

**Alison Mary Forbes** is a sixteen-year-old high-school junior. She plans to pursue a long-awaited theater degree in college. Much thanks to the wonderful Barry Weber for submitting her poem when she was too chicken to do it herself! Alison can be reached at P.O. Box 26353, Wauwatosa, WI 53226.

**Kelly Garnett** is currently a sophomore, majoring in Elementary Education at Oakland University in Michigan. She would like to thank her family and friends that have always been an inspiration—and true "chicken soup" for her soul.

**Marc Gaudioso** is an aspiring screenwriter in Hollywood, California. He has a B.A. in English with an emphasis in creative writing from the University of Southern California, where he wrote a number of short stories. He can be reached via e-mail at *slvrscrn76@aol.com.*

**Zan Gaudioso** is a freelance writer whose stories have appeared in newspapers across the country. Zan earned her degree in special education for the deaf and went on to teach sign language, as well as teaching deaf children and adults. She became part of a landmark program that was the first to utilize sign language in order to foster verbal language skills in autistic children. From there, with additional training, she went on to become a surgical nurse. With writing as an integral driving force in her life, she continued to write and be published in newspapers and in family medical journals. She currently lives with her fiancé and their dog, Delilah, in Pacific Palisades, California. She can be reached via e-mail at *justzan@usa.net.*

**Lia Gay** is eighteen and is leaving in the fall to start college at the University of Kansas, where she will major in journalism. Lia is a talented writer, whose stories in the first volume of *Chicken Soup for the Teenage Soul* were favorites with readers. Lia is certain to succeed at any writing project she undertakes, and she is certain to succeed equally well at living life to the fullest. She would like any correspondence to be sent to her care of Kimberly Kirberger, by regular mail to: P.O. Box 936, Pacific Palisades, CA 90272 or by e-mail to: *letters@teenage chickensoup.com*.

**April Joy Gazmen** is an eighteen-year-old Filipina-American attending University of Houston-Downtown. Although she participates as a volunteer and in school activities, writing and reading are her passions. She is inspired by the following people who are always in her heart: Mama, Cza, Hawke, Chino, friends and teachers. To be published in *Chicken Soup for the Teenage Soul II* is a dream come true. She can be reached at *irelandnikita@hotmail.com*.

**Celine Geday** is fourteen years old and is an honor-roll student in Washington. She enjoys writing short stories, poems and essays, reading, acting, dancing, listening to music and skateboarding. She is working on fulfilling her dreams and furthering her talents in all of these areas. She can be reached via e-mail at *NJCCGEDAY@juno.com*.

**Katie Gill** had Hodgkin's disease when she was sixteen. She is now twenty-four and pursuing a graduate degree in education. Presently she is working on a book for teens with cancer and trying to establish support networks for adult survivors of teenage cancer. Katie can be reached at 4520 Ashbury Park Dr., North Olmsted, OH 44070.

**Randy Glasbergen** has had more than twenty-five thousand cartoons published in magazines, books and greeting cards around the world. He also creates *The Better Half*, which is syndicated to newspapers by King Features Syndicate. You can find more of Randy's cartoons online at *www.glasbergen.com*.

**Miriam Goldstein**'s body cast now resides in her basement, slowly dissolving under the combined assault of dampness and insects. However, Miriam herself has no plans for dissolution in the immediate future. She is a native of Manchester, New Hampshire and is currently attending Brown University, where she is double-majoring in biology and English. She enjoys wandering through tide pools, swamps and woods, haphazardly hammering bits of wood together as a theater techie, making sounds that vaguely resemble music on the flute and tenor sax, meeting unconventional people and tweaking the nose of popular culture. She despises conformity and intolerance. She can be reached by writing c/o Martin's Associates, 817 Elm St., Manchester, NH 03104 or by e-mail at *khory@juno.com*.

**Arthur Gordon** was born in Savannah, Georgia. He has been managing editor for *Good Housekeeping*, editor in chief for *Cosmopolitan* and editorial director for *Guideposts* and *Airforce Magazine*. He has written two books, *Reprisal* and *A Touch of Wonder*.

**Luken Grace** is currently serving a two-year mission in Venezuela until August of 1999. He is a 1996 graduate of Sinagua High School in Flagstaff, Arizona. As the third child of six children, he has always enjoyed writing stories and drawing. After he graduates from college, he plans on becoming an English teacher.

**Jennie Gratton** graduated from Central High School in Manchester, New Hampshire in 1999, where she was president of the drama club and played trumpet in the band. She is currently attending Northeastern University majoring in English and theater. She has been writing on her own for years, keeping a journal and writing poetry and short stories. Jennie hopes to pursue a career in writing or costume design, and can be reached via e-mail at *Butrcup123@aol.com*.

**Cynthia Hamond** is a freelance writer. This is her second story for *Chicken Soup*. She enjoys her school visits, especially when the children react to that "A-ha" moment in a story. She and her husband, Bruce, have five children and one grandchild. Cindy volunteers at St. Henry's as a teacher and lector and visits the homebound. She can be reached at 1021 West River St., Monticello, MN 55362 or call 612-295-5049 or fax 612-295-3117.

**Barbara Hauck** is currently a sophomore in high school and enjoys her cat, athletics, music, math, computers, writing and drawing. A polo enthusiast, Barbara hopes to attend a college where she can play polo competitively.

**Jennifer Love Hewitt** is best known for her starring role as Sarah Reeves on FOX's Golden Globe-winning drama series, *Party of Five*. Love has starred in such big-screen hits as *I Know What You Did Last Summer* and *Can't Hardly Wait*. Her upcoming projects include *I Still Know What You Did Last Summer*, *The Suburbans* (with Ben Stiller), and an ABC movie-of-the-week in which she will play her idol, Audrey Hepburn.

**Margaret (Meg) Hill** writes articles, short stories and young-adult books. Recent titles are *Coping with Family Expectations* (Rosen, 1990) and *So What Do I Do About Me?* (Teacher Ideas Press, Libraries Unlimited, Englewood, Colorado, 1993). Kirk is the pen name she uses when writing from the viewpoint of a teenage boy.

**Wil Horneff** has made a name for himself on stage, screen and television. After beginning his career on Broadway, Wil starred in the feature films *Born to Be Wild*, *The Sandlot* and the upcoming *Harvest*. On television, he gave an award-winning performance as Jody Baxter in the CBS remake of *The Yearling* and costarred in Stephen King's *The Shining*. Wil is currently a freshman at the University of Pennsylvania.

**Katie E. Houston** is a sophomore in Santa Barbara, California. She loves acting, singing, dancing and has been taking piano lessons for eight years. She enjoys writing, especially realistic fiction and poetry. Katie runs track (hurdles) and she would someday like to perform on Broadway or be an English/drama teacher.

**Bret Anthony Johnston** is currently a Teaching-Writing Fellow at the Iowa Writers' Workshop. His work has twice been honored in the *Atlantic Monthly*, and has appeared in such magazines as *Glamour, Mid-American Review, Southwest Review* and *Shenandoah*, where one of his stories received the 2000 Jeanne Goodheart Prize for best fiction of the year. His stories have been anthologized in *Patterns of Exposition 16ed* and *Scribner's Best of the Fiction Workshops 1999*. He can be reached at *Bretjohnst@aol.com*.

**Randal Jones** is a professional speaker and resident of Re: Think. He teaches seminars on thinking skills and personal management, helping people live and work deliberately for maximum effectiveness and satisfaction. He can be reached at 4307 Lealand Lane, Nashville, TN 37204, or by calling 615-292-8585.

**Laurie Kalb** is a member of the Class of 2000 at the Annenberg School for Communication at the University of Pennsylvania. Writing has been a passion of hers since she was a little girl. She also enjoys running, sculpture and nature photography. Although the lifestyle of a bohemian poet will always be appealing, she ultimately hopes to utilize her interest in human behavior and interpersonal relationships to encourage others to believe in the power of their own voices. She can be reached via e-mail at *Laurie248@aol.com*.

**Andrew Keegan** is one of Hollywood's most popular young actors. Last television season, he had roles on both *Party of Five* and *7th Heaven*. Andrew will star in the upcoming Touchstone Pictures film *Ten Things I Hate About You*, which is based on William Shakespeare's *The Taming of the Shrew*. In his free time, he donates countless hours to charities that help critically and terminally ill children.

**Kendal Kelly** was born on October 2, 1982, the second of four children. She lives in Bristow, Oklahoma, near Tulsa. She is a high-school junior with a GPA of 3.97. She runs cross country and track, and plans to take state championship before she graduates. She loves little kids and babies, and writes in her spare time. She plans to attend college.

**April Kemp, M.S.,** is an award-winning motivational speaker and sales trainer. She is dynamic with a high-energy delivery style dedicated to the education of audiences nationwide. Along with her husband, April developed a motivational software product, "Motivational Mind Bytes." She can be reached at 800-307-8821.

**Hilary E. Kisch,** a resident of Toronto, Canada, has finished her first year of university as an English major. "No Longer A Child" is her first piece of work submitted to a publisher. Aside from her passion for writing, she enjoys singing, playing guitar, and participating in a variety of sports including rugby and wakeboarding. She would like to dedicate this piece to her mother and thank her friends, Meghan and Greg, for their continued support. She can be reached via e-mail at *Hilary79@excite.com*.

**Heather Klassen** is from Edmonds, Washington, and writes for children and teenagers. She has had two picture books published and over one hundred stories appear in magazines. She can be reached by e-mail at *tressen60@cs.com*.

**Mary Ellen Klee** is an acupuncturist working in Santa Monica, Calif. Since 1971, she has been a student and teacher of the Arica method and practice developed by Oscar Ichazo. She has had a home in Big Sur, Calif., for over 30 years and is a trustee of the Esalen Institute. Starting with a teenage diary, writing has been a hobby and refuge for most of her life.

**Paula (Bachleda) Koskey** is the happy mother of two wonderful hormone hostages (a.k.a. teenagers), HopeAnne and Luke, and one post teen (whew!), Jesse. She would like to thank her children for all their inspiration and encouragement—and Clairol for covering the gray. She maintains her balance by writing, walking, eating chocolate and believing in miracles. Paula is the author of a children's book entitled *Secrets of Christmas*. She can be reached by writing 1173 Cambridge, Berkley, MI 48072, or by calling 810-542-0376.

**Jonathan Krasnoff** is a junior at Kansas State University in Manhattan, Kansas. He is majoring in Public Relations and Print Journalism. Jon hopes to attend law school after graduation. This story is dedicated to the bonds of true friendship. He can be reached at *jdk9569@ksu.edu* or by writing to P. O. Box 1415, Manhattan, KS 66505-1415.

**Theresa Jensen Lacey** is a freelance writer who has authored four hundred newspaper/magazine articles and two Native American history books: *The Blackfeet* (1995) and *The Pawnee* (1996, Chelsea House). Lacey is the author of two YA novels (available), is working on a children's book and one on Native American women. The author is of Comanche and Cherokee descent. She can be reached at 112 Carney Rd., Clarksville, TN 37043, or by calling 931-358-5511, or by e-mail: *tcjl@hotmail.com*.

**Chris Laddish** is a freshman in San Rafael, Calif. He has always enjoyed writing and has won first place in the Philips Literary Writing contest two years in a row. He hopes to become a screenwriter or journalist. Chris enjoys mountain biking, in-line skating and exploring the Internet. He is the youngest of six children and has lived in San Rafael his entire life.

**Alison Lambert** is a member of the class of 2000 at the University of Pennsylvania in Philadelphia. She is a certified emergency medical technician with the Newtown Square volunteer fire company #1 in Newtown, Pennsylvania. Ali is also an ocean lifeguard in Long Beach Township, New Jersey. She can be reached by e-mail: *alambert@sas.upenn.edu*.

**Medard Laz** is a popular speaker and author of the international bestseller, *Love Adds a Little Chocolate: 100 Stories to Brighten Your Day and Sweeten Your Life*, as well as nine other books. Medard was instrumental in the development of Marriage Encounter and he cofounded (with Suzy Yehl Marta) Rainbows for All God's Children, a support group for children and teens who have experienced a divorce or death in their families. This group has ministered to over 600,000 children in sixteen countries. He also founded Joyful Again! (with Charlotte Hrubes), a support weekend for widowers and widows. Med is a highly sought-after speaker, giving presentations and workshops on a variety of marriage and family issues, as well as topics related to emotional and spiritual growth. Med lives in Chicago and is a priest of the Archdiocese of Chicago. He can be reached at 3600 S. 57th Ct., Cicero, IL, or by calling 708-656-9216, or by e-mail: *MedardLaz@aol.com.*

**Gary LeRoux** is twenty-five years old and lives in Louisiana. He is interested in reading and writing about juvenile issues. His writing skills mainly include letters and poetry concerning juvenile justice. He can be reached at P.O. Box 2103, Reserve, LA 70084.

**Brian Leykum** is a freshman at New York University. He grew up on Long Island, but his family recently moved to Massachusetts. "My Friend Mike" is Brian's first published piece. He can be reached via a-mail at *CurlyJ81@aol.com.*

**Phyllis Lin** is a fifteen-year-old freshman in high school in Bartlett, Illinois. An aspiring writer, Phyllis writes for both her school academy newsletter and for her own pleasure. In her spare time, she enjoys going out with friends, reading and playing the piano. Phyllis can be reached at e-mail: *Phyllis911@yahoo.com.*

**Kathryn Litzenberger** is a member of the Class of 2000 in Cromwell, Connecticut. This is her first published work, though she has always loved to write. In her spare time she sings, acts, writes and spends time with her friends. She dedicates this story to those who encouraged her to reach for her dreams: her friends, her family, her teachers and to the little girl who inspired her story—Rikki. She can be reached via e-mail at *Jewel0442@aol.com.*

**Laura Loken** is now a seventeen-year-old student in Crosby, North Dakota. Her story, "Don't Cry, Dad," was written on Christmas Eve in 1998 when she was sixteen years old. She enjoys singing, writing music, working in a nursing home and hanging out with friends. She is active in FCCLA, Youth Alive and her church youth group. She can be reached via e-mail at *fire_blue62@hotmail.com.*

**James Malinchak,** age twenty-seven, is the author of two books for students: *Teenagers Tips for Success* and *From College to the Real World.* He specializes in motivational and inspirational presentations for teenagers and college students worldwide and is being called "America's #1 Teen Motivator." For information on his talks or books, contact him at P.O. Box 3944, Beverly Hills, CA 90212, or call 954-796-1925, or e-mail *JamesMal@aol.com.*

**Bonnie Maloney** is a sophomore in high school in Attleboro, Massachusetts. She enjoys reading and writing, and plans to study these along with psychology in the future. She is currently employed at a local bank that operates in and out of school, and looks forward to going somewhere unexplored for college.

**Sandy Dow Mapula** is a native of El Paso, Texas. She is presently a nurse for Zach White Elementary School and loves to write in her spare time. Her two sons, Steven and Kevin, whom she describes as the joys of her life, provide her with the inspiration to write. She can be reached at 604 Tepic, El Paso, TX 79912 or by e-mail: *SMAPULA781@aol.com*.

**Jill Maxbauer** is a junior in high school. There, she is involved with theater, music, athletic training, softball and the Safe & Drug Free Schools Committee. She is the youngest of three girls and is currently deciding where she would like to go to college.

**Sarah McCann** is a sixteen-year-old student in Bedford, Nova Scotia. Her first love is dancing, but she also enjoys writing, watching movies and drawing.

**Paula McDonald** has sold over a million copies of her books on relationships and gone on to win numerous awards worldwide as a columnist, inspirational feature writer and photojournalist. She lives on the beach in Rosarito, Mexico. She can be contacted in the United States by writing PMB 724, 416 W. San Ysidro Blvd., Ste. L, San Ysidro, CA 92173 or by e-mailing *eieiho@compuserve.com*.

**Dianna McGill** was born and raised in a small town about an hour north of New York City. Her parents moved from the Bronx about two years before she was born. She is the youngest of eight born to strict Irish Catholic parents. Her family overcame many adversities together financially, as well as emotionally, and they remain close. She is thirty-two years old and works as a senior client service rep in a very large insurance agency. Reading and writing are two of her favorite hobbies and she hopes to write a novel someday.

**Emily R. Monfort** is a sophomore at South Eugene High School and International High School in Eugene, Oregon. She has never been published, but writing stories and poetry is one of her many hobbies. She plays soccer for her school, loves to snowboard, wakeboard and white-water raft with her family. She loves to read and, after finishing *Chicken Soup for the Teenage Soul*, she felt motivated to send in a story about a life experience that could be inspiring to others.

**Dan Mulhausen** is a student just graduated from Southridge High in Kennewick, Washington. After his letter was written he had foot surgery in the winter of '98, then came back and competed in his senior year of football and tennis. In football his team made the playoffs for the first time in school history and in tennis he was named team cocaptain. He awaits a response from Notre Dame University. He can be reached by e-mail at *Rudy63@aol.com*.

**Morgan Mullens-Landis** was born Morgan Nicole Maylee Mullens on December 28, 1982 in Gainesville, Florida. Her dad died a few weeks before her fourth birthday in December 1986. She was put in foster care in October 1995. She became Morgan Amithyst Landis on July 20, 1998 when she was adopted by Brian and Jackie Landis. She can be reached via e-mail at *amirose46@hotmail.com*.

**David J. Murcott** is a freelance writer who resides in San Diego, California. He has written and edited stories for *A 5th Portion of Chicken Soup for the Soul*, *Chicken Soup for the Teenage Soul* and *Stone Soup for the World*. He can be contacted at 619-590-1461.

**Sara Nachtman** is sixteen years old and is a focused student, determined athlete, with much emotional experience with trying to keep up with her competition. Sometimes she gets discouraged when her progress is slow or tiresome. These are the times when Sara writes to keep her motivation high while keeping in perspective what is really important.

**Kent Nerburn** is an author, sculptor and educator who has been deeply involved in Native American issues and education. He has served as project director for two books of oral history, *To Walk the Red Road* and *We Choose to Remember*. He has also edited three highly acclaimed books on Native American subjects. Kent won the Minnesota Book Award in 1995 for his book *Neither Wolf Nor Dog: On Forgotten Roads*. The story *Like People First* appeared in Kent's book *Letters to My Son*. Kent holds a Ph.D. in Theology and Art and lives with his family in Bemidju, Minnesota.

**Jenni Norman** is a fifteen-year-old sophomore in Albemarle, North Carolina. In addition to running cross-country and playing soccer, she is a member of the debate club and the Albemarle athletic fellowship. She loves making her friends laugh, writing, staying glued to the TV during the World Cup, trips to the beach and traveling abroad—she has been to Austria, Germany, Hungary and the Czech Republic, and plans to travel to England and France. Most of all, she loves chasing her mischievous dachshund Oscar. She can be reached at P.O. Box 550, Albemarle, NC 28002.

**Tony Overman** is a nationally known motivational youth speaker. He founded the National Youth I Care Hotline and produced *Teen Talk*, a nine-part video series. Tony conducts training workshops for teachers and motivational assemblies for schools. He can be reached at 18965 F.M. 2252, Garden Ridge, TX 78266, or by calling 800-487-8464.

**Sandy Pathe** is a junior in high school in New Jersey. She plans to continue her trips to Honduras annually and hopes her story can motivate others to put themselves out there and lend a hand. Any questions or comments are welcome at *SungirlsR@aol.com* or call 732-449-0335.

**Peer Resources** is a leading authority in peer helping services, programs, and resources for children, teens and adults. They can be contacted by e-mail at*helping@islandnet.com* or visited at *www.islandnet.com/~rcarr/peer.html*. Write to 1052 Davie St., Victoria, BC V8S 4E3 or call 800-567-3700.

**Theresa Peterson** is a high school student and an active member of her church. He spare time is spent reading, writing and having fun with her friends. She is a warmhearted person whose loyalty to her friends and family is admirable. She can be reached at P.O. Box 366, Woodstown, NJ 08098.

**Jessica Pinto** is a freshman majoring in English at the University of California, Santa Barbara. She was invited to appear on National Public Radio to read her poetry and had two poems published by the 1999 Marin Poetry Contest. She was accepted to the California State Summer School for the Arts in 1998 for creative writing, where she composed "Ode to Shoes." She can be reached at P.O. Box 202, Mill Valley, CA 94942.

**John Powell, S.J.**, is a professor at Loyola University in Chicago. He is a popular lecturer, teacher and bestselling author who effectively brings together psychology and religion in a unified approach to personal growth and spiritual development. For more information about any of John Powell's books, please call Thomas More Customer Service at 1-800-822-6701.

**Shad Powers** is a freelance writer in Battle Creek, Michigan. He has written for magazines such as *All About You, Jump* and *U. Magazine*. He is currently a sports writer for the *Battle Creek Enquirer* and can be reached via e-mail at *ShadP40@aol.com*.

**Kevin Randall** has been a leadership trainer and public speaker for the past seven years, having spoken at the National Association for Campus Activities National Convention, NACA Great Lakes Regional Conference, and to high school students across Michigan. In 1997, Kevin developed his most requested presentation, entitled Leadership as a Lifestyle, and has presented this session to rave reviews at high schools, colleges and conferences nationwide. For more information about Kevin Randall or his leadership programs contact, *Randallkev@hotmail.com*.

**Kate Reder** is seventeen years old and lives in San Francisco with her parents and her older sister, Libby. She is a senior in high school, where she is the editor of the newspaper and of a literary magazine. She recently spent a fabulous summer in a Native Alaskan village writing, thinking and doing community service.

**Rick Reed** is a business owner, franchise developer and motivational speaker, as well as a youth travel hockey coach. His story is dedicated to his loving wife, Amy, and his two awesome sons, Patrick and Calvin, to whom he commits his story as proof of a life lesson learned—one he hopes they can learn without direct involvement. He can be reached via e-mail at *RReed12879@aol.com*.

**Daphna Renan** is currently a freshman at Yale College. She moved six times before she entered sixth grade, and it was during these early years that she learned the significance of deep and enduring friendships. Daphna would like to thank those who have filled her life with love, laughter and learning.

**Sheila K. Reyman** is a certified community college instructor. The consultant/trainer for a family child care program, Sheila presents workshops throughout the state. She has also been invited to speak with teens regarding goal-setting and positive attitudes. She can be reached at P.O. Box 20987, Mesa, AZ 85277, or by calling 602-807-1965.

**Rachel Rosenberg** is fifteen years old. She wrote "Unrequited Love" in 1998 when she was fourteen. She has been writing since she was ten, and one day plans to be a writer. She also writes longer stories and poems. Rachel attends high school in Montreal, Quebec, and can be reached at *Rae_38@hotmail.com*.

**Jennifer Rosenfeld** is a career counselor and is currently authoring *Building Your Yellow Brick Road: Real Women Create Extraordinary Career Paths*. She would love to hear more inspiring career profiles and can be reached at 212-794-6050.

**Jamie Rowen** is currently a student at Swarthmore College in Pennsylvania, studying International Relations. She loves to write, especially children's stories. This is her first published poem and she dedicates it to the victims of the Columbine tragedy.

**Kimberly Russell** would like to thank her entire family for all of the continued support they have given her. She is leaving in the fall to attend Gettysberg College where she will probably major in pre-law. She would like any correspondence to be sent to her care of Kimberly Kirberger, by regular mail to: P.O. Box 936, Pacific Palisades, CA 90272 or by e-mail to: *letters@teenagechickensoup.com*.

**Michelle Sander** is the middle of three girls from a Northern California single-parent home. She graduated with honors from San Ramon Valley High School in June 2000, and began her higher education at the University of California, San Diego in the fall. She can be reached by e-mail at *dmsander@ucsd.edu*.

**Harley Schwadron** is a self-taught cartoonist living in Ann Arbor, Michigan and worked as a journalist and public relations writer before switching to cartooning full-time in 1984. His cartoons appear in *Barron's, Harvard Business Review, Wall Street Journal, National Law Journal* and many others. He can be reached at P.O. Box 1347, Ann Arbor, MI 48106 or call 313-426-8433.

**Bob Schwartz** is a freelance humor writer with a concentration in the area of family life. He has a weekly column in a Michigan newspaper and his humorous writings have appeared in many national magazines and regional parenting publications. He also provides a monthly humorous column on running for numerous regional running magazines. He lives in Huntington Woods, Michigan with his wife and three children and can be reached via e-mail at *rschwartz@s4online.com*.

**Veronica A. Shoffstall** is a member of the Baha'i faith, which teaches that all people are from one race and have been created noble by one God. She has been trying to make sense of the world through words all her life. Now in her mid-forties, she is trying to recapture the wisdom of her youth and learn the lessons expressed in her poem *After a While*, which she wrote at the age of nineteen. She can be reached at 229 East 25th Street, #4D, New York, NY 10010.

**JoLynn Shopteese** is eighteen years old and lives in Savage, Minnesota. She wrote "Forever Changed," as a speech that she was asked to give after a missions trip to Mexico. She is hoping that she can be leader on the same trip next year. In the fall, she will be a freshman at Bethel College. She is planning to major in Spanish and go into social work and maybe writing. She would like to thank her family, especially her mom for "putting up with her." She can be reached via e-mail at *volleyball13jo@mailexcite.com*.

**Ashley Sims** is seventeen and lives in Morro Bay, California. She enjoys writing in her spare time. She feels that writing allows people to get in touch with their emotions and to express them. She hopes that one day she can help make a positive difference in the world.

**Jane Denitz Smith** is the author of two young adult novels, *Mary by Myself* (1994), and *Charlie Is a Chicken* (1998), both published by HarperCollins Publishers, and both Harper Trophy paperbacks. She is also the author of a board book, *Baby and Kitty and Mommy and Daddy* (Workman Publishing, 1994) and has written several plays, as well as novels. She writes and teaches in Williamstown, Massachusetts, where she lives with her husband and three children.

**Karina Snow** lives with her husband, Mark, in Oceanside, California. She is a recent graduate of Brigham Young University and volunteers with the youth group in her church. Karina enjoys reading, cooking and playing with her two young children, Tori and Brett.

**Elizabeth Stumbo** will graduate as a member of the class of 2000. She participates in sports, scenery for school and community theaters, and is editor of her high-school yearbook. She hopes to pursue a career in the arts and communications field. She can be reached at P.O. Box 338, Ogden, IA 50212.

**Ruth Ann Supica** is a fourteen-year-old student in high school in Overland Park, Kansas. She really enjoys writing and is thrilled to have her first published piece be in *Chicken Soup for the Teenage Soul III*. This story is dedicated to her best friend, Laura Halvorson, who has stood beside her for all fourteen years of her life; to Teresa Hogan, one of her biggest inspirations; and to her wonderful family. She can be reached via e-mail at *Rootie14@aol.com*.

**Jill Thieme.** Turning "Wonder into Wonderful" was only one of the many lessons in life that Mom taught us. When we didn't have money, Mom would tell us to "Make a Memory." For several years now our holidays and birthdays have become a tradition of special activities. We'll be happy to share our creative family outings with others if you write to us at P.O. Box 381, Bridgeport, MI 48722.

**Erica Thoits** is the *Teen People* contest winner. She loves to horseback ride and swim. Her favorite pastime is going out on the family's boat. She is an avid reader and has been writing ever since she could type. Her handwriting is too sloppy to handwrite things. She loves dogs and couldn't live without her thirteen-year-old dog, who is only one year younger than she is.

**Terri Vandermark** graduated from Johnson City High School in 1983. She spent her first five years after graduation as a PCA for the elderly and continues to enjoy helping others. Today she works full-time as parts crib attendant for Felchar Mfg., a division of Shop Vac Corp. She enjoys writing, reading *Chicken Soup for the Soul*, being in love with Randy and spending time with her special friend, Tonya. Her latest dream has come true—getting her story published in *Chicken Soup for the Teenage Soul*.

**Sarah J. Vogt** was born and raised in Columbus, Indiana. Currently, she resides in South Florida and works as a PC/network analyst for a major corporation. Sarah has an undergraduate degree from Florida Atlantic University in business administration. Computers are her hobby and her livelihood and writing is her passion. She can be reached at 80 Catalpa Way, Columbus, IN 47203.

**Jodi Vesterby** was raised in Olivia, Minnesota. She currently attends Concordia College in Moorhead, Minnesota, and will graduate in 2001 with a degree in English Education. While attending Concordia, she has been involved in Campus Ministry, Habitat for Humanity and Justice Journeys. She can be reached by e-mail at *pvesterby@thurstongenetics.com*.

**Tal Vigderson** was born in San Diego, California. Tal has an undergraduate degree in film from San Diego State University. He has had careers in photography, entertainment-marketing research and teaching in several grade levels, including special education in a junior high school in south central Los Angeles. Tal attended law school at Loyola of Los Angeles and passed the California Bar. He is currently working as an entertainment attorney in Los Angeles representing filmmakers, writers, directors, producers, Internet companies and major studios in various forms of transactional work. Tal likes to travel and enjoys tennis, hiking and photography. He can be reached via e-mail at *TOV3@aol.com*.

**Christine Walsh** is a comedian and actress in the greater Boston area. She is a freelance writer who loves all genres of literature, but favors writing for children and adolescents the most because it encourages boundless creativity. This story is dedicated to Brad, the person who taught her how to believe in herself.

**Camden Watts** will graduate from high school in 1999. Camden enjoys staying busy with difficult courses, running cross country, swimming, playing soccer and dancing. She writes and draws for her school newspaper and for her nationally acclaimed literary magazine, *Opus*. Her best work comes from experiences written late in the evening.

**Mary Jane West-Delgado** is a physical therapist and author of short stories and cartoons. She is president of Toe Bumpers, Inc., creating fun and decorative safety products for the home. You can reach Mary Jane at 805-688-1372 or by e-mail at *delgado@terminus.com*.

**Kristy White** is a fifteen-year-old sophomore in high school in Grass Valley, California. She enjoys acting, writing and playing the piano. She can be reached via e-mail at *eleemosynary29@hotmail.com*.

**Sharon Whitley** is a former bilingual grade-school teacher who has also taught high-school special education. Her work has appeared in *Reader's Digest* (including eighteen international editions), *Los Angeles Times Magazine, Guideposts* and the *San Diego Union-Tribune*. She can be reached at 5666 Meredith Ave., San Diego, CA 92120, phone: 619-583-7346.

**Tom Witte** was a writer and graphic arts designer in Denver, Colorado. He wrote this poem for his nephew, Ben, on the occasion of his bar mitzvah. His "Message for Ben" was written with great love, and Ben is proud and honored to have it published in memory of Tom, who died of AIDS at the age of forty-six. Ben can be reached via e-mail at *BMR@one.net*.

**Cecile Wood** is a British citizen, studying at the College of William and Mary in Virginia. She is currently doing a semester abroad in Buenos Aires, Argentina. She is grateful to *Chicken Soup for the Soul* for giving her a chance to share her stories.

**Rebecca Woolf** is a freelance writer and photographer who has written for *Chicken Soup for the Teenage Soul II* and *III*, *Teen Love: On Relationships*, *Teen Love: On Friendship*, *Teen Love: A Journal on Friendship*, *19* (the popular UK magazine) and more. Keep your eyes out for Rebecca's first solo book of poetry titled, *Through Broken Mirrors: A Reflective Memoir*. Rebecca is the program director and newsletter editor for Lead the Star, a creative company devoted to inspiring creativity and strength in identity in young adults. To reach Rebecca, please e-mail her at *rebeccawoolf@leadthestar.com*.

**Lynne Zielinski**, mother of seven and "Nana" to thirteen grandkids, resides in Huntsville, Alabama. She believes that life is a gift from God and what we do with it is our gift to God. She tries to write accordingly. Lynne can be reached by calling 256-883-1592 or 256-880-9052.

*Owning the World.* Reprinted by permission of Mary Pat Alarie. ©2000 Mary Pat Alarie.

*My Toughest Decision.* Reprinted by permission of Kristina Dulcey. ©1998 Kristina Dulcey.

*It's Tough to Be a Teenager.* Reprinted by permission of Tony Overman. ©1998 Tony Overman.

*Four Kisses.* Reprinted by permission of Kate Reder. ©2000 Kate Reder.

*No Matter What Happens.* Reprinted by permission of Alison Mary Forbes. ©1998 Alison Mary Forbes.

*Hero of the 'Hood.* Reprinted by permission of Paula McDonald. ©1997 Paula McDonald.

*Good Night, Dad.* Reprinted by permission of Luken Grace. ©1998 Luken Grace.

*A Name in the Sand.* Reprinted by permission of Elizabeth Stumbo. ©2000 Elizabeth Stumbo.

*Tears.* Reprinted by permission of Jamie Rowen. ©2000 Jamie Rowen.

*Can That Be?* Reprinted by permission of Kelly Ann Fleming. ©2000 Kelly Ann Fleming.

*Minutes Like Hours.* Reprinted by permission of Vidhya Chandrasekaran. ©2000 Vidhya Chandrasekaran.

*The Last Song for Christy.* Reprinted by permission of Rebecca Woolf. ©2001 Rebecca Woolf.

*Defining Myself.* Reprinted by permission of Morgan Mullens-Landis. ©2000 Morgan Mullens-Landis.

*Passing the Dream.* Reprinted by permission of Penny Caldwell. ©1996 Penny Caldwell.

*The Gravediggers of Parkview Junior High.* Reprinted by permission of Kif Anderson. ©1996 Kif Anderson.

*The Boy Who Talked with Dolphins.* Reprinted by permission of Paula McDonald. Also reprinted with permission from the April 1996 *Reader's Digest.*

*For You, Dad.* Reprinted by permission of Bill Holton. Excerpted from *Woman's World Magazine.* ©1998 Bill Holton.

*Somebody Loves You.* Reprinted by permission of Wil Horneff. ©1998 Wil Horneff.

*A Street Kid's Guide.* Reprinted by permission of Jennings Michael Burch. ©1998 Jennings Michael Burch.

*An Open Heart.* Reprinted by permission of Sandy Pathe. ©1998 Sandy Pathe.

# Also Available

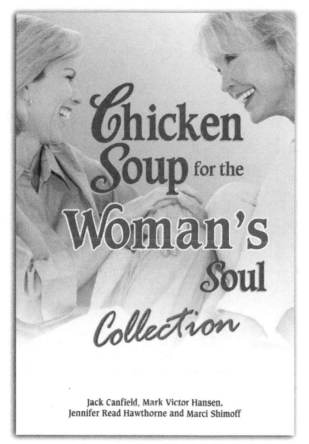

Code #3358 • hardcover • $19.95

# Also Available

Jack Canfield, Mark Victor Hansen,
Patty Hansen and Irene Dunlap

Code #3862 • hardcover • $19.95